"One L of a Year"

How to Maximize Your Success in Law School

Leah M. Christensen

CAROLINA ACADEMIC PRESS
Durham, North Carolina

Library of Congress Cataloging-in-Publication Data

Christensen, Leah M.
  One L of a year : how to maximize your success in Law school / Leah
M. Christensen.
     p. cm.
  ISBN 978-1-59460-947-3 (alk. paper)
  1. Law schools--United States. 2. Law--Study and teaching--United
States. 3. Law students--United States. I. Title.

  KF283.C485 2012
  340.071'173--dc23

                          2012010136

Carolina Academic Press
700 Kent Street
Durham, NC 27701
Telephone (919) 489-7486
Fax (919) 493-5668
www.cap-press.com

Printed in the United States of America

"One L of a Year"

This book is dedicated to Noah and Bailey, who fill my life with more joy than I ever thought possible.

Contents

Introduction

There are a number of books that give law students advice about how to navigate through the first year of law school. This book strives to be something slightly different. The purpose of this book is to provide research-based learning strategies for law students who are either just beginning law school—or for those who are in law school but find that they are struggling and need a new approach. Law school is very different than anything you have done before. You cannot use the same study and learning methods that you used in your undergraduate (or prior graduate school) education. And if you have already been through a semester or even a year of law school (and did not get the results for which you had hoped), you need a different and more proactive way of approaching the study of law. This book is geared towards helping you develop that plan.

Law school is a shock to most students in their first semester. Why? Law school requires a large volume of complex reading and analysis, and you likely have not encountered this previously in your education. Perhaps in undergraduate courses you could keep up with your schoolwork fairly easily. However, in law school, the volume of reading coupled with its inherent complexity makes 'just getting by' almost impossible. Therefore, as you think about the upcoming semester, you will need to develop different reading and study strategies to get you through your first year—and beyond. You will need to outline differently, read cases differently, and approach law school in a more active, engaged and efficient manner. The good news is you *can* learn the skills to help you succeed in law school. The key to success in law school, however, is to develop a proactive learning plan as soon as possible.

As a law professor, I have been very interested in how law students learn. I have had the opportunity to conduct empirical research on what the most successful law students do differently than the less successful law students. The good news is that even if you've struggled in law school thus far, you can still be successful in law school. But in order to achieve your goals, you may need to work differently than you have in the past.

The purpose of this book is to focus on the reading, studying and testing strategies that are particularly helpful to law students as they begin law school. This book is more than advice—it is a learning guide based upon empirical research and statistical correlations between learning strategies and law school GPAs. Further, I attempt to *show* you what the most successful law students do by using interviews from actual students. It is one thing to *read* about how to read a judicial opinion—it's another thing entirely to *see* how a first-year law student accomplishes this task. This book is full of examples of how students read, write, outline, and take exams. In addition, it also addresses the important issues of law school test anxiety and depression.

This book is divided into two parts. Part I covers issues most relevant either before you go to law school or as you begin law school. Part I explains why law school is so different than your prior schooling. Part I also addresses learning styles (what is your individual learning style), how to read a case, how to brief a case, and how to prepare for class. Part II of the book focuses very specifically on what you need to do when you are *fully engaged* in the study of law. Part II focuses on specific learning techniques to master the essentials of law school: legal writing, legal research, outlining, and exam taking (essay and multiple-choice). Part II also addresses how to use "Dead Week" effectively (the week before final exams), and how to deal with test anxiety and law school depression.

I believe that with drive and determination, *every* student can get through law school. Further, just because you may have struggled during your first semester (or your first year) does not mean that you will not become a skillful and successful lawyer. This book is meant to help you navigate through law school so that you can achieve your full potential as both a law student and a future lawyer.

Part I

Getting Used to Law School: The Basics

Chapter 1

The New World of Law School: What Makes Law School So Different?

Every year I begin the fall semester by asking my students what they know about law school. Most of them have seen television shows like *The Firm* or *Law and Order*. Even on the internet, there are numerous websites devoted to instructing students on how to manage their first year of law school, including advice on how to read an opinion or brief a case.

In addition, most of my beginning students have been very successful in their undergraduate careers. They have tested well in the past (on the LSAT or other exams) and they all believe they will be just as successful in law school. Even though law school is a new experience, almost all law students begin their experience believing that if they work just like they did in college, they will be equally successful in law school.

However, using the same reading and study strategies in law school that worked for you in college will not necessarily translate into success. Every fall semester, I watch first-year students struggle with reading a legal opinion for the first time. Despite their hard work and effort, most law students are left confused and frustrated. This confusion comes not because these students lack skills or intelligence, but because of the unique characteristics of law school—the high volume of complex reading coupled with a strange new teaching methodology called the Socratic Method.

The purpose of this first chapter is to provide you with a better understanding of how law school is unique. This chapter will describe four characteristics of law school that make it a very different experience for law students: (a) an increased workload; (b) the Socratic Method; (c) the need to direct your own learning; and (d) intense peer competition.

If you understand these unique characteristics of law school—you can be better prepared to make the transition into law school more easily.

A. The Increased Workload in Law School

You have no doubt heard tales about the amount of work expected from law students. These stories are true. You will have a great deal of reading and thinking to do in order to prepare for each of your classes. And the reading will be difficult and time-consuming—because law school reading is a whole new vocabulary and format. In your first-year courses, you will likely be assigned at least 20 pages of reading per class period—per *course*. You will likely have five courses at a time. That doesn't sound like too much, right? *Wrong.* If law school reading were like the reading you've done before, it wouldn't be a problem. However, *legal* reading, i.e., reading judicial opinions, is *very* time-consuming—particularly during your first semester.

Consider the following scenario. Typically, each law school class is between 50–80 minutes per class period (depending on whether you meet two or three times per week). And you will typically have two to three class periods per week in each course. And you may have up to five courses each semester. Therefore, you will likely be in class an average of 15 hours per week.

A law student will spend at least three to five hours of study time for each hour she is in class. Therefore, if a student is in class 15 hours per week, the student will likely need to study 45 hours per week *in addition* to the 15 hours per week she is in class. This means that a full-time law student begins law school with a 60 hour-per-week time commitment *just* for getting the basics done.

For any new law student, this is a tremendous workload. And this new time commitment can be overwhelming. The good news is that you can learn to study efficiently. However, you need to begin law school with a plan. I've seen too many students simply study for endless hours—working desperately to keep up with their classes. They think that if they can study *more* than their peers, they will succeed. But studying *more* is not always studying *better*. The actual number of hours you study is far less important than the quality of your reading and thinking.

Consider the words of one of my prior students, Annie. Although Annie became an efficient and successful law student during her second year, she felt like she studied too much during her first year of law school.

> I would say that looking back [over my first year in law school], I spent all my time studying. I thought I wasn't [just studying], but I did.

> ... I think I studied every Friday, Saturday and Sunday. And thank goodness for my "study buddies." My study buddies also studied that much. We would pick Fridays where we would go to dinner. So, we would work all Friday afternoon and then eat dinner. And that felt like we were "going out." I didn't really make a lot of friends....

> First year, we had classes at 9 a.m.... Then at 3 p.m. [after classes], I would go straight to the library. Do reading. Later in the se-

mester, I would do less reading and more just sitting and talking to the "study buddies" or something. So, I probably would
just get dinner and then come back and stay ... until like 10:30
p.m. or 12 a.m., and then go home and start all over again ... I
would do that all week. Seven days a week. I would pick one day
a week where I would go out or something like that. Later in the
semester, I would be able to go to dinner or something like that.
But, I would make sure it would be one.[1]

Annie ended up in the top 5% of her law school class. There is no
doubt that she worked incredibly hard in law school. But she also fig-
ured out how she *learned* best in law school. And *that* was the key to her
success—not her long study hours.

My main point is that many law students attempt to compensate for
the high work load of law school by simply working longer hours, reading more cases or buying more outlines, hornbooks or supplements. The
strategy of working *more* may backfire in the end.[2] The most successful
law students balance law school with their lives outside of law school.
This means that in order to allow yourself that all-too-important free
time, you need to read and study efficiently and effectively. This book
will give you some strategies for how to accomplish this task.

B. The Socratic Method, or in Other Words: The Strange Way Classes Are Taught in Law School

Another unusual aspect of law school is the strange way that many
professors teach first-year classes. It is called the "The Socratic Method."
Socrates (470–399 b.c.) was a Greek philosopher who engaged in the
questioning of his students in order to uncover "truth." He sought to get
to the foundations of his students' and colleagues' views by asking con-

---

1. This transcript was part of a larger study I completed on how law students
read judicial opinions. The students signed waivers and agreed that their comments
could be published. *See* Leah M. Christensen, *"Legal Reading and Law School Success: An Empirical Study"* 30 Seattle U. L. Rev. 603 (2007); Leah M. Christensen, *Law
Students Who Learn Differently: A Narrative Case Study of Three Law Students with Attention Deficit Disorder (ADD),* 21 J.L. & Health 45 (2008).

2. Students may spend hours in the library devoting a *substantial amount* of time
reading their assignments. But the students may not be reading *efficiently.* Are they
getting distracted? Talking to friends? Falling asleep? If you are not reading efficiently,
you are not extracting the relevant information out of the cases. Further, you may
be exhausting yourself and this inhibits effective learning. Studying more is not always better. We will discuss how to study *efficiently* throughout the next several chapters.

tinual questions until a contradiction was exposed, thus proving the fallacy of the initial assumption. This became known as the Socratic Method.[3]

In 1973, there was a movie called *The Paper Chase* in which a famous actor, John Houseman, struck fear in the hearts of all current and future law students with his portrayal of a fierce law school professor who used the Socratic Method to torment his students. Although many law professors still use the Socratic Method, they like to think of it more as a tool to engage a large group of students in a classroom discussion.

The Socratic Method is supposed to be a conversation between the law professor and the law student. During this conversation, the professor and the student assist one another in finding the answers to difficult questions. In law school, it will often play out in the following manner. The professor will stand in the front of the room and call on a student. All students are expected to have read and briefed the case or cases before class. If you are called on, you are typically "on" for a series of questions from the professor. Your professor will ask you questions about the case assigned for that day, including basic questions like which court wrote the opinion, the facts, the result or conclusion of the court, etc. In addition, your professor may ask you additional questions about the reasoning of the case or perhaps about the policy that the court used to come to its conclusion. These are often more difficult questions. Law professors use the Socratic Method in order to develop your analytical thinking skills.

In college, your job as a student was to give information *back* to your professor. You read the material, the professor lectured about it — you memorized it and then gave it back to your professor in the form of a test. However, in law school, law professors hope to teach you to 'think like lawyer.' What does this mean? It means that we want to train your brain to read judicial opinions, extract the legally relevant rules from the case, and apply those rules to new situations or hypotheticals. 'Thinking like a lawyer' is really asking you to become adept at text-based reasoning and this new skill involves a very precise method of reading and analysis.

Most law students would be able to talk to their professor about a case they had just read *if* the discussion were one-on-one with their professor. But in the law school classroom, you are discussing the case in front of 75 to 100 of your law school peers. This *is* intimidating for any law student. Not many of us are adept initially at the skill of "thinking on our feet."

Some students dislike the Socratic Method because they feel that the professor is "hiding the ball." In other words, the professor knows what he or she wants the student to say — and will keep pressing the student until the student gives the 'right' answer. But the student has no idea

---

3. Ironically, Socrates was tried, convicted, and executed for corrupting the young.

what the professor wants her to say! So first-year law students often feel like they are being lead on a fishing expedition—except that they are the fish on the hook—and it's very uncomfortable.

Here's an example of the Socratic Method used in a typical Constitutional Law class:[4]

> Professor: Ms. Smith, suppose the California state legislature passes a statute banning "the making of any statements critical of the state government." You write an editorial for the student newspaper in which you state that the members of the legislature who voted for the statute thereby violated their oath to support the Constitution. You are prosecuted for violating the statute. Do you have a constitutional defense?
>
> Student: Yes.
>
> Professor: What is your defense?
>
> Student: It violates the First Amendment.
>
> Professor: But the First Amendment says that "*Congress* shall make no law ... abridging the freedom of speech, or of the press." Is the California legislature the same body as Congress?
>
> Student: No.
>
> Professor: So is the prosecution permissible?
>
> Student: Uh ... I'm not sure. I don't think so.
>
> Professor: Why not?
>
> Student: The First Amendment applies to the states.
>
> Professor: Yes it does. We'll talk later about a series of cases in which the U.S. Supreme Court ruled that when the Fourteenth Amendment prohibits any state from denying a person "liberty" without "due process of law," it implicitly includes within "liberty" most of those rights that are spelled out in the Bill of Rights. But I'm troubled by something else today. Why should a California court have to pay any attention to what's in the Federal Constitution?
>
> Student: Um ... Perhaps because of Article VI?
>
> Professor: I assume you are referring to the portion of Article VI that says: "This Constitution ... shall be the supreme Law of

---

4. This excellent example of the Socratic Method at work in a first-year Constitutional Law class is based upon Professor Michael C. Dorf, *How To Think Like a Lawyer: Advice to New and Prospective Law Students*, at http://writ.news.findlaw.com/dorf/20010822.html (last visited October 1, 2011).

the Land; and the Judges in every State shall be bound thereby, any Thing in the Constitution or Laws of any state to the Contrary notwithstanding."

Student: Yeah, that's it.

Professor: Well, that seems rather circular doesn't it? What if I showed you a different Constitution, also labeled "the Constitution of the United States." Suppose it has a provision that states: "The form of the government of the United States shall be a dictatorship." And suppose there is another provision: "This Constitution shall be the supreme law of the land; and everybody shall be bound by it, any thing in the constitution or laws of any state or other body to the contrary notwithstanding."

Tell me Ms. Smith, why is the Constitution printed in the front of your Constitutional Law casebook more authoritative than the "Dictatorship" Constitution?

Student: Umm....

And the conversation continues. "For every answer there is another question, until the exasperated students begin to feel like the point of the Socratic [M]ethod is to show how much smarter the professor is than they are."[5]

There is one additional aspect of the Socratic Method that may be very different than your previous classroom experiences prior to law school. Although law professors call their classes "lectures," they don't typically lecture in the sense of giving you information about what the reading or assignment actually means. Instead, the professor leaves you with many different possibilities of what a case or rule *might* mean. This drives law students crazy! Law students want to know the *right* answer. But often there is no right answer. Most frequently, the answer is: "it depends." Typically the answer depends on the *arguments* you can make about the rule as applied to the specific facts in front of you. If the facts change, then the outcome changes as well.

You will likely have law professors who use the Socratic Method, particularly during your first year. Proponents of the Socratic Method argue that it is not used to intimidate or "break down" new law students; instead, it is used for the very reason Socrates developed it in the first place: to develop critical thinking skills in students and enable them to approach the law as intellectuals.

However, you will hear stories about professors who *do* abuse this method of teaching—and unfortunately, some of these stories are true. Further, although the Socratic Method may be a useful teaching method-

---

5. Inspired by Michael C. Dorf, *supra* n.5.

ology for some law students, research has shown that it actually enhances the learning of only a small percentage of students, i.e., those students who tend to learn by listening (aurally).[6]

The good news is that there are more and more progressive law schools and law school professors that are adopting teaching methodologies *in addition* to the Socratic Method. These changes are good for all students—regardless of how you learn.

Consider the comments of Katie, a first-year law student. She was shocked by her Property professor's use of the Socratic Method.

> I am petrified every time I'm there [in class] ... And, so, I'm experiencing fear ... and ... anxiety ... It's hard because I can't believe I let someone get to me like that. And why does she get to me?
>
> It's beyond [the traditional Socratic Method].... I was yelled at one day for not being prepared when I was actually fully prepared. I actually didn't say the words that she wanted me to say it.
>
> [She said:] ... "I can't believe you would come here unprepared. I can't believe you would ... not brief a paper like I told you. You know I told you what you needed [to do] and you're not doing it."
>
> ... [F]or the rest of the day, you sit there and you think about it.
>
> ... So, when I go to that course, it's like, "[I]s she going to call on me? Am I not going to know the answer?"

Another student described his initial reaction to the Socratic Method.

> The first two weeks, I felt confident coming in that I was as smart as everybody else. I really didn't think that was going to be a problem. I still don't think that's a problem. I was definitely afraid of having to give an answer "on my feet." [T]here [were] a million different things they could ask you. And the social pressure around you. Like most people, I was terrified to go to class. The reading was fine. The material was fine. But going to class was horrible.
>
> ... I think it was the whole first year just stress in general. Some professors were tougher. And I looked back at my grades and I didn't do any better or worse really. So it was just a stressful environment.
>
> And it's all new. And I don't understand that. I don't understand why when people are new at something you would grill them off the bat.

---

6. This learning style will be discussed further in Chapter 3.

The Socratic Method has been described as "mystifying and patriarchal, persisting because of the large classes and professors too lazy to adopt new teaching methods."[7] It has been found to be particularly ineffective for the teaching of women, minorities, and students who learn differently.[8] Yet this teaching methodology persists in the cultures of many law schools.[9]

The purpose of this section is to prepare you for the reality that law school may, at times, be difficult. But remember, the Socratic Method is just one part of law school. And although it will feel like a *big* part of law school initially, it becomes a much smaller part of your legal education during your second and third years.

C. But Then Again, Professors Aren't All That Important in Law School. YOU Are Ultimately Responsible for Your Own Learning!

Despite the fact that the classroom environment in law school may be challenging, the good news is that your law school professors are only a small part of your overall learning experience. Now I'm sure you're asking: "Why am I paying all this money for law school if the professors aren't really teaching me anything?"

One of the biggest mistakes I see students make in their first semester of law school is assuming that their professors will teach them everything they need to know to become good lawyers. And most first-year law students believe they are in law school to learn the "law." Students are surprised that the focus of law school classes is not really on the substantive rules of law—particularly during the first year. Yes, you will certainly learn the rules of Civil Procedure and discuss basic rules of law in Property. You will also learn a basic legal vocabulary and analytical framework in your courses. And if you're lucky, some of your professors will also teach you some important lawyering *skills* that you can apply to the actual work you will do eventually as a lawyer.

Although your professors will introduce you to cases, rules and skills, you will actually learn the details of each of those things *on your own*.

---

7. Jennifer Jolly-Ryan, *Disabilities to Exceptional Abilities, Law Students with Disabilities, Nontraditional Learners, and the Law Teacher as Learner*, 6 Nev. L.J. 116, 124–125 (2005). *See also* Paula Gaber,"*Just Trying To Be Human in This Place:" The Legal Education of Twenty Women*, 10 Yale J. L. & Feminism 165 (1998) Alice K. Dueker, *Diversity and Learning: Imagining a Pedagogy Difference*, 19 N.Y.U. Rev. L. & Soc. Change 101 (1991–92); Paul L. Caron and Rafael Gely, *Taking Back the Law School Classroom: Using Technology to Foster Active Student Learning*, 54 J. Legal Educ. 551, 554 (2004).

8. Jolly-Ryan, *supra* n.8 at 125.

9. *Id.*

There is a lot of learning that goes on in law school *outside* of the classroom. And my main point is this: ultimately, *you* are responsible for your own learning.

So one of your main tasks in the first few weeks of law school is to determine *how* you learn most effectively. And this is particularly important for you if you learn differently. Chapter 2 of this book will talk about different learning styles and, hopefully, it will give you some insight about the way in which you learn best.

Quite simply, law school seeks to help you become a legal thinker, one who is largely self-taught. And in order to teach yourself the law well, you need to know how you learn and retain information most effectively. And you need to become an active learner. If you approach law school like you approached college, you may be surprised at the dismal results. Therefore, use the first weeks of law school to become a motivated and proactive learner.

D. Friends or Competitors? Get Ready for Competition in Law School!

I am always amazed to witness how law students change during their first year of law school. Students start out friendly and collegial and they transform into competitive and (often) unhappy individuals. This has been a reality in law school for a long time: legal education thrives on competition. With my own students, I notice that they are initially friendly and hopeful, and generally happy individuals. But the intense competition in law school tends to alter their initial excitement and optimism. There have been several empirical studies that have illustrated how law school takes a negative toll on law students' emotional well-being.[10] One of the most accurate quotes about peer relationships in law school is as follows: "Relationships forged in law school are like those forged in war: what you share with these people is unlike any experience any of you have had before."[11]

---

10. Lawrence Krieger found in one study that: "The incidence of clinically elevated anxiety, hostility, depression, and other symptoms among these students ranged from eight to fifteen times that of the general population." Lawrence Krieger, *Institutional Denial About the Dark Side of Law School, and Fresh Empirical Guidance for Constructively Breaking the Silence*, 52 J. Legal Educ. 112, 114 (2002).

See also, e.g. K. M. Sheldon and Lawrence S. Krieger, *Personality and Social Psychology Bulletin, Understanding the Negative Legal Effects of Legal Education on Law Students*, http://psp.sagepub.com/cgi/content/abstract/33/6/883 (last visited 09/12/11) (finding that "law school has a corrosive effect on the well-being, values, and motivation of students, ostensibly because of its problematic institutional culture." *Id.*

11. Corrine Cooper, *Letter to a Young Law Student*, 35 Tulsa L.J. 275, 276 (2000). *See also* the advice given to first-year law students by Professor Barbara Glesner Fines, at http://www.law.umkc.edu/faculty/profiles/glesnerfines/bgf-home.html (*citing* Cor-

You will learn a great deal from your law school colleagues. Some aspects of your peer relationships will be very positive and other aspects will be negative. I *can* promise you it will be an experience you will never forget.

How does the law school curriculum breed such intense competition? Consider the following reality: law schools are filled with talented and dedicated students—all of whom have excelled in the past. Now place all of those talented, driven students into a completely performance-oriented environment. What do I mean by performance-oriented? I mean that in law school, you are judged solely based upon your *performance* on law school exams—particularly during your first year. There are no bumps in your grade for good attendance or stellar class participation. There is no extra credit for coming to office hours or just being a wonderful and insightful student. Your entire grade in a course is determined by your performance on either one or two exams (or writing projects):[12] a midterm examination and a final examination. You (and everyone else around you) will work all semester and study like crazy. And, strangely, you will go into each exam with little idea about whether or not you *really* understand the material. The exam will last for three or four hours (depending on the amount of credit assigned for the course) and you will attempt to spill out an entire semester's worth of material during that single exam period. And the exams are graded anonymously. You will receive a final score on the exam which will determine your grade in the class.

And if that weren't enough pressure on new law students, almost all law schools use a mandatory curve during the first year (and often some variation of the curve in years 2 and 3 as well). A mandatory curve means that in any given class, law professors are only *allowed* to give a certain percentage or number of students an A, B or C. In addition, law professors are also required to give a certain number of grades *below* a particular letter grade—usually below a C or C–. In a class of eighty students, if only 10% of students can receive an A, this means that only a handful of students will get A's. Likewise, a certain percentage of students (likely around 10%) *must* receive grades below a C–. You are graded against your peers and *not* against an objective "good" answer. In other words, the poorer your peers do on an exam, the better your chances of grabbing one of the top grades.

Why does legal education persist in keeping the curve despite its perverse effects? I believe that the legal job market, in part, keeps the curve in place in legal education. If law school were pass-fail, or if there were no exams at all, then competition between students would be minimal.

---

rine Cooper, *Letter to a Young Law Student,* http://www.law.umkc.edu/faculty/profiles/glesnerfines/letter.htm (last visited 9/12/11)).

12. In your legal writing or first-year skills class, your grade will be determined largely by one or two writing projects (more or less "take home" exams).

Everyone would leave law school with their diplomas and be on their way. But the competition in law school is caused, in part, by the job market. There are fewer jobs than there are lawyers. In order for law firms (and other legal employers) to determine who they will hire, legal education has created a hierarchy. Some law firms or judges only interview students who are in the top 10% or 15% of their law school classes. This means that at least 85%–90% of all law students will not have the opportunity to interview for these more exclusive positions.[13] And everyone would *like* the opportunity to interview for these types of positions.

So after first semester grades come out each year, the relationships between students often change—for the worse. Certainly, some students choose wisely not to "buy into" the ranking game. But it is very hard to resist because everyone wants to do well in law school.

Your personal experience (and happiness) in law school may be related, in part, to how you react to the inherent competition in law school. Some students allow it to motivate them; others allow it to scare them. Some students let it anger them. Interestingly, each 1L class develops its own sense of competition; some 1L groups become very supportive communities and others become groups of intensively competitive individuals. You have *control* over how you deal with the competition. Law school competition will always be there but you do not have to buy into it. In other words, try to focus on *learning* in law school and not on simply getting the "A" in a class.[14]

There is no question that legal education needs to make some changes in how we assess and evaluate students. Our students should be much more to us than merely grades or class ranks. But until law schools become more humane environments, it may be up to students individually to protect themselves against the negative effects of competition in law school. By knowing how you learn most effectively, and by having a study plan during your first year, you can succeed in law school.

---

13. This is know as "OCI" or "On Campus Interviewing." In the fall of your second year, many of the elite larger employers (those that know that they will hire 20 summer associates every year), come to campus to interview students. Because everyone wants to interview with them, they restrict who they will interview to the top students. And this same phenomenon occurs with government jobs, i.e., District Attorney Offices or Defender Offices. These are just as coveted as private law firm experiences.

14. I completed an empirical study on whether law students who thrived on competition actually did better than law students who focused on learning. *See, e.g.,* Leah M. Christensen, *Predicting Law School Success: A Study of Goal Orientations, Academic Achievement and the Declining Self-Efficacy of our Law Students,* 33 J of L. & Psych. Rev. 57, 57 (2009).

Chapter 2

Succeeding in Law School by Knowing How *You* Learn Best: What Is Your Individual Learning Style?

Each of us has a different learning style (or a combination of learning styles). A "learning style" refers to how someone processes and retains new and difficult information. There is no single *right* way to learn— there are only different *ways* to learn. Professor Michael Hunter Schwartz advocates that law students need to become *expert* learners.[1] In other words, not only do you need to know how to learn generally, but you also need to know how you "personally learn best" and how you "prefer to learn."[2]

All law students will have different learning preferences—in other words, different students will prefer some methods of learning over others. An important point, however, is that law school tends to *favor* some learning styles over others. For example, a student who learns best by *listening* to her law professor lecture may find law school classes more meaningful than a student who prefers to *see* the concepts on PowerPoint slides or graphs. As we discussed in Chapter 1, the most common approach in law school teaching is the lecture format, combined with the Socratic Method. However, this method of teaching does not always work well for every law student *because not all students learn effectively within this lecture format.* Therefore, in order to maximize your learning in law school, you need to begin by understanding more about the way in which you learn.

---

1. Michael Hunter Schwartz, *Teaching Students to Be Self-Regulated Learners,* 2003 Mich. St. DCL L. Rev. 447 (Summer 2003).

2. *Id.*

A. The Basic Learning Styles

Your learning style refers to the way in which you like to approach new information. Each of us processes information in our own way, although we may share some learning patterns, preferences, and approaches. There are five basic learning styles but most of us use a combination of more than one.[3] In the order from most common to least common, the learning styles are typically described as follows:

(1)*Verbal Learners.* These students absorb information most effectively through written text.[4] The majority of law students fall into this category.

(2)*Visual Learners.* These students tend to be more right-brain, holistic learners who absorb information as a whole, rather than in parts, and who process information best when it is presented using pictures and diagrams.[5] Students who are visual learners tend to learn most effectively by using visual aids because they remember best what they read or see.

(3)*Oral (or Auditory) Learners.* These students tend to work best when they 'talk out' their ideas.[6] In addition, these students develop their ideas or process information by participating in class discussions. Further, many students find that they learn effectively when they walk around their apartments or study rooms 'talking' out difficult concepts.

(4)*Aural Learners.* These students might learn best by listening to lectures, class discussions, study group discussions, or tapes.[7] The student who tapes his or her lecture to listen to it again may be an aural learner.

(5)*Tactile and Kinesthetic Learners.* These students tend to learn material by touching and experiencing what they need to absorb.[8] In the law school environment, these students tend to learn most effectively by writing and taking good notes, and through "learning by doing," which might include role-playing, simulations, clinical experiences, or hands-on research exercises.

There are many different "learning style" inventories that can assess how you learn most effectively. It may be beneficial to you to spend some time filling out one of these detailed questionnaires. One example of a

---

3. There are many excellent articles and books analyzing law students' learning styles. *See* Michael Hunter Schwartz, Expert Learning for Law Students. 2nd edition. (Carolina Academic Press, 2008); *see also* Vernellia R. Randall, *The Myers-Briggs Type Indicator, First Year Law Students and Performance*, 26 Cumb. L. Rev. 63, 68–74 (1995); M.H. Sam Jacobson, *A Primer on Learning Styles: Reaching Every Student*, 25 Seattle U. L. Rev. 139, 142–143 (2001).

4. Anthony S. Niedwiecki, *Lawyers and Learning: A Metacognitive Approach to Legal Education*, 13 Widener L. Rev. 33, 34 (2006), n.6 (*citing* Jacobson, *supra* n.3 at 151).

5. *Jacobson, supra* n.3 at 152.

6. *Id.* at 154.

7. *Id.* at 155.

8. *Id.*

simplified "learning styles" questionnaire can be found in the chart on the next page. This chart asks a series of questions that relate to three of the most common learning styles: visual; auditory; and kinesthetic. For each question in the left-hand column, choose the response that best describes your learning preference. When you select an answer, give yourself a point for that column. The column with the highest total represents your primary processing style. The column with the second-most choices is your secondary style.[9]

If most of your responses fall within the first category, you may tend to be a visual learner. If most of your responses fall in the second column, you may prefer an auditory or aural learning style. And if most of your responses fall within the third category, you might prefer a tactile or kinesthetic learning style. Although this chart provides only a snapshot of an in-depth learning profile, the types of questions will allow you to begin thinking about your individual learning style.

After you have a sense of your learning style, consider how you might *use* your learning style to study more effectively in law school. For example, consider how the three different learning styles described above might affect how you read a case in preparation for class. If your primary learning style is visual, you might find yourself drawing pictures in the margins of the case as you read. Perhaps you *see* the facts of the case play out as if you are watching a movie.

In contrast, if your primary learning style is auditory, you may understand the text best when you *listen* to the words you read. Perhaps you carry on an internal conversation between yourself and the text, or you read the text aloud.

Or if your primary learning style is tactile/kinesthetic, you may find yourself using a highlighter to mark passages that are meaningful to you. You may also like to take notes or even walk around as you read so that you are both mentally and physically engaged in the learning task.

The main point of this exercise is to recognize that there are many different ways in which we learn. One key to academic success in law school is to understand your individual learning preferences so that you can maximize your learning in law school.

B. Applying Your Learning Style to Law School

In an ideal world, your professors in each of your law school classes would adapt their *teaching* styles to meet as many diverse learning styles as possible. However, you should be prepared to have several classes in

---

9. This learning inventory was taken from the Ageless Learner website, under the link for "Learning Style Assessment," at http://agelesslearner.com/assess/learning style.html (last visited on 01/06/12).

Learning Styles Questionnaire

1. When I try to **concentrate** …	I grow distracted by clutter or movement, and I notice things around me other people don't notice.	I get distracted by sounds, and I attempt to control the amount and type of noise around me.	I become distracted by commotion, and I tend to retreat inside myself.
2. When I **visualize** …	I see vivid, detailed pictures in my thoughts.	I think in voices and sounds.	I see images in my thoughts that involve movement.
3. When I **talk with others** …	I find it difficult to listen for very long.	I enjoy listening, or I get impatient to talk myself.	I gesture and communicate with my hands.
4. When I **contact people** …	I prefer face-to-face meetings.	I prefer speaking by telephone for serious conversations.	I prefer to interact while walking or participating in some activity.
5. When I **see an acquaintance** …	I forget names but remember faces, and I tend to replay where we met for the first time.	I know people's names and I can usually quote what we discussed.	I remember what we did together and I may almost "feel" our time together.
6. When I **relax** …	I watch TV, see a play, visit an exhibit, or go to a movie.	I listen to the radio, play music, read, or talk with a friend.	I play sports, make crafts, or build something with my hands.
7. When I **read** …	I like descriptive examples and I may pause to imagine the scene.	I enjoy the narrative most and I can almost "hear" the characters talk.	I prefer action-oriented stories, but I do not often read for pleasure.
8. When I **spell** …	I envision the word in my mind or imagine what the word looks like when written.	I sound out the word, sometimes aloud, and tend to recall rules about letter order.	I get a feel for the word by writing it out or pretending to type it.
9. When I **do something new** …	I seek out demonstrations, pictures, or diagrams.	I want verbal and written instructions, and to talk it over with someone else.	I jump right in to try it, keep trying, and try different approaches.
10. When I **assemble an object** …	I look at the picture first and then, maybe, read the directions.	I read the directions, or I talk aloud as I work.	I usually ignore the directions and figure it out as I go along.
11. When I **interpret someone's mood** …	I examine facial expressions.	I rely on listening to tone of voice.	I focus on body language.
12. When I **teach other people** …	I show them.	I tell them, write it out, or I ask them a series of questions.	I demonstrate how it is done and then ask them to try.
Total	Visual: _____	Auditory: _____	Tactile/Kinesthetic _____

law school where your professor teaches in a way that does not necessarily meet your individual learning needs. Therefore, you must be prepared to take on some of the responsibility for your own learning in law school. You will be more successful in law school if you know how *you* learn best. This is called "meta-cognition" and this involves "self-regulation of cognitive activities through monitoring and making appropriate adjustments" in one's learning.[10] In other words, you need to teach yourself *how* to learn.

If you know your learning style, you can adjust your approach to classroom learning and studying as you need to (depending on your professor). You can also challenge yourself to become more adept at learning in different ways, thereby becoming a more successful independent learner. For example, if you are a verbal learner, you probably will learn by reading your casebook and supplementary materials. If you are a visual learner, you will likely want to supplement your learning in the regular classroom by creating charts or other visual aids. You may make detailed, color-coded outlines or use other visual cues to assist your learning. If you are an aural learner, you may feel comfortable engaging in class discussions. You may also like to read aloud or become involved in several study groups so you can talk over the concepts in detail. If you are an auditory or aural learner, you will probably enjoy the lecture format of the law school classroom. You might consider asking your professor's permission to audiotape the lecture. Finally, if you are a tactile or kinesthetic learner, you may find yourself taking notes or using index cards, creating your own essay and multiple-choice questions. You may also find that you love law school most when you are working in a clinical program or engaged in experiential learning.

Remember that law school learning requires *more* than just memorization skills that may have worked for you before. You need to become more involved in your learning — devising a study plan that utilizes your learning strengths.

Of course, learning styles are also affected by personal characteristics such as intelligence and personality, which are least subject to change, and information processing (right brain/left brain functions), social interaction (motivation, values, and social milieu), and instructional preferences (e.g., light, temperature, sound, design), which can and do change.[11]

Although these specific issues of personal and social characteristics are beyond the scope of this book, they may indeed affect how you learn. For example, you will want to determine whether forming or joining a study group is a good use of your time. The answer depends on how you

---

10. Niedwiecki, *supra* n.4 at 35.
11. Jacobson, *supra* n.3 at 146–147.

learn best. Some students become distracted if they study with others. Other students find it incredibly helpful. For example, an oral learner, who learns by *participating* in discussions, or an aural learner, who learns by *listening* to discussions, may find study groups an ideal way to learn material. But this method may be less helpful for the verbal, visual, tactile, or kinesthetic learner. Deciding whether a study group is for you also depends on the social milieu in which you operate best and within which you are most comfortable. If you decide to form or join a study group, get to know your colleagues first and choose the group members with care. If they are of the same mindset and work ethic as you, you are more likely to have a successful study group experience.

Finally, knowing one's learning style is also integral to your ability to process the large volumes of information that you must digest in law school. Keep in mind that some courses give law professors more opportunities than others to meet the learning styles of their students, and often class size is an important factor in the number of active, experiential activities that will occur in a class. For example, you may find that you thrive in your Legal Research and Writing course, a required course in most law schools during the first year. These types of smaller classes that focus on learning skills (research and writing) in combination with substance can give professors more opportunities to teach to diverse learning styles. In addition, these types of classes often give law students the opportunity to learn in a variety of ways, such that the learning style of almost every student can be satisfied in these classes. For this reason, students who perhaps struggle in the more traditional law school classes might excel in these types of hands-on, skills classes.[12] If you find that you do like these smaller, experiential classes, you may want to select as many of these classes as possible throughout law school.

As you begin your first semester of law school (or as you begin a new year in law school), determine if you have a specific learning style. Consider which classes seem easier for you and which ones feel more challenging. For those classes that are more challenging, consider how you will supplement your learning in those classes. Perhaps you can buy review tapes or listen to lectures. Or maybe you can create note cards for each rule and diagram the rule with different colors. Perhaps you will create flowcharts to help you organize the information in a class. The key is to begin early and to have a plan for using your learning style to maximize your academic success. The remaining chapters of this book will provide you with specific ways you can maximize your learning strengths in the law school classroom and on exams.

---

12. These classes tend to be legal writing classes, law school clinical programs, trial advocacy, contract drafting, mediation, appellate advocacy, etc. In these classes, you focus on both doctrine and the skills of applying the doctrine to client-type situations.

Chapter 3

Legal Reading: The Key to Law School Success

Through my research, I have learned the importance of *how* law students read judicial opinions. Although many professors assume that students come to law school knowing how to read a case well—legal reading is very different than any other type of reading you have done before. The most successful law students read cases differently than law students who tend to struggle during their first year. In an empirical study on legal reading, I found that law students in the top 50% of their class read cases very differently than law students in the bottom 50% of their class. This Chapter will discuss the results of the legal reading study and the correlation between how a student reads a case and her law school GPA. My research has shown that legal reading is one of the *most* important skills to master in law school.

A. Legal Reading and Law School Success

You will spend thousands of hours in law school reading judicial opinions. Yet rarely will your law professors discuss *how* you should approach legal reading. Instead, law professors will assume that you are an excellent reader because you have obviously been successful as a student before getting into law school. However, legal reading is a particularly challenging task. In order for you to fully comprehend *legal* text, you need knowledge of legal terminology and an understanding of both case structure and legal theory.[1] One of my favorite quotes about legal reading comes from Scott Turow describing his first year at Harvard Law School. He compared reading cases to "something like stirring concrete with my eyelashes."[2]

---

1. Peter Dewitz, *Legal Education: A Problem of Learning From Text*, 23 N.Y.U. Rev. L. & Soc. Change 225, 226 (1997).

2. Mary A. Lundeberg, *Metacognitive Aspects of Reading Comprehension: Studying Understanding in Legal Case Analysis*, 22 Reading Res. Q. 407, 409 (1987) (*citing* Scott Turow, One L 30–31 (1978)).

Although many law students adapt quickly to legal reading, other students struggle with legal reading throughout law school. Sometimes struggling students simply take *longer* to read through the dense material found in a typical law school case. Other students read the cases quickly but they fail to take *out* of the case what the professor sees as the most important material or essence of the case. I believe that every law student can learn to be an effective legal reader. But like any other skill, you may need to practice *how* to read a legal case more effectively.

In 2007, I completed an empirical study that examined whether the way in which law students read a judicial opinion impacted their law school success.[3] Specifically, I questioned whether there was a correlation between the way in which first-year law students in the top 50% and bottom 50% of their class read a judicial opinion and whether the students' use of particular reading strategies impacted their law school grades. I found that even when students went through the same first-semester classes, the more successful law students read judicial opinions differently from those students who were less successful. Further, the study suggested there was a correlation between the reading strategies of the top law students and their first-semester grades.

Before you can improve your reading skills, however, you need to understand what happens in good readers' minds while they read. You probably do many of these things already. Good readers have developed *habits* when they read. We call these habits "strategies." Reading strategies help legal readers understand, connect to, and determine the importance of *what* they are reading. Let's first examine the three categories of reading strategies that are used most frequently.

B. Three Types of Reading Strategies

There are three main types of reading strategies: (1) default reading strategies; (2) problematizing reading strategies; and (3) rhetorical reading strategies.[4]

The first type of reading strategy is called a *default* reading strategy. Default reading strategies represent the basic strategies that any of us use

---

3. Leah M. Christensen, *Legal Reading and Law School Success: An Empirical Study,* 30 Seattle U. L. Rev. 603, 603 (2007).

4. Dorothy Deegan (Evenson), one of the first researchers to examine how law students read legal text, used the results of her reading study to construct three categories or types of reading strategies: problematizing strategies, default strategies, and rhetorical strategies. Dorothy H. Deegan, *Exploring Individual Differences Among Novices Reading in a Specific Domain: The Case of Law,* 30 Reading Res. Q. 154 (1995), at 161. In the present study, I adopted these categories to define and analyze the way in which my students read a judicial opinion.

to move through legal text, including paraphrasing, rereading, noting certain structural elements of text, underlining text and making margin notes.[5] The research has shown that when readers use default strategies, they move through the text in a linear progression.[6] Dorothy Deegan Evenson, an expert on legal reading, describes default reading strategies as follows:

> Typically, readers would restate or paraphrase portions of the information, often underlining and/or making margin notes. What differentiated these moves from the ones associated with [other] strategies was the unproblematic nature of the process. In other words, these verbalizations were not specifically initiated from or tied to explicit questions or hypotheses.[7]

Beginning readers tend to rely more heavily on default reading strategies because these strategies are both accessible and familiar. If you are new to legal reading, it makes sense for you to begin reading by underlining or highlighting the opinion because these are the same types of reading strategies that you used earlier in your academic careers.

In the reading study, readers used default reading strategies when they moved through the text in a linear progression.[8] For example, readers used default strategies when they "paraphrased" or "underlined" text. Default strategies also included "making margin notes," "noting aspects of structure" and "highlighting" text.

The following example illustrates a student using default reading strategies as the student read through the case for the first time. For the purposes of my study, I had the students perform a "think aloud," where the study participants would read a portion of the opinion out loud, and then stop and reflect upon what they were thinking at that point in their reading. The regular text is the student's thoughts or "think aloud." The highlights and margin comments indicate which reading strategy the student was using.

Ok. So it is a disciplinary proceeding action, —— noting important detail

and the main issue is the attorney's failure to dis- ┐

close material information that was known to ┘ —— noting aspect of structure

him. Um—and it was directly adverse to his —— paraphrasing

client's position. He didn't advise the client

hrasing— and he didn't advise the court and so there was

a public reprimand and admonishment. Um— —— noting factual detail

5. Dewitz, *supra* n.1 at 228–229; Deegan, *supra* n.5 at 161.
6. Deegan, *supra* n.4, at 160.
7. *Id.* at 161.
8. Deegan, *supra* n.4, at 160–161.

skimming —— just briefly skimming the, um, keynotes, the —— noting aspect of structure

paraphrasing —⎡ Attorney and Client, failure to disclose au-
              ⎢ thority in the Rules of Professional Conduct
              ⎣ there would be Rule 1.4 and 3.3. I'm skimming —— skimming

with that.[9]

These twelve moves represented the use of default reading strategies.[10]

The second type of reading strategy is called a *problematizing* reading strategy.[11] Problematizing reading strategies contain techniques to help readers solve *problems* within the text. "Readers use problem formation strategies to set expectations for a text. They ask themselves questions, make predictions, and hypothesize about developing meaning."[12] Prior research in reading has found that problematizing strategies involve "strategic behavior" on the part of the reader, in that the reader's behavior can be described as purposeful.[13] Various studies have associated the use of problematizing strategies with high performing student readers and expert/lawyer readers.[14] These readers asked questions; they talked back to the text, made predictions, hypothesized about meaning, and connected with the overall purpose of their reading.[15]

The following provides an example of a law student reading using problematizing strategies. Once again, the regular text in the paragraph below represents the student's thoughts about the case. The highlights and margin comments indicate the particular reading strategy used by the student. And the italicized text is the actual text of the case.

connecting with prior text —⎡ So now I'm just going to go back to where they
                            ⎣ started talking about the facts. Because I'm more ⎤
                              concerned about the videotape as I think that's ⎥—hypoth•
                              going to be an issue. *Prior to the client's initial* ⎦

---

9. Transcript of Interview with Student 105 at 1 (on file with the author).

10. Deegan, *supra* n.4 at 161 (*citing* R.J. Spiro, B. Bertram & W. Brewer, eds., *Constructive Processes in Prose Comprehension and Recall*, in Theoretical Issues in Reading Comprehension 1, 256 (1980)). Deegan relied on Spiro's theory that "the default assignment process … probably forms the basis for a large part of construction in comprehension." *Id.*

11. Deegan, *supra* n.4, at 161. In the present study, I adopted these categories to define and analyze the way in which my students read a judicial opinion *See also* Michael Pressley & Peter Afflerbach, *Verbal Protocols of Reading: The Nature of Constructively Responsive Reading* 1–14, 119–40 (1995).

12. Dewitz, *supra* n.1, at 228–229 (describing his definition of Deegan's problematizing strategies).

13. Deegan, *supra* n.4, at 160.

14. See Deegan, *supra* n.4, at 163–165; Laurel Currie Oates & Anne Enquist, Legal Writing Handbook: Analysis, Research, and Writing 37 (4th ed., Aspen Publishers, 2006) at 159; Lundeberg, *supra* n.2 at 417.

15. Oates, *supra* n.14, at 159–160.

hearing, and before the client met with or hired a
lawyer, the client was advised by videotape of his
evaluating ——*rights.* So this is curious. Um—I guess it's so un-
voicing confusion ——clear to me. Apparently at the first appearance, ⎤
⎬ synthesizing
the client viewed the videotape and pled guilty. ⎦
But I guess it's a little unclear and apparently he —— evaluating
distinguishing ——wasn't represented at that time.[16]

Note how the student is actively working through the text—grappling with the potential legal issues in the opinion.

Finally, the third type of reading strategy is called a *rhetorical* reading strategy.[17] While using rhetorical reading strategies, readers move through the text in an evaluative manner or in way that synthesizes what is being read with the reader's own experiences.[18] Rhetorical strategies "represented points where the reader engaged in the kind of practices where the reader took a step beyond the text itself. They [were] concerned with constructing a rhetorical situation for the text, trying to account for the author's purpose, context and effect on the audience."[19]

In the study, law students used rhetorical reading strategies when they examined text in an "evaluative" way or when they moved outside of the text "into the realm of […] personal knowledge."[20] In my study, I categorized the following moves as rhetorical: "evaluating," "connecting with prior experience," "contextualizing" and "connecting with purpose."[21]

This last example illustrates a law student using rhetorical reading strategies. Note in particular how the reader evaluated the case and actively read the case to prepare for a client interview.[22]

evaluating ⎡ Here we have a legal professional who is sup-
⎢ posed to be giving the best information to his
⎣ client to make informed decisions and that's —— evaluating
the basis for this rule. And so in our case, be- —— connecting to purpose
cause the client may be coming into us, we have —— connecting with purpose

---

16. Transcript of Interview with Student 109 at 3 (on file with the author).

17. Deegan, *supra* n.4, at 161.

18. *Id.*

19. *Id.* (citing C. Haas & L. Flower, *Rhetorical Reading Strategies and the Construction of Meaning*, 39 College Composition and Communication 167, 176 (1988)).

20. *Id.* at 161.

21. *Id.*

22. I asked the study participants to read the case with a specific purpose in mind: prepare for a client interview. When students used this purpose in their reading, I coded their move as "connecting with purpose" which is a rhetorical reading strategy.

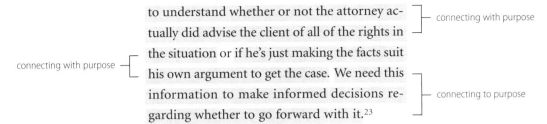

to understand whether or not the attorney ac-   ⎤ — connecting with purpose
tually did advise the client of all of the rights in   ⎦

connecting with purpose ⎤ the situation or if he's just making the facts suit
                        ⎦ his own argument to get the case. We need this   ⎤
information to make informed decisions re-   ⎦ — connecting to purpose
garding whether to go forward with it.[23]

These examples illustrated the three types of reading strategies used by law students in the study: (1) default reading strategies; (2) problematizing reading strategies; and (3) rhetorical reading strategies. The next section of this Chapter will explore the study background and results in more detail.

C. The Legal Reading Study: Background and Results

My study examined the way 24 first-year law students read a legal case using these three types of reading strategies. Each of the students volunteered to participate in the study. Specifically, I asked the law students to read a judicial opinion authored by the Indiana Supreme Court, *In Re Thonert*, 733 N.E.2d 932 (Ind. 2000).[24] The students were instructed to read the text of the case aloud, stop every sentence or two and tell me what they were thinking. In psychological research, this type of activity is called a 'think aloud.' I recorded the students as they read and had the recordings transcribed.

Before I had the students read the opinion, I instructed the students to read the case with a particular purpose in mind:

> **Read the following legal text assuming that you are a practicing attorney and that you are reading the opinion to prepare for a meeting with a client who has a case that is similar to the facts of case you are reading.**

I gave them this specific purpose because I wanted to find out whether reading with the purpose of preparing for a client meeting changed the way in which students read the case.[25]

---

23. Transcript of Interview with Student 105 at 4 (on file with the author).

24. The opinion, *In Re Thonert*, was a *per curiam* decision by the Indiana Supreme Court reviewing a disciplinary proceeding against an attorney. *In Re Thonert*, 733 N.E. 2d. 932, 932 (Ind. 2000).

25. I did not give the students any particular facts to suggest their client's issue. I left the client's legal problem purposefully vague.

The introductory portion of *In Re Thonert* is printed below.[26] You may want to skim the case yourself to see how *you* read the judicial opinion before you consider the study results.

---

733 N.E.2d 932

Supreme Court of Indiana.
In the Matter of Richard J. THONERT.

No. 02S00-9902-DI-151.
Aug. 22, 2000.

Disciplinary proceeding was brought against attorney, in which Disciplinary Commission and attorney entered Statement of Circumstances and Conditional Agreement for Discipline. The Supreme Court held that attorney's failure to disclose to appellate tribunal controlling authority which was known to him, and had not been disclosed by opposing counsel, that was directly adverse to his client's position, and to advise client of the adverse authority, warranted public reprimand and admonishment.

So ordered.

* * *

PER CURIAM.

The respondent in this attorney disciplinary matter is charged with failing to disclose to an appellate tribunal controlling authority known to him, not disclosed by opposing counsel, that was directly adverse to his client's position. He also failed to advise his client of the adverse authority when his client was contemplating his legal options.

This matter is presented to this Court upon the Disciplinary Commission's and the respondent's *Statement of Circumstances and Conditional Agreement for Discipline,* entered pursuant to Ind.Admission and Discipline Rule 23(11)(c), in resolution of this matter. That agreement is before us now for approval. We note that our jurisdiction of this matter derives from the respondent's admission to the practice of law in this state in 1974.

The parties agree that the respondent represented a client charged with operating a motor vehicle while intoxicated. Prior to the client's initial hearing and before the client met with or hired the respondent, the client was advised by videotape of his rights. He pleaded guilty to the charge, and the matter was set for sentencing hearing. Prior to that hearing, the client met with the respondent to discuss the possibility of withdrawing his guilty plea. During their meeting, the respondent told the client of another criminal case, *Snowe v. State,* 533 N.E.2d 613 (Ind.Ct.App.1989), in which the respondent had prevailed on appeal for the defendant. He provided a copy of the Indiana Court

---

26. The full text of the opinion can be found in Appendix A at the back of this book.

of Appeals decision to his new client. The respondent agreed to represent the client for $5,000, which the client paid.

Snowe also involved a prerecorded videotaped televised advisement of rights, but the record in that case failed to indicate whether the defendant had ever viewed the tape advising him of his rights. Further, the opinion held that a trial court judge cannot rely solely on displaying a videotape advisement of rights, but instead must also determine whether the defendant knows of and understands his rights, the nature of the charge or charges against him, the full import of the rights waiver in his guilty plea, and the sentencing possibilities for the charges against him. *Snowe,* 533 N.E.2d at 617.

At the client's initial hearing, it was established that he had viewed the videotape, that the videotape advised him of his rights and the sentencing possibilities under the charges filed against him, that he understood the charge against him and his rights as explained in the videotape, and that he voluntarily waived those rights and pleaded guilty.

On May 30, 1996, the respondent entered an appearance on behalf of the client and filed a motion to withdraw the guilty plea. The trial court denied the motion without hearing. The respondent appealed that ruling, alleging that his client had a right to withdraw the plea because, due to the absence of counsel at the time he entered it and the fact that the record did not reflect that the trial court properly examined the client as to waiver of his rights, the client had not made it knowingly, intelligently, or voluntarily. The respondent further argued that the client had a right to a hearing on his motion to withdraw the plea.

The respondent represented the defendant in *Fletcher v. State,* 649 N.E.2d 1022 (Ind.1995). In that case, this Court addressed the questions that the respondent raised in his client's case. The ruling in *Fletcher* was adverse to the arguments that the respondent offered on appeal of his client's case. The respondent had served as counsel of record for defendant Fletcher in the appeal before this Court. This Court's ruling in *Fletcher* was issued on May 1, 1995, over one year before the respondent filed his appeal on behalf of the client. In his appellate brief filed on behalf of the client, the respondent failed to cite to *Fletcher* or argue that its holding was not controlling authority in the client's case. The respondent also failed to argue that the holding in *Fletcher* should be changed or extended. Although he advised his client of the *Snowe* case, he failed to advise him of *Fletcher* or explain any impact *Fletcher* might have on his case. Opposing counsel had not previously disclosed *Fletcher* to the Court of Appeals.[27]

* * *

The results of the study were very interesting. I found that there were significant differences between how the Higher Performing Students

---

27. *In re Thonert* 733 N.E.2d 932, 932–933 (Ind. 2000).

(HP)[28] and the Lower Performing Students (LP) read the text.[29] The HP students spent more time engaged in problematizing and rhetorical strategies, and significantly less time engaged in default reading strategies. In contrast, the LP students spent the majority of their time using default strategies, and only a small percentage of their time using problematizing and rhetorical reading strategies.

Consider the following graph, which illustrates the results of the study.

Table 1: Results of the Christensen Study

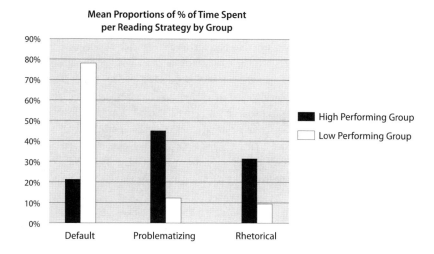

The HP students spent only 20% of their reading time engaged in default strategies. In contrast, the HP students spent 46% of their reading time engaged in problematizing strategies and 33% in rhetorical strategies. Accordingly, the HP readers spent almost 80% of their reading time using problematizing and rhetorical reading strategies.

In contrast, the LP students spent the majority of their reading time, i.e., almost 77%, using default strategies. LP students spent only 13% of their reading time engaged in problematizing strategies and 10% of their reading time using rhetorical reading strategies.

These results showed that although the most successful law students used all three types of reading strategies, they spent much more of their reading time engaged in high-level, analytical reading, i.e., problematiz-

---

28. The Higher Performing Students (HP) were in the Top 50% of their law school class.

29. The Lower Performing Students (LP) were in the Bottom 50% of their law school class.

ing and rhetorical reading strategies. In contrast, LP students failed to utilize the higher-level reading strategies to the same extent; instead, LP students spent most of their reading time using default reading strategies.

The other significant finding in this study was a statistical correlation between the way in which the law students read, i.e., their use of reading strategies, and their law school GPA.[30] Notably, there was no correlation between undergraduate GPA (UGPA) and LSAT scores with the use of any particular reading strategy. In other words, when students entered law school with high UGPA and strong LSAT scores, these scores did not appear to correlate to high grades in law school.

However, there *was* a correlation between law students' use of problematizing and rhetorical reading strategies and law school grades. In other words, the more time a student spent using problematizing and rhetorical reading strategies, the higher the student's law school, first-semester GPA. Therefore, in my study, the way in which a student read a judicial opinion was a more accurate predictor of law school success than the student's undergraduate GPA or LSAT scores.

These results are important: even if you didn't come to law school with high undergraduate grades or a high LSAT score, you can still achieve success in law school by learning how to read like the most successful law students. The next section of this chapter will discuss in greater detail how the HP law students read differently than the LP students.

D. What Did the Successful Law Students Do Differently?

The HP law students read differently in four distinct ways. First, the most successful law students "connected with the purpose" of the case reading more frequently. Second, the most successful law students established the "context" of the case before they began to read. Third, the most successful law students worked actively to "resolve their confusion" before they moved on to another section of the case. Fourth, and finally, the most successful law students did not overuse any one reading strategy—instead, they utilized all three types of reading strategies as they moved through the text.

This section will explore more specifically how the HP readers approached case reading.

---

30. Pearson *r* correlations were used to determine the correlation, if any, between grades, LSAT scores, and reading strategies. Law school GPA was correlated with the use of problematizing (.646), rhetoric (.632) and default strategies (-.710), all at the .001 level. There were insignificant correlations between the use of reading strategies and UGPA and LSAT scores.

1. The HP Law Students Connected with a Purpose

The HP law students who connected with the purpose of preparing for a client meeting were more engaged and active in their case reading than the law students who read without noting a specific purpose. The HP students as a group connected to the purpose of their reading more frequently than the LP students. I asked each of the students in the study to read the judicial opinion as if they were a practicing lawyer who was preparing for a client meeting. Those students who internalized this purpose seemed to do several things very differently as they read: first, they read the facts of the opinion more closely (to determine whether their client's case might be analogous to the facts of the opinion); second, they noted the defendant's punishment (to inform their client of potential consequences); and third, the students noted the procedural posture of the case more accurately (understanding that the court was reviewing a mutual agreement).

Consider the following examples from the reading transcripts of two law students as they connected to the purpose of the reading, i.e., reading the case to prepare for a client meeting. For these examples, the bolded text illustrates the students' responses and the italicized text is the language from the actual opinion.

A female in the HP group (who was in the top 3% of her law school class) began her case reading by taking note of her overall purpose.

> **"All right. I am a practicing attorney and I'm reading the opinion to prepare for a meeting with a client and they have a case that is similar to the facts that I am reading."**[31]

About mid-way through the facts of the opinion, she once again related her reading to her purpose, i.e., analyzing the case to counsel her client:

> **"So going back to** *Fletcher v. State.…* **So** *Fletcher,* **if we're basing our arguments on** *Fletcher,* **that is not good for our client's case."**[32]

This student connected with purpose consistently throughout her reading, assuming the role of an attorney as she moved through the text.

In contrast, here's an example of a student in the LP group who failed to connect with the given purpose during any part of his case reading. As a result, this student was more distracted as he read and he appeared to be overwhelmed by the details of the text.

> *On May 30, 1996, the respondent entered an appearance on behalf of the client and filed a motion to withdraw the guilty plea.* **So I'm going to write that in my facts. "30, May." I don't like all the numbers next to each other so I put "May" after.** *The respon-*

---

31. Transcript of Interview with Student 134 (on file with the author).

32. *Id.* at p. 2.

dent entered an appearance on behalf of the client and filed a motion to withdraw. Attempt to withdraw guilty plea. The trial court denied the motion without hearing. **Ok. So — I'm going to put that up in procedural history. I'm going to put it above the appellate court. Trial court denied motion. And I'm going to make a line connecting them. Ok. Now I'm thinking what I'd like to purchase on eBay. I actually stopped drafting my briefs on the computer because I would become distracted by eBay. Ok.**[33]

Reading the case as if he were a practicing attorney (or assuming any other active role) may have helped this student focus more on the details of the case. After his first semester of law school, this student was in the bottom 10% of his law school class.[34]

2. Successful Law Students Established the Context of Case

The second factor that influenced the way top law students read a case was that the HP students paid close attention to the context of the case both before and during their case reading. By in large, students in the HP group *contextualized* the opinion more frequently than LP students. Specifically, the HP law students noted which court wrote the decision, the year of the decision, and the historical/legal significance of the decision as they read the case.

Table 2: Amount of Time Spent Contextualizing

Table 2 illustrates that the HP students as a group noted the context of the case close to 68 times during their reading protocols (almost five times

---

33. Transcript of Interview with Student 100 at 6 (on file with the author).

34. Certainly there could be several reasons why this student struggled in law school. It is certainly possible that this student may have had an undiagnosed learning disability. However, this student struggled *at least* in part because of the way in which he read his cases.

per student); in contrast, the LP students as a group noted the context of the opinion only eight times total (or less than one time per student).

For example, the HP students noted that the case was decided by the Indiana Supreme Court; that the case was a recent decision; and that it was a *Per Curiam* decision.[35]

In reviewing the student protocols, I noticed that when law students took the time to understand the context of the case *before* they began to read, they improved their overall comprehension of the case. The case had context. The students understood whether or not it had precedential value as compared to other cases.

Consider the following examples taken from the student protocols as they related to the context of the opinion.

A female in the HP group (in the top 10% of her class at the end of her first semester) began her reading by noting the context of the case.

> **All right this case is in Indiana and it comes from the north-eastern quarter** *in the matter of Victor H. S. 02S009902 VI 151. The Supreme Court of Indiana.* **So this would be the highest court.**[36]

Similarly, another female participant (also in the top 10% of her class) began her reading as follows:

> **Ok. This case is from the Supreme Court of Indiana. August 22, 2000.** *It's in the matter of Richard J. Thonert. Disciplinary proceeding was brought against attorney in which disciplinary commission and attorney entered statement of circumstances and conditional agreement for discipline.* **It sounds a little juicy. Attorney on trial.**[37]

In contrast, a male in the LP group jumped right into the text of the opinion without noting anything about the date, type or subject matter of the opinion. Instead, this student spent his time highlighting and noting the structural components of the opinion as opposed to the deeper substantive issues. As this student read, he became very confused about what was actually happening in the case.

> **The first thing is I would take out—I would take out my green marker, which means [holding] and I very rarely use it; it only**

---

35. A *Per Curiam* decision is a ruling issued by an appellate court with multiple judges in which the decision rendered was made by the court acting as a whole, anonymously, as compared to a more typical judicial opinion which is authored by a named judge or justice. *Per Curiam* decisions tend to be brief in length, and usually deal with relatively non-controversial issues. The designation is stated at the beginning of the opinion.

36. Transcript of Interview with Student 103 (on file with the author).

37. Transcript of Interview with Student 102 (on file with the author).

means holding and I would mark—the Supreme Court would get a thick line and then I would try to break up the different phrases of that sentence so that it would be easier to pick up with the explanation, but it's all in one sentence and it's kind of confusingly written. So the Supreme Court, and then one line is:*Held that attorney's failure to disclose appellate tribunal controlling authority, which was known to him* and then I would be done at this comment. I would put a thick line through and because connecting word—*had not been disclosed by opposing counsel* and I'd stop at that comment again.*That was directly adverse to his client's position.* I'd stop at that comment again.[38]

This student continued to skim and mark the case as he read it—spending a great deal of time highlighting the text. However, the student's actions seemed to overshadow his real understanding of the case. At the conclusion of his case reading, the student was confused as to what the attorney did wrong. Although it was fairly clear in the opinion that the attorney would be sanctioned for his breach of the rules of professional responsibility, the student may not have grasped this important conclusion of the court. He ended his case reading as follows:

Right now I'm thinking to myself, I don't know exactly what happened here. I know that they didn't tell. Something has not been disclosed to the client. I'm not exactly positive what that thing is. I'm still not sure what this adverse authority or counsel is.[39]

Although this student seemed to work very hard to understand the text—highlighting and noting details in the text, the student failed to grasp a larger sense of what the case was about. This student may have improved his comprehension of the case by taking a few moments before diving into the text to note the context of the case, including the type of opinion, the procedural posture of the case and the court that rendered the opinion. Establishing the context of any case you read is a simple but important technique to use whenever you begin to read a new case.

3. Successful Law Students Resolved Their Confusion before They Moved on to the Next Paragraph in the Case

Another interesting difference between the HP and LP students was how they handled their confusion as they read. Almost every student in the study was confused at some point in time during their reading. This happens to practically everyone when they read an unfamiliar case. But what I noticed in particular is that the HP students dealt with their confusion

---

38. Transcript of Interview with Student 114 (on file with the author).
39. *Id.*

very differently than the LP students. The HP students resolved their confusion early on. In other words, when the HP students got stuck, they would page back and figure out the answer to their question before moving on to the next paragraph. In contrast, the LP students tended to leave their questions hanging. Instead of figuring out the answers, the LP students simply moved on through the text hoping that the opinion would eventually make sense in the end.

Let's turn to a specific example. A male participant in the LP group began his reading protocol by making an incorrect assumption about the subject matter of the case. Although the introductory portion of the opinion was indeed confusing (the headnotes[40] characterized the case as involving an attorney-client issue), the opinion clarified early on that the legal issue in the case was actually an attorney disciplinary issue. Like many of the students who read the *In Re Thonert* case for the first time, this LP student began his case reading thinking that the central issue dealt with the attorney-client privilege.

> **This is an issue of—I'm seeing this as an attorney-client privilege. Maybe professional conduct rules kind of a case? The second note here is—the keynote is Attorney and Client.[41]**

As the student read a few more paragraphs, he questioned whether the case really dealt with the attorney-client privilege. The student had a hunch that the case was really about the attorney's breach of the rules of professional conduct. However, instead of going back to re-read the text to confirm this hunch, the student simply kept reading on hoping that his confusion would eventually resolve. However, this didn't happen. The student ended his reading protocol just as confused as he began it. Consider the end of his reading protocol.

> *It is therefore, ordered that the respondent, Richard J. Thonert, is hereby reprimanded and admonished for his violations of Professional Conduct.* **That is—it's not clear to me quite what the outcome is at this point other than to say that whatever the agreement the parties have reached and discipline that's called for from that agreement is what the appellate court agrees should happen. Okay, I'm going to read on.** *The Clerk of this court is directed to provide notice of this order ... and to provide the Clerk of the United States Court of Appeals for the Seventh Circuit. The Clerk of each*

---

40. A headnote is a short synopsis and/or excerpt from a court's written opinion on a specific point of law. The headnote is created by the publisher of the case, for example, Westlaw, and aids the reader in understanding isolated segments of the court's opinion. Additionally, headnotes from all decisions (published by Westlaw) are organized by a key number system that assist people in doing research.

41. Transcript of Interview with Student 113 at 1 (on file with the author).

> *of the United States District Courts in this state and the Clerks of*
> *the United States Bankruptcy Court in this state with the last known*
> *address of respondent as reflected in the records of the Clerk. Costs*
> *are assessed against the respondent.* **So with regard to the actual**
> **punishment, I'm assuming that there was some actual public**
> **reprimand. What that is I am not exactly sure. It's also as the**
> **punishment costs are assessed to the attorney. And that was it.**[42]

In reviewing this student's think-aloud, I found that he really struggled with being able to choose between relevant and irrelevant information within the text. This student seemed to believe that all the details in the text were equally important. In addition, this student spent 68.65% of his reading time using default reading strategies and he paraphrased the text most of the time. The student evaluated the text only two times during his reading protocol and he failed to connect with the purpose of the text at all. In short, the student never gained a full understanding of what was occurring in the case. And it became clear to me that the way in which this student read cases affected his law school performance overall. This law student's GPA was in the bottom 2% of his class after the first semester of law school. Further, this student *knew* that his reading strategies were not working for him. He felt very frustrated after his first semester of law school. In a follow-up interview, the student described his method of reading cases as follows:

Student:	Ah—Ideally, I try and read cases twice. Realistically that doesn't happen as often as I'd like it to. My goal is through the first reading to get to understand what the case is about. Who the main players are? To basically—to understand the case and to get an idea of what I would need to put together in a basic brief. If I can't read for the second time, … I try and skim through and pick out perfect details …
Interviewer:	Has this been successful for you?
Student:	Arguably, no. No.
Interviewer:	Where do you feel you get stuck?
Student:	Just it's very time-consuming. I feel like I'm a slow reader and even to read it once and to go back through even to skim it for the details that I'm looking for, I feel that I'm not getting through the material as quickly as I would like to and to grasp as much as I would like. To retain as much. The retention.[43]

---

42. *Id.*
43. *Id.* at 6.

This student needed to figure out how to read cases more efficiently and effectively. It is quite possible that this student may have had a learning disability or may have simply needed to learn additional reading strategies to help him read faster and retain more information. There is no doubt that this student was spending a great deal of time and effort reading cases for class, but he was not extracting the *right* information out of the cases. In other words, the student was not seeing the deeper legal arguments within the court's opinion. It is quite possible that using different reading strategies would have improved this student's classroom and exam performance.

In contrast, consider the following example that illustrates how a student in the HP group resolved his confusion. Note how this student really stuck with the legal text until he understood the key facts and concepts. This HP student evaluated the text and related what he read back to his own personal experience (a rhetorical reading strategy). Further, he was actively engaged in "talk[ing] back to the text."[44] As a result, this student appeared to have a better comprehension of the court's decision overall.

> **Boy, that first paragraph was a little thick for me. It sounds like there is a lot going on. It sounds like neither party was forthcoming with a controlled issue.** *Failure to disclose to appellate tribunal controlling authority, which was known to him.* **So he had knowledge and didn't disclose it. It sounds like he is in trouble. There are about four different keynotes. All of them are titled attorney and client. I'm just going to read two of them. Because if I read too many of them it sort of taints my reading. And I'd rather just—so this is keynote.**[45]

Note how this HP student was actively involved in the text. His reading continued.

> **Ok. So here, this is probably the third or fourth time that I read this sentence. And now, it's finally clear what's going on. So Thonert, he is a pro se for the respondent because he is an attorney himself and it's an attorney disciplinary action. He was involved in an appeal and he had information that's pertinent in his client's case. The opposing counsel didn't reveal it. So, he had an ethical duty to review it. That's the issue. It's probably— I'm just going to speculate about the matter—how big of a wrap are we going to give this guy because he didn't adhere to ethical standards to the profession. And I'm going to assume that they're talking about the facts. This accusation that he didn't disclose information, that it was known, and that the only con-**

---

44. Elizabeth Fajans & Mary Falk, *Against the Tyranny of the Paraphrase: Talking Back to Texts*, 78 Cornell L. Rev. 163, 163 (1993).

45. Transcript of Interview with Student 102 at 1 (on file with the author).

siSeration the court could find is what is the appropriate punishment. Oh, here is another top to it. He also failed to advise
his client of the adverse authority when his client was contemplating his legal options.... So here is a case in which omissions
of the lawyer are represented.[46]

This student re-read various parts of the case to make sure he understood the facts before moving on. In addition, although this student took
the same amount of time overall to read the opinion as the LP student
above, his effort paid off. This HP student finished the opinion having
an excellent understanding of the case. Further, this student ended up
in the top 10% of his law school class at the end of the first semester.

4. The Overuse of Default Strategies

Finally, I noted that LP students as a group relied too heavily on default reading strategies which included things like highlighting text, paraphrasing, or writing notes in the margin. In contrast, the HP law students
as a group used a variety of reading strategies throughout their reading
protocols. Table 3 illustrates the amount of time each group spent using
default reading strategies.

Table 3: HP and LP Students Using Default Strategies

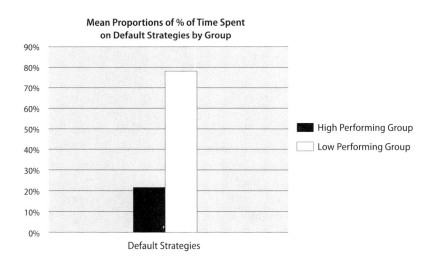

The LP law students (as a group) spent almost 78% of their reading time
using default reading strategies. Although we all use default reading strategies at some point in time when reading new material, never going *beyond*

---

46. *Id.* at 2.

default reading strategies does not work in law school. Law professors want you to go deeper into the case. The students in the LP group approached the case as if there were simply 'filling in the blanks' of a standard case brief: facts, issue, holding, and reasoning. Although you certainly need to be able to articulate the facts, issue and holding of any case, you also need to understand how the case relates to the other cases you've read in the class. For what proposition does the case stand? How does the case change the law? Using problematizing and rhetorical strategies in *addition to* default reading strategies will allow you to go deeper into the court's analysis.

Consider the following example of a female LP student at the beginning of her reading protocol:

> **Ok. I have my headnotes in my computer and I'll probably read over them again so that I understand what important rules or professional conduct that they are talking about.** *And when the attorney failed*—**why is he going against the rules of professional conduct? So I'll probably read over those again and make sure I've got them in my head and then I'll go onto the case.** *The respondent in this attorney disciplinary matter is charged with failing to disclose to an appellate tribunal controlling authority known to him not disclosed by opposing counsel, but was directly adverse to his client's position.* **So I would underline that what he was charged with and then in the margin I would put—I would just write the words "charge." "Charged." And then I'd put "failure to disclose." And I wouldn't write out the whole thing because I'm going to go back. I'm just putting in the margin so that I have kind of like reference points and I go back to the case. I don't have to reread the entire paragraph. I've got the whole margins to tell me that kind of pinpoint to me what that paragraph is about. So when I go back into my computer I will—I will do the briefing of the case, but I will do that at the end after I've read the entire case. So I just put notes in the margin so that when I go to brief the case I can just refer back to these margins to find the stuff I need.** *He also failed to advise his client of the adverse authority when his client was contemplating his legal options. He failed to advise his client of adverse authority.* **I would underline that. On legal options. So that's a paragraph of what he was charged with. So that's where I put "charge with failure to disclose" in the margin.**

Notice that this LP student spent most of her time paraphrasing the text as she read. Although she clearly had a system for reading the case, it was unclear whether her system improved her comprehension of the case. This student spent 85% of her reading time using default reading strategies; only 2.91% of her time using problematizing strategies and 11.65% of her time using rhetorical strategies. Although she was able to recognize the distinct parts of the case, i.e., facts, issue, holding, and reasoning, she failed to hypothesize, synthesize facts with rules in the case, evaluate the court's result or connect with the underlying purpose of the reading. In this sense, the student missed many of the nuances of the court's decision.

The next example shows how a male student in the LP group overrelied on the use of "highlighting." This student had a very intricate system of using different colored highlighters to represent the structural components of a case. Although highlighting can be helpful as a way of designating important text, a successful law student needs to do more than simply filling up the page with highlighted text. A representative portion of this student's reading protocol is as follows:

> So this is getting confusing because they are talking about different clients over and over and they are not saying last names. They could be much more helpful. But this is going to get a green line again because it's a ruling. So the ruling in *Fletcher* was adverse to the argument that the respondent offered on appeal to the client's case. That is in green. *The respondent had served as counsel of record for the defendant in Fletcher in the appeal before this Court. The court ruling in Fletcher was issued on May 1, 1995.* So now I'm going to use a big yellow highlighter for May 1, 1995 and I'm going to put a line through the court's ruling of *Fletcher* that was issued on that date and that way I can look on this page and there is only a few spots where there is big yellow line and only two of them are numbered, so it is very easy for me to see that this was a year apart.

Although this student used other reading strategies as he read, he highlighted almost every paragraph of the decision. Once again, although highlighting is both common and helpful, law professors want you to go beyond simply noting important text. Minimally, we want you to put the text into your *own* words. If you only highlight the text (and don't take the next step of rewriting the text in your own words), you are taking a shortcut that may backfire in the end.

What can you learn from these reading protocols? The HP students developed their own opinions about the law. Further, successful law students (and lawyers) questioned the decisions they read; they evaluated the results of any case, and they considered the implications of any rule as applied to the facts. Reading the law is far more than simply making notes or highlighting text. As law professors, we want you to read the law critically and efficiently.

Although there will be many things you can do to enhance your success in law school, becoming an efficient and capable legal reader is probably the most important skill to develop during your first year. If you are concerned about your reading, you may want to get help sooner rather than later. The best thing you can do is make an appointment with your Academic Support Program. Typically, the professors that work in the Academic Support Program will have specific exercises to assess your reading problems. In addition, they may have ways that you can improve your reading speed, accuracy, vocabulary, etc.

E. When Might You Need Additional Reading Help?

Reading legal text well occurs when you can use "a number of inter-related skills" when you read, and "when the reader chooses among these skills wisely in light of the purpose of the reading being tackled."[47] If you find yourself taking a very long time to read your assignments (and your reading speed does not improve within the first month of law school), you may need to get some additional help with your legal reading.

The research has shown that poor readers make more oral reading errors[48] that can affect the meaning of texts than good readers.[49] This danger is particularly acute in law school: if you are misreading or skipping words as you read, you are at risk of miscomprehending whatever you are reading and this will only hurt you in law school.

And it may not be enough that you are a careful and accurate reader—you must also be an efficient reader so that you can devote your mental energies toward reading comprehension. Reading research illustrates that good readers store words and word parts in their memories as visual orthographic images.[50] Such storage allows readers to bypass the decoding stage to quickly retrieve words from memory. For skilled readers, this process takes place within 250 milliseconds of encountering most words.[51] This automaticity allows readers to devote their focus toward comprehension.[52] In contrast, slower reading poses two major threats to comprehension. First, slower readers must dedicate their mental efforts toward decoding (figuring out the meaning of the text), leaving limited cognitive resources for meaning-making.[53] Secondly, slow reading taxes short-term memory, as it is more difficult to retain the long and complicated sentences often found in higher level texts at slow reading rates than at rapid speeds.[54]

This can be particularly problematic in law school reading. In light of the typical law school workload, this choppy and hesitant reading

---

47. Ruth Ann McKinney, READING LIKE A LAWYER: TIME-SAVING STRATE-GIES FOR READING LAW LIKE AN EXPERT (Carolina Academic Press)(2005), at 267. 34

48. "Oral reading errors" is when readers make errors while reading out loud.

49. Lauren Capotosto, *Decoding and Fluency Problems of Poor College Readers* at http://www.collegetransition.org/promising/rtp8decodingandfluency.doc (last visited on 01/05/12).

50. *Id.*

51. *Id.*

52. *Id.*

53. *Id.*

54. *Id.*

poses a very real and practical challenge. If you are assigned 60 pages of reading per week in *each* course, this reading load is substantial for even the most effective legal reader. However, this amount of reading will likely be overwhelming for a law student with a slow reading rate. An average college student's reading rate is around 263 words per minute.[55] If your reading speed is less than 250 words per minute in law school, you may need to get some additional help to improve your reading speed.[56]

How can you determine your average reading speed? Adopting the advice from Professor Ruth Ann McKinney, choose anything around the house that you'd like to read (although not likely law-related because that will be too difficult).[57] Also avoid newspaper articles where the text is printed in columns. And read something you haven't read before.

Read for five minutes and accurately time yourself (or have a friend do so).[58] Mark where you started and where you stopped in the text. Calculate how many words you read in total and divide by five. This number is your average number of words per minute. If you are reading less than 250 words per minute, you likely need to speed up your reading in general.

Luckily, there are likely resources available to you if your law school is associated with a university campus.[59] Most campuses have reading centers and reading specialists that can help you. If you do not have access to a formal reading center, consider using a good book with exercises to help improve your reading speed.[60] You can improve your reading speed markedly by doing simple exercises over a period of a few months. As your speed increases, this will open up more time in your reading to do all those things that the most successful law students accomplish in their case reading. If you are no longer stumbling over words and phrases, you can take the time to consider and evaluate the court's opinion.

The good news is that legal reading is a skill you can develop over time. You don't need to withdraw from law school if you are a slow reader or if you have some reading issues. But you do need to be honest with yourself and work to develop the leading reading skill set that will *help* you in law school—not hold you back.

There is no doubt, however, that legal reading is very important to *any* new law student's success. Paying attention to the way in which you read will allow you not only to become a better law student, but a better lawyer as well.

---

55. *Id.*
56. McKinney, *supra* note 47 at 276.
57. *Id.*
58. *Id.*
59. *Id.*
60. *Id.*

Chapter 4

Going Beyond the Traditional Case Brief

Now that we've discussed the importance of legal reading, it is time to discuss how you can use case briefing to help you get more out of your casebook reading in law school. During your first week in law school, you will likely be given a template for a traditional case brief. In addition, you will be told that you need to brief every case in order to prepare well for your law school classes. However, you are not always told *why* you need to brief your cases. This chapter will explain the *why* of case briefing and give you some tips to get the most out of briefing your cases.

First and foremost, you should know that case briefing is based *in part* on a template for legal analysis called IRAC. You may have already been introduced to this formula.[1] IRAC is a formula for the way you will frame a legal argument in law school. "IRAC" is an acronym for Issue, Rule, Analysis and Conclusion.

The "I" in IRAC stands for *Issue* and this part of the formula identifies the questions (or legal issues) raised by a fact pattern. Any one or sometimes several of the legal arguments discussed in a case may give rise to a legal issue. How do you *find* "issues"? Some will jump out at you, even on the first read of the case. Sometimes the court states the issue specifically. For other legal issues, you will need to work harder to uncover them by asking yourself *why* each fact is present and then *testing* that fact against the rules that are articulated in the case. Any time you read and brief a judicial opinion, you will need to identify the legal issues.

Next comes "R" in IRAC which stands for the *Rule*. Your job is to determine which rule or rules govern the court's decision. Typically you want to write a succinct, clear rule statement of the precise law that governs the issue that you stated above. You will recognize the rule because there is usually a specific rule statement or a legal citation in a case that the court uses to identify the rule.

The "A" in IRAC stands for the *Application* or *Analysis* of the issue and this is often the most important part of the formula. In the context of case briefing, you will be looking for the court's *reasoning* here. In an exam

---

1. The IRAC paradigm is particularly helpful to writing coherent exam answers and in formulating legal arguments for your legal writing classes.

context, the "A" is your opportunity to say *why* the facts either meet or don't meet the elements of the rules you stated. (More on this part of the "A" later). Sometimes, there are good arguments to be made on both sides of a legal issue and the court will discuss both before coming to a conclusion. Certain facts may point to the satisfaction of a particular element, while other facts indicate that element is not met. In the "A" section of a case brief, you want to describe how the court argues and supports its position with regard to the legal issues raised by the parties.

Finally, the "C" in IRAC stands for the Conclusion. The Conclusion is the wrap-up where you will resolve the issues or questions you have raised earlier. In the context of case briefing, the Conclusion is typically the conclusion of the court. What was the court's final decision? Did it agree with one party over another? What happened to the case? Did it go back for another trial or was a claim dismissed? Try to figure out not only the legal conclusion but also the *procedural* disposition of the court, i.e., what did the court do with the case?

You will likely receive a copy of a traditional case brief that contains several sections which are enumerated below. See if you can identify the IRAC formula within the components of the case brief provided below.

Title (e.g., Patty v. Smitty)
Citation (e.g., 500 U.S. 100 (1987))

Facts: Summarize the facts of the case. Focus on the facts that you need to understand the holding and reasoning of the case.

Procedural Posture: Most of the cases that you'll read in law school will be appellate court decisions. In this section, list what happened at the lower court level. Although you don't have to go into too much detail, you do need to understand how the case came to the present court. One or two sentences are sufficient for this section.

Issue(s): What is/are the legal question(s) facing the court? Form the issue questions in a way that they can be answered by **yes** or **no**. Often you can find the issue statement within the initial paragraphs of the opinion.

Holding: How did the court answer the issue question(s)? First, answer this question with either a yes or no, and then provide a short statement as to why the court so held.

Reasoning: This is the most important section of your case brief. Here you want to list in more detail the reasoning of the court in reaching its decision. Be detailed in this section but try not to simply rewrite the opinion. Restate the reasoning in your own words. List what the law was before this case was decided and how the law has changed after this decision. **Important note: Law professors tend to focus on the reasoning of a case in class discussions.**

Concurring/dissenting opinions: Make a note as to the basic arguments of any concurring/dissenting opinions but this section should be fairly short.

Although this template is a good start to help you extract the necessary information out of a case, it may not go far enough. Before you begin briefing all of your cases using this template, I would like you to consider how case briefing helps you work through your case reading.

A. Case Briefing Provides a Cognitive Schema

As discussed in Chapter 3, legal reading is very difficult. The vocabulary is unfamiliar and the structure of a judicial opinion is strange. Legal text is unique in both its form and content; it is its own special genre. The case brief serves as an effective cognitive "schema" to provide you with a framework within which to analyze a legal opinion.

What is a schema? "A schema is a cluster of information that we hold in our mind about a subject."[2] In simple terms, a schema is stored knowledge. During reading, comprehension occurs when the reader can match the text information to a pre-existing schema.[3] The new information is compared against the old.[4] The existing schema fills in the gaps in the text and allows for many kinds of inferences.[5]

Schemas are "critical building blocks of the human cognitive process."[6] They permit us to process the never-ending amount of information we encounter each day.[7] Categories and schemas affect not only what information receives our attention, but how we categorize it and what we re-

---

2. RUTH ANN MCKINNEY, READING LIKE A LAWYER: TIME-SAVING STRATEGIES FOR READING LIKE AN EXPERT, 17 (Carolina Academic Press 2005). *See also,* Leah M. Christensen, *The Psychology of Case Briefing: A Powerful Cognitive Schema,"* 29 CAMP. L. REV. 5, 5–6 (2006).

3. Christensen, *supra* n.2 at 11 (*citing* Peter Dewitz, *Reading Law: Three Suggestions for Legal Education,* 27 U. TOL L. REV. 657, 660 (1996)).

4. *Id.*

5. *Id.*

6. Christensen, *supra* n.2 at 11 (*citing* Ronald Chen & Jon Hanson, *Categorically Biased: The Influence of Knowledge Structures on Law and Legal Theory,* 77 S. CAL. L. REV. 1103, 1131 (2004)).

7. *Id.*

member about it.[8] Without prior experience in the law, you have no schemata to deal with legal reading, and your ability to read and analyze the law is often inefficient and overwhelming.[9]

Case briefing gives you the framework within which to enter into the discourse of law. A case brief is nothing more than a schema. Especially in the first semester of law school, case briefs can help you preserve your thoughts and observations as you begin to organize the content of the cases you read. By going through the process of drafting a case brief, you will free up your short term memory which will allow you to think about what the case actually means.[10]

Note, however, that you are not likely to receive feedback on your case briefs. Your case briefs are for your own benefit; law professors do not ask you to hand them in. Therefore, you will need to evaluate whether you are briefing correctly largely on your own. If you would like additional help on case briefing, you can go to the instructors and professors in your Academic Support Program. This is precisely the type of feedback that they can give you early on in law school.

Most law students prepare their case briefs on their laptop computer. As illustrated above, a typical brief contains the following components: case heading; parties' names; procedural history; facts; issues or questions presented; holding; reasoning/rationale; and perhaps a separate section for the reader's own thoughts.[11]

Law students are particularly diligent during their first semester of law school and they figure out how to "fill in" the parts of a case brief fairly quickly. However, all too often, students stop at that point. In fact, many law students stop briefing cases altogether because they consider it too time-consuming. Consider the words of a first-year law student:

Interviewer: Do you use case briefs as a study strategy?

Student: No, I used it in the first week. I had a hard time writing out the holdings. I actually have a hard time when I'm writing out the brief. Not concentrating …. It's time consuming and inefficient.[12]

---

8. *Id.* at 11–12.

9. Christensen, *supra* n.2 at 12 (*citing* McKinney, *supra* n.2, at 18–19). Further, traditional law school teaching usually concentrates on only one learning style; it does not address the varied cognitive styles represented in each entering class. Students who have different cognitive styles than the typical "Socratic" method will have to learn legal reasoning on their own.

10. *Id.* at 13 (*citing* McKinney, *supra* n.2 at 23).

11. Note that most traditional case briefs do not have a section for your own thoughts. I believe that you should add this section. Evaluating the case and forming your own opinion about the result allows you to more actively participate in the case reading/briefing.

12. Transcript of Interview with Student 102 at 10 (on file with the author).

By giving up case briefing so soon in her law school career, this student may have missed out on the benefits of the case brief as a cognitive schema. Although a brief will help you organize a judicial opinion, it also serves as a way to help you think critically and creatively about the law. This is a key aspect of case briefing that often goes unrecognized by most students. Further, those students who continue to brief their cases into their second year of law school may have an academic edge over those students who have stopped briefing cases.

One student in the top 5% of her class after the first semester of law school disclosed that she still briefs every case before class. Although she highlights text and writes in the margins during her initial read-through of the case, she briefs the case during her second reading. She appeared to recognize that the process of briefing a case enhanced her overall case analysis.

Interviewer: Tell me a little bit about what reading strategies you use [in general]?

Student: Um, typically I start by reading the case once through. I highlight what I think is the issue, rule of reasoning, procedural history all in the margin. I highlight it and then put the "R" next to it. I read it through that one time and depending when it's due for class, I'll either brief it right after that or wait until the next day. When I brief it is when I really understand it. I understand it the first time through, but when I brief it, it really solidifies in my head.[13]

    . . . .

Interviewer: Do you still brief cases after you read them?

Student: Yeah. Everything. Well, there are rare occasions where I don't need to or I'm too lazy. But, yeah, I still brief pretty much everything including the notes after the case and everything. Um, just because that's my way of understanding it. That's my "learning." When I write it down is when it solidified in my head. So, I'll read it through the first time carefully and then, based upon what I highlighted, I usually do end up rereading the whole case. I don't just read what I've highlighted because it's not always correct. Or I miss something. So, I go through and write down everything that I think

---

13. Transcript of Interview with Student 111 at 7 (on file with the author).

> is important, mostly the reasoning and rule of law.
> I don't spend a lot of time on the facts.

Interviewer: Have you felt that these strategies have been successful for you?

Student: Yeah. Extremely successful. Because when I read it through—I mean for me, that's pretty passive. I mean, yeah, I'm trying to mark out what the issue and the holding is and everything, but I won't remember it the next day. Now, if I brief it, then I do remember it the next day. And, plus, its right in front of me. I don't like paging through the case and trying to find where I put my "H." So, I like having it all in front of me and I think it's been really successful. I mean I always—I won't say never. But I hardly ever feel lost in class, and if anything, I might do it too thoroughly, because I just know everything.[14]

This student possessed a sophisticated understanding of both how she learned most effectively and the underlying benefits of case briefing. She understood that she did not learn the case until she "briefed" it. Law professors often forget to discuss case briefing after the first week of law school. Yet I've found that the way in which law students use their case briefs evolves over the course of their law school career. When asked to describe how her case briefing strategies changed throughout the course of her first year of law school, the above-student responded:

> My briefing has gotten a lot better. I mean it's—before I just didn't know—when I started law school, I did not know what was important at all. Because of the certain tone of judicial opinions, I think when you first start out you think everything is important and it sounds so above your head. So you're like, well, if I don't understand this, it must be important. But, now I can just pick out right away—this has nothing to do with what we're talking about or this is definitely what this court finds to be the most important issue that the case turns on or the most important fact .... And I definitely can pick out the rule of law so much faster.[15]

This student, like so many of my first-year students, began to develop her own cognitive schema about the law. As her legal vocabulary increased and her understanding of an opinion's unique structure became more refined, her case analysis also improved.

---

14. Christensen, *supra* n.2 at 15–16.
15. Transcript of Interview with Student 111 at 8 (on file with the author).

B. Taking Your Case Briefs Beyond Your Yellow Highlighter

By the end of the first semester of law school, most students choose to "book brief" their cases by underlining or highlighting components of a legal opinion. This is a good start, but it is rarely enough. You might think you are saving time by simply marking your casebooks with a highlighter. However, using the highlighter to move through the assigned reading rarely accomplishes what a new legal reader needs at this point in your law school career.[16]

One first-year student who was still struggling with case analysis after first semester admitted she spent a great deal of time highlighting cases as she read. She used a color-coded system of highlighting, using a different color to represent the different structural components of a judicial opinion.

Interviewer:	Tell me a little bit about what reading strategies you use?
Student:	[I] summarize as I go. Like, reread, because there is a lot of stuff in here that I just don't get the first time. I understand the words, but I have no idea what the meaning is so I have to read it two or three times and underline.
	....
Interviewer:	So you highlight?
Student:	Oh, I highlight a lot. I underline. I tend to write a lot of words in the margins in pencil.... If it's a rule of law, I'll highlight in a certain color. So I use orange for a rule of law. The reason I use different colors a lot of time is just because I'll use all one and I stop looking at it.[17]

If possible, try not to fall into this habit. Blindly highlighting your casebook or simply briefing on your computer without doing something more will hold you back. If you only highlight text in your casebook, you are simply marking what has been written by the author.[18] You are failing to engage in your own analysis or evaluation. Even the best highlighting only "capture[s] the author's words."[19] Effective case analysis re-

---

16. Christensen, *supra* n.2 at 16 *(citing,* McKinney, *supra* note 2, at 176.)
17. Transcript of Interview with Student 112 at p. 6 (on file with the author).
18. Christensen, *supra* n.2 at 17 *(citing* McKinney, *supra* n.2, at 176).
19. *Id.*

quires more than simply highlighting the author's language. One of the most important functions of a good case brief schema is to force you to consider your *own* thoughts and reactions to the case.[20]

Further, while most students would agree that case briefing helps them prepare for class, it does more than that. Not only does writing a case brief help you understand the case, it is also a way of "chunking" information to free up working memory so you can think about the main idea of a case. In other words, a case brief is not simply an end in and of itself.

C. Case Briefing Promotes "Chunking"

Law professors want you to think about the "chunks" of information you have written in your briefs so you can analyze the case on your own and see how it fits into the context of the course. This is where your learning truly occurs. In addition, this is a key facet of case analysis. Experts in any field have ways of chunking information into rational groups.[21] Once clumped in a rational group, the same amount of information takes up less storage space in working memory, thus freeing more space in working memory for the challenging task of actually thinking about the material.[22] The ability to recall more information is, therefore, a function of the size and information content of the individual chunks.[23]

Case briefing is the beginning of your journey toward a fuller understanding of the nuances and flexibility of legal text. How can you make this happen? The remaining section of this chapter will provide an example of how to expand your traditional case brief to get more out of your case reading.

---

20. Your model case brief should contain a section for the student's own thoughts and/or conclusions.

21. Christensen, *supra* n.2 at 18 (*citing* McKinney, *supra* n.2, at 174). Cognitive scientists understand that knowledge is structured in memory like cohesive groups of concepts or "chunking." In turn this "chunking" of knowledge makes information meaningful. Information, including facts, figures, and beliefs, is organized into clusters of knowledge. "The concept of knowledge, as distinguished from information, implies understanding." Paula Lustbader, *Construction Sites, Building Types, and Bridging Gaps: A Cognitive Theory of the Learning Progression of Law Students*, 33 Willamette L. Rev. 315, 320 (1997).

22. Christensen, *supra* n.2 at 18 (*citing* McKinney, *supra* n.2, at 175).

23. Christensen, *supra* n.2 at 18 (*citing* Gary L. Blasi, *What Lawyers Know: Lawyering Expertise, Cognitive Science, and the Functions of Theory*, 45 J. Legal Educ. 313, 344 (1995)). Blasi cites the following example: "Most people who glance at the following string of symbols will have some difficulty remembering it: WYSIWYG/P6/QWERTY/AS400. To a person with limited knowledge of computers, this is a string of twenty-three individual symbols, possibly bearing an encrypted message. But a more computer-literate person will quickly recognize this string of symbols as four discrete chunks, each representing a known concept or object, and will easily remember it." *Id.* at 343.

D. A First-Year Student's Example Case Brief

I would like to provide you with an example of an actual first-year law student's case brief. This student sought out comments from my writing assistant about whether he provided enough detail in his brief to really aid him in understanding the case. My writing assistant provided detailed comments back to the student on how he might improve his case briefing.

Note how the student used the traditional case brief template. Although the student was on the right track, he needed to go a bit farther into the reasoning and details of the case. The student's case brief with my research assistant's comments are provided on the next page. Read the student's case brief critically to determine what, if anything, you would do differently. This section ends with some very useful advice given to the student by my writing assistant (from her perspective as a third-year law student).

Sample First-Year Case Brief with Comments

United States v. Jewell
(US Court of Appeals, 1976)

Parties: Π/respondent- US; Δ/appellant- Stoner

Procedural History:

Π sued Δ for smuggling drugs. Judgment for Π. Δ appealed.

T.A. Comment: Generally speaking, you may want to include a little more specific information for your procedural history (in this case specifically, it's not really necessary). But, it will help you tremendously in all areas of the law to understand what really happened — and a good majority of the tricky legal terms/concepts will appear in the procedure sections.

Facts:

- Δ drove into the US in an automobile and claims to have "<u>unknowingly</u>" transported illegal drugs

- Question of whether defendant "knew" he was transporting illegal drugs

- Jury found that Δ had positive knowledge of marijuana,

- (Deliberate ignorance)

Isn't this really the "issue" in the case? If you put this down as a "fact" on an exam, it would likely be marked wrong. The fact is only what actually happened — D drove across the border with drugs in his glove compartment. His claim of "unknowingly" transported illegal drugs is really the defendant's argument or legal issue.

Make sure to distinguish what is a fact and what is an issue. They are very different things.

This is a case on appeal, which doesn't have a jury. The appellate court is looking at this from a court record. You may want to distinguish procedural facts (of the appellate court) from these underlying facts (which is what happened at the lower court level).

This part of "deliberate ignorance" is good — were you asking yourself why the jury found that he behaved knowingly, and therefore violated the statute? Good.

Legal Issue:

- Can deliberately turning a blind eye to illegal activity that you know is likely to be going on be construed as "knowledge"?

I would restate this to be clearer. The issue looks correct but you want it to read smoothly.

Rule:

- Deliberate ignorance = positive knowledge (high probability).

This is a good rule statement for the purpose of being prepared for class, but think about using your brief to help you with future exam-writing as well. Write out a more formal rule statement.

My Reasoning:

Why? Make sure to create that analytical bridge for your reader, even if you think the point seems obvious.

- According to the facts, Δ had entertained the knowledge, in high probability that marijuana was in his automobile. If Δ knew that he was transporting illegal, but instead covered his eyes, then defendant has knowledge.

Courts Reasoning:

Be more specific in pointing to which facts demonstrate that he knew of the high probability that he was transporting drugs.

- The defendant knew of the high probability that he was smuggling drugs and therefore, based on the rule, certain "knowledge" can be imputed to the defendant and he is therefore guilty.

Disposition: Affirmed

In your first semester, the process of case briefing has two (if not more) important purposes. First, it will help you test your ability to recognize and isolate the different elements of IRAC by having to compartmentalize them in a written format. Additionally, it will give you an outlet to practice writing out your rule statements and your analysis. This practice will be very valuable when it comes time to write an exam. Make sure that your case brief uses as many facts from the case at hand as possible and ask yourself why a particular fact is significant to the outcome of a case. It is likely, especially in the beginning—your case brief will not hit on the issues discussed in class. Don't be discouraged by this! You may have simply articulated things in a different way or gotten to the correct conclusion by taking a different road. Either way, make sure to seek out some one-on-one time with your professor to discuss case briefing. You may want to ask that they comment on your analysis, clarity of your writing, and organizational structure. If you don't take a proactive approach to getting feedback on your briefs, you may miss an opportunity to improve your skill set.

E. Going Beyond the Traditional Case Brief

After you receive your traditional case brief template, consider revising the template to incorporate more of the types of questions that your law professors want you to consider as you read through a case for class.[24] The following example provides a revised case brief format that poses

---

24. Note how many of these questions in this case brief are the types of questions the Higher Performing law students noted in their think-alouds as a part of the reading study described in Chapter 3.

the types of questions you should be able to answer if you have read the case well.

1. **CONTEXTUALIZE THE CASE**[25]

   Where is the case from?

   What court wrote the opinion?

   What year was the opinion written?

   How will this case act as precedent to your issue?

   Why are you reading the case?

   What is your purpose for reading the case?

   What should you focus on?

2. **OVERVIEW**

   Briefly skim the synopsis of the case.

   What is the subject matter?

   What are the keynotes?

   What are the main issues?

3. **READ THE CASE**

   What's the procedural posture?

   What is the summary of legal proceedings?

   What are the issues in dispute?

   Outline the facts.

   Who are the parties and what do they want?

   Create a picture of the facts.

   Identify the key issues.

   What issues is the court deciding and/or reviewing?

   What did the court decide?

   Identify the holding and the rule/s applied by the court.

   Why did the court so hold?

   What occurred in the case procedurally? Is the judgment reversed or affirmed, or is the motion denied?

4. **REREAD TO GET THE BIG PICTURE**

   Make sure you understand all the legal terms.

   Distinguish relevant from irrelevant facts.

   Using the issue and holding, note which facts are legally relevant to the court's decision.

   Understand the court's rationale. Can you write it out in your own words?

   What is the court's reasoning? What is dicta?

   What rules is the court applying? What is the policy behind the rules?

5. **EVALUATE THE CASE**

   Do you agree with the decision?

   Was it well-written? Well-reasoned?

---

25. Christensen, *supra* n.2 at 24–25 (citing Mary A. Lundeberg, *Metacognitive Aspects of Reading Comprehension: Studying Understanding in Legal Case Analysis*, 22 Reading Res. Q. 430–432 (1987)). This example is based in part on Lundeberg's suggestions about revising the typical brief format.

Why are you reading the case, i.e., why is it in your casebook?
Why did the court come to this conclusion?

6. MAKE NOTES

Summarize the case in your own words.

In the margin or in a separate case brief, use your own words to summarize the case, its facts, the law, and the law as applied to the facts. Why is the case important? Is the judge correct? What influenced the judge's decision? Were facts or law more important to the outcome? How will this decision serve as precedent for future cases?

Hopefully, if you adopt this revised case brief template, you will begin to understand that there are many facets to case analysis. It is all too easy to read a case only to plug its components into the corresponding section of the case brief. You cannot stop there. Case briefing is only the *beginning* of case analysis, not the end. If your case analysis never develops beyond identifying the structural components of a case, your full understanding of any case will be limited. As law professors, we want you to have your own opinions about cases and about the law.

One successful first-year student in the top 10% of her law school class understood this concept well. In an interview, I asked her to consider what advice she would give to a beginning law student about to start his or her first semester:

> We're often taught to believe that because there is a holding in a case, there is a right answer. And I really don't believe that you can do well in law school if you just accept that. I think you should always be open and never discount your reaction because if you feel it, then you can make an argument for it. Don't back down just because the holding is a position that the majority of the court took. Use your own thoughts and ideas, and intuition.[26]

Remember that when you brief a case, you need to go beyond merely paraphrasing the text. Try to become open to more than one argument in the judicial opinion. Good lawyers and law students question the decisions they read; they evaluate the results of the case, and they consider the implications of any rule. This is precisely what law professors *test* in exams. We want you to read the law creatively, as well as critically. A good case brief can help you accomplish this task more effectively.

---

26. Transcript of Interview with Student 102 at 11 (on file with the author).

Chapter 5

How to Prepare for Class: What Does Your Professor *Really* Want from You?

Your main task in your first-year classes is to read a series of cases that discuss a specific rule of law. From the cases, you will distill a legal rule or holding. The professor expects you to read and understand the cases *before* you come to class. The actual classroom experience will not tend to focus upon the facts, issue, and holding of the case (although you will likely cover these basics in the first part of class). Instead, after an introductory discussion of the case, your professor will pose a hypothetical. A hypothetical is a new factual situation that will contain a similar legal issue. Your job is to apply the rule (from the first case) to the new factual situation and determine the likely outcome. If your professor uses the Socratic Method, the professor will choose a student from the class and hold a "conversation" with the student focusing on this new hypothetical. The purpose of this conversation is to point out the nuances of the court's reasoning and to consider how the case might apply to this new set of facts.

In law school, we assume that you have read and understood the cases before you come to class. The classroom experience *applies* that information and reasoning. The purpose of law school classes is to expand upon that information; to test the credibility of the court's reasoning; to discuss the policy implications of the court's decision, etc. You can prepare for class most effectively by thinking about the difference between what the professor wants you to do *before* class as compared to what the professor expects you to do *in* class. This next section will provide you with a list of suggestions to help you through the three stages of the law school classroom experience: (1) what to do *before* class; (2) what to do *in* class; and (3) what to do *after* class.

A. Things to Do before Class

1. Before You Begin Reading, Determine *Why* You Are Reading the Case!

As you sit down to prepare for your first several assignments, one of your tasks is to figure out *why* your professor is having you read that case. As we've already discussed, good reading entails active, careful reading of the cases in your textbooks. This is easier said than done. You need to consider *why* you are reading the case. Why did the casebook author select *that* particular case to illustrate a particular rule or concept?

Before you dive into reading the case, take a moment to check the table of contents of your casebook. Try to understand what topic or subject matter the case covers. Is the author trying to illustrate a particular rule of causation? The table of contents will give you a good idea of what rule the case is meant to illustrate. In addition, check your syllabus. Your professor may have given you a hint about why he or she is having you read *that* case at that particular time in the course. If you can begin your class preparation with some idea of the *context* of a case—both in terms of why you're reading the case at this time in the course and the context of the case itself—you've given yourself a leg up on what you will be asked in class.[1] After you understand the basics of the case, try to focus on the part of the case that discusses the rule or theory most relevant to that section in the book.

2. Go to Class!

First and foremost, make sure you attend class. Have your homework done *before* class. If you cannot complete the full reading assignment, you want to minimally skim the reading and/or use a commercial outline to get a sense of the basics of the cases.

3. Schedule Your Study Time

You will need to schedule your study time. Be prepared to feel like you should spend every minute of your day studying the law. And you could try to do that but you'd burn out in a week. Taking regular breaks helps you learn by giving your mind, eyes and body a rest. Then you can return to your work refreshed and able to comprehend more information.

You need to schedule your study time for another reason as well. Depending on how you learn, you may find that you become too immersed

---

1. Remember that knowing the context of the case was something that the most successful law students did as they read a case.

in a single course or a particular reading assignment. Perhaps you are spending too much time on one subject and failing to get to the assignments in another class.

There is something to be said about scheduling law school like you would organize a workday for your job. Consider that law school *is* your job right now. You should assume you will work reasonably hard during your first year at your new job. Therefore, you should schedule 50 hours a week of study time (in addition to class time). Plot out exactly how much time you will spend on each reading assignment. If you have three classes to prepare for in one evening, then you need to assess realistically how much time you have. If you have 6 hours in that evening, you should schedule two hours per class. This allows you to attack your studying very purposefully and carefully so that you can cover as much of the reading as possible in your allotted time.

4. Use Commercial Outlines and Study Guides Strategically

Commercial law school outlines[2] tend to be comprehensive guides that cover the cases and legal rules applicable to a given course. Commercial outlines can be helpful to students because they present the 'big picture.' In some first-year courses, like Torts for example, it can take several weeks to cover all the elements of negligence. By referring to a commercial outline (or another type of study aid), you can gain a helpful perspective about how the individual pieces of the law fit into the larger whole. Commercial outlines and other study materials present material in a condensed, highly structured fashion, and they are often designed to parallel the materials presented in popular casebooks.

There are many different types of study aids that include commercial outlines, treatises, or hornbooks. During my first year of law school, my professors told us *not* to buy any study aids. I dutifully listened to their advice and used only my casebook and class notes to create my outlines during the first year. On my exams, I very carefully regurgitated all the cases we discussed in class. But I missed seeing the forest through the trees. I failed to understand the bigger picture of how the individual cases formed larger concepts or doctrines, and I lost points because I missed this larger perspective. During my second year of law school, I used com-

---

2. There are a whole host of supplementary materials available. You can choose from outlines, flashcards, nutshells (short mini-books that give concise explanations), etc. There are also the "Examples and Explanations" series or a "Question and Answer" series, as well as longer treatises (more descriptive statements of the law) and hornbooks (typically written by the casebook author to provide background information in the law). I have also suggested that students use bar review materials and/or tapes, particularly if they are auditory learners. You will want to choose a study aid that matches with your learning style. Try a few out. You do *not* need to buy them all.

mercial outlines. The outlines allowed me to do two things: first, I was able to preview the cases before I read them in my casebook; second, the outlines allowed me to see the big picture of how the cases fit into the full context of the course.

Commercial outlines or other study aids, however, cannot substitute for your course materials. You need to go to class (because your professor will test you on the material you've covered in class). Study aids *can* be an important resource to help you prepare for classes and exams. Anything you do to improve your understanding of the basics of the case gives you 'context' to help your case reading. Study aids also provide you with various hypotheticals or examples of how the rules apply to real-life situations. These examples are important to your classroom (and exam) preparation. Although you will discuss the basics of the cases and their holdings in class, most of your class time will be spent discussing the application of the case rules to new hypotheticals. If you've already considered possible examples as you've prepared for class, you will be one step ahead of your peers. And you will be better prepared for your exams as well.

Table 1 will help you become familiar with the different types of study aids available to you. Your school library will likely have many of these, so you may want to see what your library carries before you spend extra money on study aids. Note also that different study aids may work more effectively for different types of learning styles. Keep your learning style in mind when you choose a study aid.

Table 1: Study Aids

Type of Study Aid	Description	Strengths	Drawbacks	When to use this type of aid	Example of this type of aid
Canned Briefs	Provide you with a one-page case brief similar to what you will need to prepare for class. Includes the rule, facts, parties' arguments, and court's holding and reasoning in a concise format.	Good resource for first semester as a 1L when you will struggle more with legal reading.	Cannot use INSTEAD of reading cases. May give you a false sense of security about your understanding of the case. Professors tend to dislike pre-prepared briefs.	After you've read a case or towards the end of the semester for review. Learning Styles: Visual, Read-Write	High Court Case Summaries
Hornbooks or Treatises	Longer, text-based books that very thoroughly explain a concept in the law. Contain narrative explanations with some examples.	In-depth coverage; detailed explanations. Professors tend to prefer these.	Lengthy, expensive and boring. Often provide too much information and minute detail.	Can use throughout the semester. Learning Styles: Visual, Read-Write, Auditory/Oral Examples and Explanations	Prosser and Keeton Dobbs on Torts

Type of Study Aid	Description	Strengths	Drawbacks	When to use this type of aid	Example of this type of aid
Commercial Outlines	Cover all the material presented in a course in an outline format. Will have black letter law broken down into elements; include examples and brief explanations of key concepts and cases.	Can be very useful to see the 'big' picture; help to synthesize the different concepts introduced in a course. May come with practice essay and multiple-choice questions.	Less detailed than class notes and will not follow the structure of your class. Use only to supplement class notes; do not use a commercial outline in place of creating your own outline.	Use throughout the semester. Start by glancing at the large-scale outline in this supplement before you begin classes to learn the vocabulary, general rules, and elements most pertinent to the course. Revisit the outline throughout course to help you put concepts together. Use at the end of the course to supplement your outlining. Learning Styles: Visual, Kinesthetic (doing practice exams, problems); Read/Write	Gilberts (uses charts, graphs, flow charts, etc.) Emanuels Legalines Roadmap
Audio recordings	Recorded lectures on a particular subject. A spoken version of a commercial outline.	Flexible; can use in your car, at the gym, in iPod. Some also come with a corresponding workbook of examples.	Can be expensive (but can purchase used). Suited primarily for one specific type of learning style (auditory/oral).	Use any time during semester; good for synthesizing at end of semester; use before you get to a concept in class for general overview. Learning Styles: Auditory/Oral; Kinesthetic (can move around while listening)	Flemings PMBR Bar Review
Exam Preparation Materials	Geared toward helping you prepare for final exams; use flow charts; checklists; tree diagrams, and capsule summaries	Concise; incorporate visuals for all different learning styles.	May not provide in depth coverage of issues and/or courses.	Geared toward exam preparation toward the end of the semester versus class preparation Learning Styles: Visual; Read/Write; Kinesthetic	CrunchTime PMBR Finals — Law School Exams Series Law In a Flash-Flash-cards
Bar Preparation Materials	Examine black letter law for multi-state bar subjects	Concise and fairly general; provide good '"big picture" review of specific courses/subject matters	Examine concepts more than cases; may not follow your course outlines.	Geared toward bar exam preparation; big picture. Learning Styles: Visual (charts, flow charts); Auditory (tapes, computer cd's); Kinesthetic (review questions)	PMBR Bar Charts Flashcards

5. Create Your Own Case Briefs When You Can

As we discussed in Chapter 4, case briefing is a way to help you figure out what's going on in the case more quickly. Doing a separate case brief for your cases is very important in the early weeks of law school. As you progress through law school, many students find that they simply do not have enough time to create separate case briefs for every case in an assignment. If you are not creating separate case briefs, you need to *minimally* make notes in the margins of the case *in your own words*. Take the concepts that you've read and internalize them into concepts that you understand. At the very least, write out portions of the case in your own words.[3]

6. Read the Case Notes at the End of Each Chapter of Your Casebook

Along the lines of knowing *why* you're reading the cases—you should also make time to read the case notes *following* the major cases (or a series of cases) in your casebook.[4] Sometimes it's good to skim the cases notes *before* you read the actual case. The case notes, like the table of contents, can give you a sense of why the case is important and how the rule has been applied more recently.

In addition, it is possible that your professor will actually spend class time discussing the case notes. After the professor has gotten through the basic aspects of the case, the professor will begin asking you how the particular rule of law from the case will apply to a different fact situation or hypothetical. The case notes and problems will help you prepare for this important aspect of the class.

---

3. There are canned briefs (briefs already written for you) likely available on most of the major cases you read. These are not necessarily bad study aids—*if* you use them appropriately. Canned briefs can be a useful way of getting oriented quickly to a case—particularly to an older case whose language is unfamiliar. Canned briefs give you a basic summary of the facts of the case, the procedural posture and the court's holding. Once you've read the canned brief, you can then read the actual case having had the additional background and context. Canned briefs can be a good place to begin if you find you're having trouble getting through your course material.

4. The case notes are questions at the end of a case that are meant to make you think about the principles. These questions can sometimes be frustrating to students because they are often ambiguous and difficult to address given your present knowledge of the material. However, they also replicate the types of questions that may be on an essay exam. Try to take the time to go through some of these examples. This teaches you to apply the rules to a new set of facts—which is what you will be asked to do on an exam.

B. Things to Do in Class

1. Arrive on Time

Law professors want you to arrive to class on time. If you are prone to being late, set your clock back! Some law professors will ban you from class if you arrive more than five minutes late. Perhaps in your undergraduate courses you could slink in late in a large lecture—that's almost impossible in law school.

2. Sit Strategically in the Classroom

Consider where you will learn most effectively in the classroom. Is it close to the professor? Do you need to be by the door to take a break during class? Do you need to minimize noise from other students? Do you need to position yourself away from your friends so you can prevent yourself from being distracted by comments and/or jokes? We all have our own learning styles. Try to do what is best for your learning style. If you tend to get distracted, you may want to stay up towards the front of the classroom. In law school, you want to do everything possible to create an environment that is conducive to learning.

3. Use Your Laptop for Notes Only!

Laptop computers can be a very distracting element in the classroom. Although you might believe you can multi-task, the truth is that you cannot learn as effectively when you are multi-tasking. As you begin law school, you need your full concentration. Give yourself the opportunity to fully engage in your classes.

4. Take Effective Notes

After the first week of law school, you will develop your own style of taking notes in class. Initially, you'll probably feel like you want to write down everything that goes on in class. Your notes will resemble a transcript of everything your professor discussed and everything your classmates said in response to the professor's questions. You will learn to be more discerning in what you write down. Many times the answer your classmate gives may *not* be the right answer.

One key strategy is to write down the *questions* your professor asks during the class. As you go back through your notes after class, you will start to get a sense of what your professor thinks is important about the case.

In addition, evaluate what you hear in class—both from your peers and your professor. You won't agree with everything discussed in class—but if you don't agree—be able to articulate *why* you disagree.

Another effective strategy for taking notes is to create an electronic template for your class notes. Consider the template at the bottom of this section. A template will allow you to take notes consistently throughout the semester and save them in a single document for each class, which will make them easier to review.[5] After every two or three classes, review your notes—reorganize them and revise them. This will make outlining easier as the semester progresses.[6]

Note Taking Template

Class:
Date/Time:
Reading Assignment:

Main Lecture/Note Taking Area

In this section, record the lecture as meaningfully as possible. Try *not* to just script or write down *everything* your professor says.

Questions

The *Questions* section is likely the most *important* aspect of your note taking. Write down the professor's questions about a particular case or concept. This gives you a sense of what the professor sees as important in the case. Try to write down a good answer for the question as well. In addition, consider writing down good questions by other students if it helps your understanding.

Summaries

The Summaries section can be filled in when you review your notes between classes. Try to summarize key points from that lecture in a sentence or two. Also note additional questions you may have or additional readings.

---

5. It is essential to devise a good back-up system for your computer files. Many students have computer problems at some point during law school. Use flashdrives, send to your email account, etc. Devise a way to protect your data. You won't have extra time to recreate it!

6. Outlining, a way to distill a law school course down to its essential elements, will be discussed in Chapter 8.

5. Review Class Notes

Because of the large volume of material you will learn each semester, you need to review your class notes regularly. You cannot cram all that information into your brain during finals. Therefore, take time to review class material. You should also highlight or note questions that you still had even after you reviewed the material. These will be concepts you'll want to review with your professor.

If you get to class five minutes early, review your notes from the last class. Ideally, your professor will recap the highlights of the last class at the beginning of the new class, but this is not always the case. Reviewing material from the prior class will help you transition and make connections with the new cases. Learning the law is not a series of discrete lectures and elements; everything builds upon a rule or skill that you have mastered previously. By conducting a five-minute review before each class, you are ensuring that you have mastered one concept before moving on to a new one.

6. Organize Your Class Notes

After every one to two weeks, organize your class notes by using a method that works with your learning style. You might try using flow-charts, graphic organizers or spatial learning strategies. In talking to successful law students, each student had his or her own way of organizing class material. Some students liked to learn by using audiotapes. Other students were more visual learners. Many of these students used graphic organizers. Graphic organizers (or spatial learning strategies) provide a visual and holistic representation of facts and concepts and their relationships within an organized frame. Graphic organizers can often be an effective tool for enhancing their thinking and learning. Specifically, graphic organizers can help you represent abstract or implicit concepts in more concrete and explicit forms.

Examples of graphic organizers include charts, maps and flowcharts. Sometimes you will see graphic organizers referred to as "Mind mapping."[7] These graphics rely on the use of arrows or geometric shapes and spatial arrangements to describe the text content and to structure key conceptual relationships.

---

7. "A Mind map is a thinking tool that reflects externally what goes on inside your head," Tony Buzan, *Maximize the Power of Your Brain,* http://www.youtube.com/watch?v=MlabrWv25qQ, (last visited 01/06/12). For information on software that can be purchased to assist in creating a mind map, *see,* Mind Technologies, http://www.visual-mind.com/concept_edu.html.

Here is a typical graphic organizer that uses a combination of "Mind mapping" and a flowchart.[8]

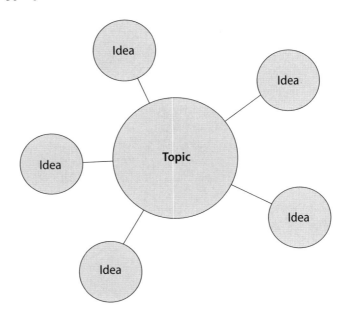

Here is a graphic organizer called a web flow chart.[9]

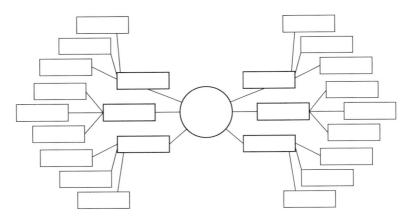

Traditional law school outlines have you look at your courses in a linear fashion and in the context of narrative text. Graphic organizers allow you to create visual images of the handful of core principles that link

---

8. ASCD, http://www.ascd.org/ASCD/images/publications/books/marzano2001a_fig6.2.gif (last visited 01/06/12).

9. *Printables for Teachers,* http://www.resources-teachers.com/img/graphic-organizers.jpg (last visited 01/06/12).

seemingly unrelated bits of information.[10] Further, by converting the material you discuss in class to something visual, you begin the process of absorbing it, processing the information and retaining. It is as much the process of *making* a flow chart or a graphic organizer that helps learning as much as it is the end product.

Consider the example of a First Amendment flow chart.[11]

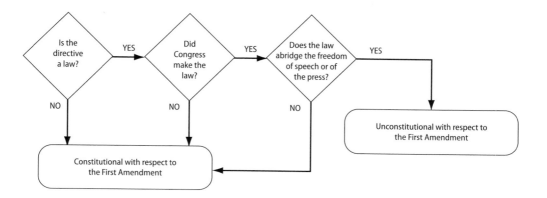

If you are willing to spend a little time on the web, you can find a software program that will help you create a variety of graphic organizers.[12] If you learn visually, then a picture is truly worth a thousand words. If you have a different learning style, then search for a method that allows you to learn most efficiently and effectively.

7. Study Groups

Outside of class time, you will also have the option of joining a study group. A study group is just that—a small group of students that meets together to discuss and review concepts from your classes. Members of study groups often share class notes and/or outlines. Study groups often work together to go over old exams. Many students find study groups helpful *if* you happen to pair up with students who learn in the same way that you do.

What makes for a good study group experience? In addition to finding students with similar learning styles, choose people with similar per-

---

10. Adapted from Study Guides and Strategies, The University of St. Thomas, St. Paul, MN.

11. From http://www.krusch.com/real/flow2.html (last visited 01/06/12).

12. For more information visit: Write Design Online, http://www.writedesignonline.com/organizers/ (last visited 01/06/12; Houghton Mifflin Harcourt, *Education Place,* http://www.eduplace.com/ss/maps/ (last visited 01/06/12; Graphic.org, *Graphic Organizers,* http://www.graphic.org/goindex.html (last visited 01/06/12).

sonality styles as well. For example, you want to avoid "moochers" if you are not a "moocher." Set objectives each week. Assign specific tasks for each member of the group. Use practice exam questions; invent your own multiple-choice questions and/or use flashcards. All of these activities replicate the law school exam experience.

Note that you do not *have* to join a study group to succeed in law school. In fact, some law students find that study groups do not benefit them enough to justify the amount of time they take. For example, if you need to learn the material by making your own flowcharts, then a study group that simply "talks out" problems may not be a good use of your study time. If you are having trouble simply getting through your course material, focus on *that* aspect of law school before joining a study group. You will likely hear other students talk about their study groups—which may make you feel like you will not do as well on exams without joining one. But be true to yourself and your learning style! If it isn't benefiting you, then don't spend time doing it!

Part II

Maximizing Your Academic Success While You're Deep *IN* the Trenches

While the first part of this book introduced you to various learning and study strategies that will benefit you in law school, the second part of this book looks more specifically at how to succeed in the law school classroom and in your exams. This part of the book also provides you with strategies for how to navigate successfully through your legal writing and legal research class. Further, Part II discusses the topics of outlining, multiple-choice exams, essay exams, test anxiety, planning for "deadweek" (the week immediately before exams) and law school depression. While Part I of this book introduced you to learning more *generally* in the law school environment, Part II focuses on the specific writing and testing-taking strategies that will help you succeed in your classes and on your exams.

So let's begin the next part of our journey: how to maximize your success while you're in the trenches of law school!

Chapter 6

Writing in Law School: Legal Structure, IRAC (No, Not the Country ...) and TREAC

Every law school has an introductory class focused on teaching you how to research and communicate the law. The most typical form of this class is "Legal Writing" or "Lawyering Skills" or "Legal Rhetoric." Whatever the name of the course, this is one of the most important classes in law school and it focuses on teaching you the unique analytical structure of a legal argument. Legal Writing demands that you *do* the work of a lawyer: you research the law, communicate the law and predict a result on behalf of your client.

There is no doubt that learning how to write within the required structure of legal writing is challenging, but it is also one of the most important skills you will master in law school. Even if you struggle with writing generally, you should make this class a priority because it is foundational: it teaches you the essence of being a lawyer—how to find the law, how to conceptualize a legal issue, and how to communicate the result to your client.

There are many benefits to your legal writing class (and other skills classes as well). For example, your legal writing class will tend to be smaller than your other law school classes. Therefore, there will be more opportunities for you to contribute your ideas and experiences on a topic because more class time is spent in discussion versus in a lecture. Second, you will have opportunities to conference one-on-one with your writing professor. This is how you will truly learn the craft of legal writing. Accordingly, you will have opportunities to talk with your professor about different ways of approaching legal research and writing. You should take these opportunities whenever they are presented to you. Make an appointment to talk to your writing professor. Perhaps the conversation will start out about your writing assignment but it may also cover learning strategies, study strategies, or any number of subjects. You have a rare opportunity in your legal writing classes to have a law school professor get to know you well! Email your professor and set up an appointment early on in the semester!

Finally, another distinctive aspect of your legal writing course is that you will have far *more* control over your work product than in your other classes. For example, you will get your writing problems several weeks before they are due. You will have time to perfect your work product *if* you use your time wisely. You may also have the opportunity to get feedback on your drafts before you turn them in. Again, ask your professor if he/she will review one of your drafts. If you can get feedback about your legal analysis before your assignments are due, you have the opportunity to excel in this class. Good writing is all about rewriting—you simply need to allow yourself the opportunity to rewrite!

There are many excellent books devoted specifically to the art of legal writing and analysis, and this chapter will not attempt to cover the material in those books. However, this chapter *will* approach legal writing and analysis very practically with a focus towards helping students who may find this class challenging at first. For some students, they get "stuck" in this class because they are not sure what their professor "wants." The format of the writing—and the assignments themselves—are unfamiliar. Many law students get stuck because they fail to adopt the formula for good legal structure. What do I mean by legal structure? I mean the formula or paradigm for a legal argument—typically called IRAC or TREAC. These are simply acronyms to help students remember that a legal argument is made up of several important parts.

This chapter will begin by focusing on legal structure—specifically how to use IRAC and TREAC to outline your arguments. This chapter will show you examples of actual law student writing. What did these students do correctly? Where did they fall astray? My hope is that by critiquing *real* examples, you will start to become more comfortable with the structure of a legal argument—which forms the basis of all legal writing (and law school exam writing as well!).

A. The Process of Writing

Writing is hard work—particularly when you are learning a new structure within which to write. So if you've had trouble writing in the past, you may think that you're not good at it. But the reality is that it's a skill—like anything else. And with effort, guidance and practice, you can learn how to write effectively as a lawyer.

The key to success in Legal Writing is to approach it with deference. It will be difficult—probably more so if you haven't written a lot in your prior education. It will take a lot of time (all writing does). But you *can* learn it. Sometimes, those students that have the *most* writing experience often struggle more with legal writing than less-experienced students because legal writing focuses (initially) on a rigid structure. Many English majors cringe at the idea of incorporating their wonderful and creative ideas into what they feel is a confining and rigid structure. But the structure is just the beginning—and a necessary one at that. Up until law school, you may not have done analytical writing before. Writing to present an *argument* is a different type of writing altogether. You are *reasoning* within your writing—and in order to do this in a convincing manner, you need to become comfortable with the structure for legal analysis.

B. The Structure of Legal Writing = Lasagna

Legal writing is like lasagna.[2] (Stay with me—it really *is* like lasagna!) Consider the typical legal reader—a busy judge or another lawyer. The legal reader has certain expectations about the structure of legal writing.[3] The legal reader wants a familiar organization; she wants vocabulary that she recognizes and understands. If you meet the legal reader's expectations regarding structure, then the legal reader (the judge or lawyer) is comfortable and open to your arguments.

Consider that this situation is very much like making lasagna for your friends or family. If you come home from work one night and tell your family that you're making lasagna, they have certain expectations about what lasagna should look and taste like. Your friends or family would expect cooked noodles, red sauce and melted cheese in defined layers. What would happen if you changed the structure of your lasagna? Suppose you didn't cook the noodles and you simply put the sauce on the side of the uncooked noodles. Your friends or family would be angry—"this is not the lasagna we expected at all!" And they would not want to eat your lasagna. They would rather throw it away and eat leftovers for dinner.

This same situation occurs for the legal reader. If a judge or lawyer has specific expectations about what your legal memorandum should look like and the type of language you should use, you want to meet those expectations. If you meet the legal reader's expectations, the judge will consider your arguments. But if you present the judge with a memorandum or brief that looks and sounds strange, the judge may not even bother to read your document. Busy legal readers do not have the time to wade through sloppy poorly written writing. And in the end, this hurts your client.

---

2. This analogy is widely used in the legal writing curriculum but it was made famous by Professor Sheila Simon, Clinical Professor of Law, University of Southern Illinois Law School. Professor Sheila Simon and Professor Richard Neumann use this analogy (and have a video clip) in their book, Richard K. Neumann and Sheila Simon, *Legal Writing*, (1st ed., Aspen Publishers 2008) and on the publisher's website.

3. The most typical types of legal writing are a legal memorandum (a memorandum drafted to explain research results and how the cases apply to your factual situation) and a brief (a type of adversarial document written by lawyers and submitted to the court advocating that the court make a particular ruling).

So although the structure I'm about to discuss will seem foreign to you (and likely bothersome as well), you will need to become comfortable with this new way of writing. If this is difficult for you (and it *is* for a lot of students), give yourself a bit more time than you *think* you need to complete your legal writing assignments. Start early and submit multiple drafts to your professor to receive feedback on your progress. In legal writing, the student who gets the first draft done early (to leave more time for revisions) typically is the student who is most successful in the class overall.

C. Structure = IRAC

In an earlier chapter, I introduced the basic legal formula or paradigm for a legal argument: IRAC. This acronym stands for the following: I = Issue; R = Rule; A = Application (or Analysis); and C = Conclusion.

This formula is a way to *begin* thinking about the structure of a legal argument. We will expand upon this formula when we discuss TREAC. However, let's begin by considering the meaning of each letter of the phrase IRAC.

I: Issue. The issue is the question that you're being asked to address— typically there may be a main issue and several sub-issues. When you brief a case, you seek out the legal issue which is typically the question being resolved by the court. When you write a legal memorandum, the attorney for whom you are writing may give you the legal issue that you need to address. The legal issue is comprised of the legal question combined with the client's unique facts. One of your first tasks in legal writing is to discern (1) the legal question; and (2) the relevant facts that apply to the question or issue.

R: Rule. The rule is most typically the law that applies to the particular legal issue. The rule can either come from a statute or a case—or a series of cases. You want to state the rule clearly and concisely, and there should always be a citation after the rule! (Lawyers love legal citations; law professors love legal citations, and judges love legal citations. And even though they are a pain to put into your writing, citations give your writing credibility and support.)

A: Application. The application section is the rule (that you've discerned from the law) as it is *applied* to the facts of your particular problem or case. This is the heart of your legal analysis. Your job is to take the rule and analyze how the rule applies to the facts of your case. You will develop possible arguments in favor of your client's position and against your client's position. You will support your arguments with cases and citations that support one position and then another. And you will come to some sort of conclusion or prediction as to the likely outcome of the legal issue. In other words, how would a court likely conclude and why?

C: Conclusion. Lastly, you will conclude ... again. Legal readers like conclusions (they like to be reminded of your prediction) and they like your conclusions to be clear and concise.

Here's a simple example of how IRAC works. The paragraph below uses the IRAC structure. Examine how the different sentences fall into the categories of IRAC. The appropriate label comes *before* each sentence.

ISSUE. In *Smith v. Jones*, 123 F.2d 456 (1st Cir. 1993), the court examined the issue of complete diversity of the parties. **RULE.** In *Smith*, the court relied upon the rule that stated that for diversity to be complete, every plaintiff must hold citizenship in a state that is different, or diverse, from every defendant's citizenship. **APPLICATION.** In the present case, the plaintiff, Doe, and the defendant, Moe, are both citizens of the same state, California. The plaintiff and the defendant do not hold diverse citizenship for purposes of diversity jurisdiction. Complete diversity of citizenship is lacking and the federal court may not assert subject matter jurisdiction based on diversity of citizenship. **CONCLUSION.** A court will likely dismiss the claim for lack of subject matter jurisdiction.

D. A More Advanced Formula: TREAC

IRAC is a simple formula and it ensures that you have all the parts of a legal argument. When I teach legal writing to students, I like to expand on the IRAC structure. Whereas IRAC is good for exam answers or case briefs, it is not detailed enough for more complex legal writing. I like to think about legal writing in terms of an expanded version of the IRAC structure called: TREAC.

The TREAC formula is comprised of the following parts: T = Thesis sentence (or topic sentence); R = Rule Statement; E = Explanation of the Rule; A = Application of Rule to Facts; and C = Conclusion.

The purpose behind TREAC is very similar to the purpose behind IRAC (to ensure you have all the parts of a good legal argument) but it offers more detail in two important respects. First, TREAC begins with a "T" for a "thesis sentence" which reminds you to state your main point about the paragraph or section very clearly. A thesis sentence tells the reader what the paragraph is about—the legal reader appreciates and *expects* this type of guidance. Further, the topic sentence often states your conclusion on the issue as well.

Second, in TREAC, the "R" of IRAC is subdivided into two separate concepts: "R" = Rule Statement; and "E" = Explanation of the Rule or Law. The Rule Statement is the same as in IRAC—it states the rule concisely and clearly. The "E" for Explanation is an important addition. The Explanation requires that you explain where the rule came from. Typically, in an Explanation section, you discuss the various cases that created the rule.

Finally, the "C" for Conclusion is the same in both IRAC and TREAC—it sums up your prediction clearly and concisely.

Let's consider TREAC specifically as it helps you think about how to formulate a strong argument within your legal writing assignment.

> **T = Thesis Sentence.** Begin your paragraph with a strong, clear thesis statement of your main point or likely result.
>
>> Example: *"Maddie Rice has a strong argument for showing that she and her step-mother have a 'close personal relationship.'"*
>
> **R = Rule Statement.** The Rule Statement is a concise statement of the rule (or element) that applies to this part of the problem.
>
>> Example: *"Under Marchetti v. Parsons, the plaintiff must be a 'close relative' of the victim in order to recover for Negligent Infliction of Emotional Distress."*
>
> **E = Explanation of the Rule.** The Explanation of the Rule tells the reader where the rule comes from. Usually, this section describes the cases that describe the rule. When you discuss a case (or cases) that help explain a rule, you will explain the facts, issue, holding and reasoning of the case (like a mini-case brief). In this section, you will not delve into your *arguments* about the cases or about the facts of your client's case. This section is purely for the lawyer or judge to *see* the law— and only the law. If you're discussing your client's facts in this section, you are mixing explanation and application. Make sure to only discuss the law in this section. Do NOT discuss the application of the law to YOUR case here!!!!
>
>> Example: *"In Marchetti v. Parsons, the Rhode Island Supreme Court clarified the requirements for a party to bring a claim for Bystander Negligent Infliction of Emotional Distress. In Marchetti, the parents of a child injured in accident brought action against driver who struck child. The court found ... [The Explanation continues laying out the facts, issue, holding and reasoning of the court]."*
>
> **A = Application.** The application section is where you do the work of a lawyer. In this section, you will take the law you have just discussed

and apply it to the facts of your particular case. This is where you bring in the facts of YOUR case. Sometimes I tell my students to *talk* this section out. If you were in front of the judge, what three points would you want to make about your case? Write those points down. Then find support for them. Is there a case that holds similarly? If so, state it and describe how it's similar. Are there opposing arguments? You'll want to have a paragraph dedicated to opposing arguments or counter-arguments. Typically you want to analyze all possibilities and discuss their strengths and their weaknesses in this section.

> Example: *"Maddie and Mary's relationship likely would meet the 'close relative' standard. Mary is the only mother figure Mary has ever known and has been in her life for two years. They clearly have a parent-child relationship that has been consistently found to meet the first element of negligent infliction of emotional distress. For example, in the <u>Rodrick v. Parsons</u> case, ... [describe the case as it relates to the issue; quote and cite to the court's language that defines a "parent-child" relationship]. Therefore, the present case is very similar to <u>Rodrick</u>. [cite]. The defense might argue that Mary is not Maddie's natural or adopted mother, but in all other ways Mary is Maddie's parent. Their involvement in each other's lives and Maddie's dependency on Mary will discount the technical aspects they are missing and allow Maddie to be defined as a close relative of her stepmother."*

C= Conclusion. Your conclusion is a restatement of your prediction or conclusion on the issue. It is a nicely constructed sentence that re-states your thesis sentence in a more concise form.

> Example: *"Maddie's physical symptoms will likely fulfill the second requirement easily."*

The TREAC formula is the key to strong legal writing. In my opinion, TREAC works better for legal writing (than IRAC) because legal writing is more detailed and complex than writing an exam answer. Your professors may suggest that you use IRAC in an exam answer and this is good advice. You have limited time in an exam situation and you are writing quickly. Using IRAC for an exam ensures that you will address all the main components of a legal argument—in other words, it prevents you from skipping an important component of your analysis and losing points!

But Legal Writing tries to accomplish *far more* in terms of detail and depth of arguments and counterarguments than writing a one-page exam answer. So a more detailed structure, like TREAC, is usually required. Think about TREAC as a building block to your legal writing. The next part of this chapter will walk you through the steps of how you would outline (and use TREAC) for a typical one-issue, legal memorandum assignment.

E. Beginning Your Legal Writing Assignment: Creating the Large-Scale Outline

Before you begin to implement TREAC, you should have worked through your legal writing problem in a detailed way, including reading and briefing the cases (that you've either researched yourself and chosen—or the ones given to you if this is a "closed universe" memorandum).[4] In addition, you should be able to articulate the major legal issues in your assignment. In other words, can you tell a friend what the legal issues are in the problem? Can you draft your Questions Presented?[5]

In creating your large-scale outline, your main or most significant legal issues will become the main headings in your legal memorandum (or brief). Your sub-issues will follow under these main headings. When you have completed a large scale outline of your issues, you *then* begin to form the structure of your argument by using TREAC.[6]

Below you will find an example of a first-year law student's large-scale outline for a legal memorandum. The student was asked to write a predictive legal memorandum analyzing whether the client could recover for Negligent Infliction of Emotional Distress after witnessing her stepmother's car accident. The main issue in the case was whether or not the client, Maddie Rice, could meet the specific elements of this tort claim. The elements for this cause of action came from Rhode Island common law. In other words, the Rhode Island Supreme Court issued an opinion that set out the elements for recovery for Bystander Negligent Infliction of Emotional Distress.

The following example is a first-year student's actual draft memorandum. Note in particular how the student uses the main legal issue and the elements of the Negligent Infliction of Emotional Distress claim to create the headings and subheadings/issues of the legal memorandum.[7] My comments are beside the memorandum and they describe in more detail the different elements of the large-scale outline.

---

4. A closed universe means that you are not allowed to do any of your own research.

5. The Question Presented is one initial component in a Legal Memorandum. A Question Presented is a statement of the legal issue in the case posed as a Question. It typically contains a statement of the rule, the legal question, and the legally significant facts. The Question Presented is followed by a Brief Answer.

6. Note that this method may not make sense for everyone, particularly if you happen to be a "free-flowing" writer. But if you're stuck with the structure of your legal writing, you might try this technique to at least begin to outline the major issues and sub-issues of your assignment.

Large-Scale Outline of NIED Assignment

File: Maddie Rice

I. Whether Maddie Rice Can Recover for Negligent Infliction of Emotional Distress

> This is the main legal issue students have been asked to address in the Legal Memorandum.

    A. Elements of Claim: Introduction/Thesis paragraph stating issues in case.

       "Relying upon the reasoning of our previous cases and our discussion today, we hold that in order to recover for a negligent infliction of emotional distress, a party must (1) be a close relative of the victim, (2) be present at the scene of the accident and be aware that the victim is being injured, and (3) as a result of experiencing the accident, suffer serious emotional injury that is accompanied by physical symptomatology." <u>Marchetti v. Parsons</u>, 638 A.2d 1052, 1053 (1994),

> This is what is commonly called a Thesis paragraph or an Umbrella paragraph. It lays out the main issues of the memorandum. I recommend to students that this is where they should lay out the elements of the NIED claim.

    B. Main Discussion of NIED Issue:

> Now we break down the elements of NIED and these elements become our sub-issues.

       1. Must be a Close Relative of the Victim.

       2. Must Be Present at the Scene of the Accident and Be Aware that the Victim is Being Injured.

       3. As a Result of Experiencing the Accident, Must suffer Serious Emotional Injury that is Accompanied by Physical Symptomatology.

    C. Conclusion

F. Filling in the TREAC

After creating a large-scale outline, fill in the details under each section and create sub-issues where necessary. This next example shows how the student filled in the large-scale outline with the TREAC components. In essence, the student created a mini-TREAC within each major element of the Negligent Infliction of Emotional Distress claim.[8] Again, using a TREAC for each element ensures that you have all the parts for a strong legal argument as it relates to that element.

---

7. Keep in mind that this is a student's *rough* outline—so there are sentence fragments, technically imperfect citations, etc. The purpose of this example, however, is to show you one way to beginning outlining the structure of a legal memorandum.

8. Note that there is no right or wrong way to outline a legal issue. As long as you are using the right elements for the claim—you can format your outline in many different ways. The main point is to begin to organize *something!*

Outline of NIED Assignment

I. Whether Maddie Rice Can Recover for Negligent Infliction of Emotional Distress

A. Introduction/Thesis paragraph stating issues in case.

"Relying upon the reasoning of our previous cases and our discussion today, we hold that in order to recover for a negligent infliction of emotional distress, a party must (1) be a close relative of the victim, (2) be present at the scene of the accident and be aware that the victim is being injured, and (3) as a result of experiencing the accident, suffer serious emotional injury that is accompanied by physical symptomatology." Marchetti v. Parsons, 638 A. 2d 1052, 1053 (1994).

1. **T: Thesis Statement:** Maddie Rice Can Likely Prove She Was a "Close Relative" of Her Stepmother, Mary Rice.

2. **R: Rule Statement:** The first element of NIED is that there must be a close relationship between plaintiff and the victim of negligence. (cite to *Marchetti*).

3. **E: Rule Explanation:** Explain *Marchetti* (facts, issue, holding, reasoning). Must be at Accident Scene and must be aware that the victim is being injured. (Witnessing the Accident is not a prerequisite): Parents of a child injured in accident brought action against driver who struck child. Court held that parents could not recover for negligent infliction of emotional distress because parents were not present at the scene of the accident. Child was crossing the street and struck by a car driven by defendant. She was transported to hospital. Parents saw her on a stretcher in the hallway of the emergency room. She had not yet been treated; "appeared lifeless, was immobile and bloodied, and had a tube in her throat."

The *Marchetti* rule came from *D'Ambra*: the court "identified a number of factors to be considered in determining the scope of a defendant's liability for negligent infliction of emotional distress to an accident bystander. These factors included "physical proximity [to the accident], the actual witnessing of the accident, and the personal relationship existing between the bystander-plaintiff and the victim." 338 A.2d at 531. "We went on to state, however, that there are "other factors which, given the right circumstances, may be of major importance in determining whether an adequate relation exits between the defendant's conduct and the plaintiff's injury." *Id*.

The *Marchetti* court also discussed *D'Ambra*. The *D'Ambra* court stated: "We consider today whether witnessing an accident is a prerequisite to recovering for negligent infliction of emotional distress or, instead, whether it is a nonessential factor — one among many to be considered by a trial justice in determining if a defendant owes a duty to the emotionally injured plaintiff. We hold that in order to recover, a party must be present at the scene of the accident and be aware that the victim is being injured." 338 A.2d at 531.

Note how the student begins to put short summaries of the significant facts. The student also uses quotes from the most important part of the case. This technique allows the student to add the necessary legal support to the arguments.

It is a great idea to use actual quotes and citations in your detailed outline; it saves time because you don't have to search for the cites/quotes later as you write.

Marchetti Holding: In order to recover for negligent infliction of emotional distress, a party must (1) be a close relative of the victim; (2) be present at the scene of the accident and be aware that the victim is being injured, and (3) as a result of experiencing the accident, suffer serious emotional injury that is accompanied by physical symptomatology. Absent these three elements, a plaintiff who seeks to recover for emotional distress arising out of an injury to a relative may not recover for negligent infliction of emotional distress.

4. **A: Application.** Applying the rule to the facts of this case:

In this case, a court would likely rule that Maddie and Mary Rice were "close relatives" under the *Marchetti* holding. They were step-daughter/step-parent. Mary would have adopted Maddie but for grandparents' concern. Mary was the only mother Maddie had known. Like parents in both *D'Ambra* and *Marchetti,* there is a similar-type relationship. (cite to facts of both *D'Ambra* and *Marchetti*).

Counterargument: The definition of "relative" implies a close familial relationship. Extending this definition to include step-parent/step-child relationship is too far. Likelihood for success: Not likely a successful counterargument because purpose of NIED is to compensate for loss of a close relationship. Maddie and her step-mother have that.

5. **C = Conclusion:** Accordingly, Maddie will likely satisfy this first element of NIED.

B. Must Be Present at the Scene of the Accident and Be Aware that the Victim is Being Injured.

1. **T: Thesis Sentence:** Maddie can likely prove the second element of bystander NIED, that she was "present at the scene of the accident and aware the victim was being injured." [cite to case]. Although this may be a more difficult element to prove, Maddie can make a strong argument that she satisfies this element of NIED.

2. **R: Rule Statement:** The current rule is from *Marchetti* which states that a party must be "present at the scene of the accident and be aware that the victim is being injured." [cite].

3. **E: Rule Explanation:** Start with *D'Ambra* to show chronology: *D'Ambra* originally required that the victim actually witness the accident. However, the *Marchetti* court interpreted *D'Ambra* to require only an examination of several factors — not to require that the victim witness the accident. *Marchetti* required that "a party must be present at the scene of the accident and be aware that the victim is being injured." However, the *Marchetti* court was not entirely clear on what this language means. Expand on possible interpretations.

4. **A: Application:** Maddie certainly was present at the accident scene and saw her mother in the ambulance, on the stretcher and covered with a blanket. She saw her mother's car. She was aware her mother had been badly hurt in the accident. However, the phrase "be aware

Here, the student begins to develop the arguments. The writer is applying the rule (related to the 'close relative' element) to the facts of the case.

Make sure not to forget counterarguments. Also provide an assessment of whether you think they are viable arguments.

that the victim is being injured" seems to imply that the party view the injury as it is occurring. However, given that *Marchetti* looks at many factors, Maddie can make a convincing argument that she was at the scene and saw her mother in an injured condition. If the policy behind this requirement is to prevent fraudulent claims, this interpretation would seem to keep that in place.

<u>Counterargument</u>: *Marchetti* is simply interpreting *D'Ambra*—but not really changing the requirement of the court wanting the victim to be at the scene and essentially witness the accident. Additionally, the facts in *Marchetti* involved parents who weren't at the scene. Court dismissed the claim based upon those facts. The court's discussion on what the *D'Ambra* court meant is simply dicta. Must go back to the requirement in *D'Ambra* and *Caparco* that require witnessing the accident. And, the language "is aware victim is being injured" requires the literal interpretation of being at the scene and witnessing part of the injury. This was not the case here.

At this stage of your outline, your writing does not have to be perfect. But having a detailed outline and using TREAC helps you strengthen and maintain your organization as you begin to write.

Hopefully, this outline gives you a sense of how you can build your analysis in a legal memorandum by starting with a broad outline and then filling in the different parts with TREAC. And then—magically, you have completed several pages of your outline and analysis, and you can begin writing the narrative.

G. Filling in Your TREAC — Part II: Adding Arguments and Detail

The next step in your writing process is to fill in the parts of your outline (and TREAC) in more detail. Specifically, you will want to focus on your Application section—the part of the outline where you address your client's strongest arguments and the possible counterarguments of the opposition. Have you used the facts of your case to support your client's argument? Begin to flush out your client's strongest arguments. Have you analogized or distinguished the cases that you discussed in your Explanation section? Law professors like to see some cites back to cases in your analysis section—combined with the facts of your case. This is a section that mixes fact and law—so make sure you have both.

And if you're really stuck on your memo, try to at least get working on one section—perhaps the Fact Statement. In a Legal Memorandum, the fact statement is comprised of the story of your client's case. Using the documents in your case file or your Assignment Memo, you can create a concise, well-written fact statement. The fact statement is often the easiest place to start when you experience writer's block.

I have found that the biggest hurdle in legal writing for law students who learn differently is to *get something on paper*. Your initial draft does not have to be brilliant or even passable. Good writing is all about re-writing! Your goal is to get a first draft done, i.e., put something down for each section in your outline. Then you can move onto the revising stage. The revising stage is typically the *longest* stage in the writing process.

H. Beginning to Write: Possible Challenges in Legal Writing for Beginning Law Students

In legal writing, you will develop and organize what you want to say and then put it down on paper (or in the computer). For beginning law students, having to organize a complicated assignment with many parts can be challenging. A typical legal writing assignment will take several weeks to complete, and it often requires a series of stages including planning, writing, and revising. These steps are part of a *recursive* rather than a linear process, i.e., each step is revisited during the writing process and the steps do not always proceed in the same order. The following suggestions may help you avoid the common pitfalls of beginning law students specifically as they apply to legal writing.

1. **Have a Plan of Action.** Have a well-developed plan of action for your writing. Make a calendar starting with the due date and work backwards to the present date. Plan out every specific stage of the writing process, including researching, outlining, writing, revising, citing, proofreading, etc., and write it on your calendar. Stick to the plan! Your plan will serve as a concrete step to allow you to *engage* in the writing process and it may help you move forward when you feel stuck. A plan also provides a permanent reminder about the content and structure of the writing task.

2. **Create a First Draft.** This is a very important step. Choose a specific date by which you will produce a first draft and stick to it! By giving yourself a firm deadline for a first draft, you can prevent procrastination problems. Some students wait until the last minute. You cannot do this and succeed in law school. Legal writing is too complicated and takes too much time.

3. **Revising and Editing.** Revising and editing skills are critical to effective legal writing. You need to leave ample time (at least several days) so you can revise and edit your work. Plan to complete at least

three complete drafts. You will need to revise each of those drafts. In addition, plan to leave one day for proofreading and citation. In my experience, many law students begin the revising stage of their writing too late. As a result, these students turn in a paper that could have been great but was only average because of a lack of revising, editing and proofreading.

4. **Obtain Feedback.** If possible, try to obtain written feedback from your professor during the different stages of your writing process (and drafts). Many students are reluctant to ask for feedback — perhaps they don't want to bother their professor or they don't want to talk about their struggles with writing. But receiving feedback is *how you learn.* Frequent feedback can make a huge difference in the quality of your writing. Meet with your professor early on. (This will help you stay with the different stages of writing). Bring your drafts to a meeting and discuss your work to make sure you are not missing critical elements and/or cases. What are the assignment's strengths? What are its weaknesses? Ask your professor to give you feedback. Although this may be difficult at first, this can also open up an important dialogue between you and your professor. Having this dialogue (and relationship) with your professor can significantly enhance your success.

I. Checking Your Structure

Now that you've completed a draft (and revised, and revised ...), it is time to check your legal writing structure. This occurs before your final 'proofing' stage. This section will end by simulating an important exercise I have my students complete prior to handing in their final memoranda in their Legal Writing I class. This exercise forces students to check their own legal structure within TREAC. Do they have a rule for every section? Have they addressed counterarguments in the application section?

I direct my students to color-code the TREAC formula in their legal writing assignment.[9] In other words, I have them bring their colored highlighters to class. After they have completed a second or third draft of their writing assignment, I ask them to make sure they have all the components of good legal structure.

Using their highlighters, I ask them to highlight each component of the TREAC structure within the assignment.

---

9. This assignment is particularly helpful for visual learners and kinesthetic learners because you are seeing the elements and moving your highlighter over the words.

The example that begins on the following page is the first section of a first-year law student's motion brief (a brief submitted to a trial court).[10] This assignment involved a motion *in limine*[11]—a trial-level motion that asked the court to exclude a particular piece of evidence. This issue was governed by a state rule of evidence (Rhode Island Rule of Evidence 403) and several cases interpreting the rule.

In this example, see if you can identify the different components of TREAC within a fully written assignment. As you read through the comments (and the highlighted sections), evaluate the student's writing. Did the student explain the law well enough? Were you persuaded by the student's arguments in the Application section? Did the student address the counter-arguments thoroughly? These are the types of questions that you will use to evaluate your *own* writing as well.

---

10. Note that this is an example of persuasive writing—which is usually covered during the second part of your first year (or during your second year). During your first semester of legal writing, you will focus on predictive writing (which is more objective, with the purpose of evaluating a legal question and predicting a result). Persuasive writing advocates for a particular position. Therefore, it tends to be more one-sided in its exploration of the possible arguments, i.e., there may be less time devoted to articulating the counter-analysis.

11. *In limine* means "at the threshold." A motion *in limine* is a pre-trial evidentiary motion that litigants file in order to have the court rule on the admissibility of evidence before trial.

DISCUSSION

A. The Photograph of Ross Gellar Offers Relevant Evidence of Plaintiff's Emotional Distress Under Rule 402 and Proves Material Facts Essential to Ms. Green's Bystander Negligent Infliction of Emotional Distress and Wrongful Death Claims.

Good use of a heading to state the issue clearly and guide the reader.

Good thesis sentence/s. This clearly sets out the main point in this paragraph.

T H E S I S

T: The photograph of Plaintiff's husband, Ross Gellar, is necessary to demonstrate Ms. Green's experience to the jury. It is relevant to Ms. Green's bystander negligent infliction of emotional distress (henceforth NIED) claim and proves contested elements of material fact. Aside from some cleaning done by the Coroner to make the body less gruesome, the photograph shows Mr. Gellar's body as Rachel Green saw it on May 24, 2006. The injuries to Mr. Gellar's right shoulder and right torso are also apparent in the photograph.

This quote is helpful as it tells the reader very specifically what the Rhode Island courts look at with regard to photographs.

R U L E

R: Under Rhode Island Rules of Evidence 402 and 403, all relevant evidence is admissible unless its probative value is outweighed by the danger of unfair prejudice … or needless presentation of cumulative evidence. R.I. R. Evid. 402,403. The court has wide discretion in deciding whether photographs are relevant under Rule 402 and admissible under Rule 403. **E:** The Rhode Island Supreme Court has declared, "a photograph of a murder victim is admissible so long as it is competent evidence which reasonably tends to prove or disprove some material fact at issue, provided it is not offered for the sole purpose of arising the passions of the jury." *State v. Bowden*. 324 A.2d 631, 637 (R.I. 1974).

T: Thesis Sentence
R: Rule Statement
E: Explanation of the Rule
A: Analysis
C: Conclusion

E X P L A N A T I O N O F R U L E

The Rhode Island Supreme Court has generally allowed photographs as evidence under a test for admissibility developed in *State v. Belloli:* "If a photograph is of such a nature as to inflame the jurors and therefore prejudice them beyond the ordinary prejudice always sustained by the introduction of relevant evidence intended to prove guilt," then its probative value is outweighed by the danger of unfair prejudice under Rhode Island's Rule of Evidence 403. 776 A.2d 928, 930 (R.I. 2001). In *State v. Belloli*, the court allowed enlarged, gruesome autopsy photographs as evidence in order to illustrate the medical examiner's testimony and assist the state in establishing elements of torture and aggravated battery for first-degree murder. *Id.* at 931. The court held that the photographs provided "a proper understanding of the corpus delicti, the extent of the injury, the condition and identification of the body" and were relevant to the question of the degree of atrociousness of the crime." *Id.*

Similarly, in *State v. Bowden*, the Rhode Island Supreme Court held that a photograph of a gruesome, water-distorted body was admissible in order to prove material facts of the State's claims. If the photograph proves a material fact in issue, "it is of no concern that a photograph may be unpleasant to view or that it may have influence beyond the strict limits or the purpose for which it was introduced." *Bowden*, 324 A.2d at 637. The court ruled that the photograph of a murder victim was admissible to assist in establishing that the corpse was that of the victim.

A: The photograph of Ross Gellar, though gruesome, invokes the ordinary prejudice necessary to establish Ms. Green's NIED claim. It is not offered for the sole purpose of arousing the passions of the jury. In order for the jury to determine whether Ms. Green can recover for NIED, they must understand what Ms. Green experienced at the time. Ms. Green fainted upon witnessing her husband's body. Other evidence indicates that she was in optimal health prior to witnessing the accident. While Atlantis Resorts admits breach of the duty of care in negligence, Ms. Green must prove that it was this breach of duty that caused her to experience emotional distress and, subsequently, go into acute hypertensive crisis that led to the loss of her child.

> Good, strong thesis sentence that begins the Application section. The reader clearly knows the writer's position.

Even though other forms of evidence are available, the jury could not fully understand the extent of the emotional trauma that Ms. Green experienced on May 24, 2006 without seeing a close representation of what Ms. Green witnessed before she fainted. The photograph is the only evidence available for this purpose. The photograph is a less-gruesome representation of what Ms. Green experienced at the accident. Ross Gellar's body has been partially cleaned up by the coroner, and thus gives a less-gruesome, less-prejudicial representation of what Ms. Green witnessed. Although less-gruesome, the image of Ross Gellar properly represents Mr. Gellar's injuries and is suitable evidence of what Ms. Green saw at the accident. Furthermore, in *State v. Belloli*, the photographs were enlargements of photographs already available as evidence and more gruesome than those presented in the present case. *Belloli*, 776 A.2d at 930. Yet, though cumulative, the court allowed the photographs as evidence to establish elements essential to the state's claims. *Id.* In the instant case, the photographs are equally essential to establish Ms. Green's bystander NIED claim.

> Good factual analysis, but still try to link the arguments back to the cases that were explained above. The writer does it below in the next paragraph, which is great. But, any time one can draw a comparison, the better. Be very specific with factual analogies. "Like *Belloli*, where the evidence was relevant because it proved an element in issue, the photo in the present case shows ..."

While this is not a prosecution for murder, and elements such as atrociousness of the crime and condition of the body are not generally necessary to NIED claims, the condition of the body and extent of the injury are essential to understand Ms. Green's negative reaction that led to her acute hypertensive crisis. The jury must decide that the accident could create similar reactions in reasonable people.

> By rearranging slightly, the student can make this first sentence SO much more persuasive. Start with the strong assertion, as this is the first thing the judge sees: "The condition of the body and extent of the injury are essential to understanding ...," and then end with ".. despite the fact that it was a murder.... "

Finally, the photograph of Ross Gellar proves contested material facts in the case, including the location of the injuries, and is thus relevant to Ms. Green's wrongful death claim. The photograph shows the shark bites and is a faithful representation of the victim, Ross Gellar. Photographs that show faithful representations of victims are generally admissible to aid the jury in arriving at the proper understanding of the events in question, especially when some principle facts are in dispute. *Bowden*, 324 A.2d at 637. The court in Bowden highlights that evidence having a natural tendency to establish the facts in controversy should be admitted. *Id.*

> Good concluding sentence here. Link the conclusion on this issue with the rules again. Remember, you are always tying your arguments back with the law the court will apply.

C: The Plaintiff asks the to court admit the coroner's photograph of Ross Gellar to aid the jury in establishing whether Ms. Green can recover for Bystander NIED and wrongful death.

APPLICATION

CONCLUSION

The previous example represents a good start to the Discussion section (the argument section of the brief). The student followed the TREAC structure well.

As you read through examples of legal writing, train yourself to critically evaluate the writing. We learn the most about writing when we critique what we've read. Even the published opinions that you read each day for class could use further revisions. As you've probably gathered by this point in your law school career, judicial opinions are *not* always well-written!

J. When the TREAC Structure Is Missing

The prior example illustrated what a Discussion section looks like when a writer uses the TREAC structure. But what does it *look* like (and how does it *read*) when a student fails to conform to the ideal legal structure? Many law students' first or second (or even third) legal memoranda will lack a coherent legal structure. How does this adversely affect the clarity and credibility of the writing? Would you as a lawyer *trust* the writer's assessment?

In this next example, the student writer does not follow the TREAC structure. Read through this example. Can you identify the parts of TREAC formula? Although the writer certainly has some aspects of TREAC, consider how missing *some* elements (or changing their order) affects the overall writing. Evaluate the following example focusing on how the writer incorporated the TREAC formula.

DISCUSSION

I. EXHIBIT 24 IS A PROTECTED DOCUMENT PURSUANT TO THE LAWYER-CLIENT PRIVILEGE.

Good to use the actual law here. Typically, the rule should be introduced with some text before jumping into a quote.

A. The Lawyer-Client Privilege in Wisconsin Statute § 905.03 applies to Exhibit 24.

R: Section 905.03 (2) provides as follows:

(2) General rule of privilege. A client has a privilege to refuse to disclose and to prevent any other person from disclosing confidential communications made for the purpose of facilitating the rendition of professional legal services to the client.

True, but what are the decisions and what's the cases' relevance to the client? This is an important thesis sentence and I think MORE can be done with it. It should say something about the interpretation of the case law.

E: Wisconsin has decided cases regarding protected information. *Dudek v. Circuit Court for Milwaukee County*, 150 N.W.2d 387, 398. In *Dudek,* attorney Dudek was subpoenaed as a witness against his client. Dudek refused to reveal certain information he had because, "the questions inquire into matters that are privileged as attorney-client communications." *Id.* at 393–394. Although the court (insert how the court reacted to this) the Supreme Court went on to say of the issue of attorney-client privilege:

This seems like the writer is talking about policy here, and she may want to introduce it as such. Use the cases to set out the policy behind the attorney-client privilege.

"The administration of justice is thought best promoted by a rule which encourages clients to reveal the facts fully to their attorneys. By encouraging revelation of the facts to the attorney, the privilege is also calculated to serve the basic objective of the jurisprudential system. Without the rule, parties would not reveal all of the facts because of fear of detriment or embarrassment. It is better to have otherwise concealed facts within the knowledge of the person charged with the direction of the lawsuit, even though he must not reveal the communication, than to have those facts or opinions buried within the knowledge of the client."

I'm not sure what this means. Transparency? Does the writer mean "communication" or "relationship"? Try to be very precise with the use of words.

Id. at 398. The purpose behind Wisconsin Statute § 905.03(2) is to protect transparency between attorney and client. This transparency is necessary for an attorney to advocate on behalf of their client's interests.

T: **Missing Thesis Sentence!** The reader has to jump immediately to the law without a reference to the purpose of the law.

T: Thesis Sentence
R: Rule Statement
E: Explanation of the Rule
A: Analysis
C: Conclusion

A: Missing Application of the law. This section simply ends without an actual application of the law/rule just discussed to the facts of the case. The Application section is perhaps the most important section of the brief.
C: Missing Conclusion.

T: Missing Thesis. Usually, a writer wants to have a thesis sentence that states the main point before jumping into the rule/statute. It lets the reader know the overall framework of the section and why the statute is relevant.

E: Missing Explanation of Rule and/or Discussion of Cases. Once again, this is a substantive omission. What cases have discussed and/or interpreted this rule? The judge needs to see how the law has been applied in this jurisdiction.

Typically, introduce the reader to your application/ analysis by starting with a strong thesis sentence to organize the paragraph. Further, address the first element of this analysis more explicitly: make the point here or earlier that Exhibit 24 *IS* a confidential communication. State the law first, facts/analysis second.

Substantive concern: Note that the Explanation of the rule, i.e., the case discussion, is missing above.

B. Exhibit 24 Is a "Confidential Communication" Made For the Purpose of Facilitating Professional Legal Services in accordance with Wisconsin Statute §905.03(d).

Section 905.03(1)(d) provides as follows:

R U L E

(d) A communication is "confidential" if not intended to be disclosed to 3rd persons other than those to whom disclosure is in furtherance of the rendition of professional legal services to the client or those reasonably necessary for the transmission of the communication.

A P P L I C A T I O N

A: In his affidavit, Jon Peters specified to attorney Block that "These, [the statements] are for your eyes only." (Affidavit 2). Mr. Peters further commented, "I left [attorney Block's office] believing that I had handed over my communications to Sam Block and that they were confidential communications." (Affidavit 2). Sam Block corroborates Mr. Peters' statement in his affidavit noting that he heard Mr. Peters say something to him to the effect of, "Here you go … these are for your eyes only …" (Affidavit 1) once Mr. Peters handed him the document.

Additionally, Exhibit 24 was produced 'in furtherance of the rendition of professional legal services to the client.' Section 905.03(1)(d). In his affidavit, Jon Peters stated, "I wrote the documents for the sole purpose of communicating this information to my attorney in preparation for the deposition." (Affidavit 2). This deposition was being taken in light of a divorce action which was under way between Jon Peters and his wife Macy Peters.

Without proof to the contrary, Exhibit 24 is a "confidential communication" within the spirit of Section 905.03(1)(d) because Jon Peters had not intended the document to be disclosed to 3rd persons.

C O N C L U S I O N

C: Additionally, Jon Peters made Exhibit 24 exclusively for the purpose of rendering professional legal service in the spirit of Wisconsin Statute 905.03(1)(d) and Exhibit 24 should therefore be barred from the case at hand.

Good use of the facts of the case. Weave in the law/cases as well. The judge is interested in the facts, but the writer's job is to persuade the judge by illustrating how the law supports the case as well as the facts. Compare (analogize) the facts of the case to like cases in the jurisdiction. This is the heart of persuasion. Is the case similar or different from the *Dudek* case discussed above? How?

What did you think of this argument section? Did it persuade you that the writer's position was supported by the law? This paper was missing some very important substantive discussion, including the explanation of the cases that discuss the attorney-client privilege and the application of the law to the facts of the present case. With some additional effort, this student's paper could certainly be revised to minimally include all the elements of the TREAC formula. However, if this were the student's final draft, the student would receive a lower grade because so much of the substance is missing from the assignment.

Note also that whenever an essential element of the TREAC structure is missing in a legal argument, the argument is far less complete and persuasive. Even if you are writing an objective (or predictive) legal memorandum, your writing lacks support and credibility without each element of the TREAC formula.

As you begin to write your first legal writing assignment, try to become comfortable with this type of legal structure. It is difficult at first, but it is also something that will help you in every aspect of law school. As you progress as a legal writer, you will be able to stray from this structure when appropriate. However, as a new legal writer, the structure of TREAC helps make sure that your legal argument on an issue contains all the relevant parts. Remember that your legal reader expects a certain structure! Try your best to incorporate that structure as you write your assignments in law school.

Chapter 7

Tips for Organizing Your Legal Research

This chapter will offer several tips for how to begin your legal research projects in an organized and efficient manner. Legal research is most typically a component of your Legal Writing course in law school although some law schools teach legal research as a separate course. Legal research is another topic (like legal writing) that warrants an entire book (and there are several excellent legal research textbooks out there already).

Therefore, the purpose of this chapter is offer a few suggestions that will help you organize and complete your legal research assignments more efficiently. Over the years, I've seen that students who struggle with legal research seem to get stuck in similar places. For example, many students find that they love to research the law. They get lost in the cases and enjoy formulating arguments. However, sometimes these students cannot *stop* researching! In other words, these students get stuck in the process of legal research—they continue looking for cases believing that there must be a perfect case out there. Accordingly, these students spend too much time on the research phase of an assignment and too little time on the writing and revising stages of an assignment.

This chapter will provide you with a plan of action (and a research outline) to help you make your legal research more manageable and efficient.

A. Organizing Your Legal Research: Using a Research Log

For many beginning law students, legal research may be initially overwhelming. With the advent of electronic research, i.e., specific research databases such as Westlaw, Lexis or LoisLaw, legal research is faster than ever before. But legal research is also exponentially more abundant—meaning that you have access to thousands of cases and sources. If you have problems processing and organizing information, you may find yourself getting *too much* information too quickly. Further, many students begin their legal research too quickly—in other words, they jump onto the computer immediately and input searches without truly identifying the specific questions or research terms that apply to their client's case. Using imprecise or haphazard search terms can lead to imprecise and inefficient search results. In the end, this wastes time because you have to sort through the irrelevant search results before you begin to narrow down the correct legal issue.

When you begin working on your first legal research assignment, you need a game plan — just like the process for legal writing. For the first several research assignments in my class, I have my students complete a Research Log. The purpose of the Research Log is to organize the legal issues and to systemize the way you search for legal sources. The Research Log gives you a concrete plan of action. Filling out a Research Log may seem tedious at first. Eventually, however, you will become familiar with the steps of legal research and you will perform these steps automatically. Until this happens, however, you want to approach legal research with the following plan.

The example that begins on the next page shows an initial research project in a first-year Legal Writing Class. The first part of the assignment presents the Research Log. I instruct my students to fill out the different parts of the Research Log as they complete their legal research for this assignment. I also require my students to use both electronic resources and print resources from the library. You should do this as well. Verifying your research results with both types of research allows you to 'check' your research!

In addition, I ask the students to create a statement of the legal issue by answering important questions in the Preliminary Steps portion of the Research Log. Students then identify the Primary Sources of Law and move to the Secondary Sources of Law. Although you may research the law in any order, i.e., go to secondary sources first, the Research Log ensures that you check both types of sources.

Research Log 1 : Assignment and Template

Bystander NIED in California

Prof. Christensen

Legal Writing I

We will be representing Rachel Gellar, a young woman who was on a boat while her fiancé, Ross Gellar, received fatal injuries as a result of a shark bite (during a shark dive hosted by the Atlantis Resort). Among other claims, Rachel would like to bring suit against Atlantis Resorts for Bystander Negligent Infliction of Emotional Distress for the distress she suffered as a result of viewing a portion of the accident which caused the death of her fiancé. Rachel lives in Los Angeles and we will bring suit in California state court (Atlantis Resorts is incorporated in California). Therefore, please research what is required in California for our client to recover for Bystander Negligent Infliction of Emotional Distress. I will provide additional facts after receiving your initial research log.

Requirements: This research journal should be the product of your own effort. Although you may talk with others in the class about the process of research, what you've found, etc., all written work (and decisions about how and why the authority is relevant) the actual writing MUST be your own work.

Please also note that I am requesting you provide two *sources from the library*, i.e., proof that you have gone to the library and copied directly from the reporters and/or other sources from the library. Please attach the copies of the sources to the Research Log when you hand it in. For your other research, you may use either electronic resources or book research, or a combination of both (i.e., find a case from the digests in the library and print them off from the electronic resources).

I. Preliminary Steps:

    A. Before you start to research, **record** your preliminary steps. This section will describe the preliminary steps you've taken for this assignment before you've begun researching. Make sure you understand the research question and the issues that are presented by the problem.

       Please respond specifically to the questions listed below.

          Is this problem an issue of state or federal law?

          What authority will be mandatory?

          What authority will be persuasive?

          What jurisdiction am I in?

          What are potential research/search terms?

          Where do I think I'm going to look first?

          Where should I start, the library or the computer?

    B. **Prepare a preliminary statement of what you believe the issue/s to be at this point.**

II. Primary Authority Research:

This is an issue governed by common-law, so there are no applicable statutes. Therefore, you can proceed to identify the relevant cases.

A. **Five Most Relevant Cases and Your Analysis of Them:**

Select and describe the five best cases you have found (not the first five cases you have found). Provide a *full and correct* citation to the case and briefly describe how each case may be useful to our situation (and specifically what issue to which it may apply). Your descriptions should include a brief statement of the facts, issue and holding of the case, and you should explain how the case is helpful or harmful to the issues in your case, etc. Note also whether the cases are mandatory or persuasive authority.

1.

2.

3.

4.

5.

B. **Other cases.**

Provide a list of other cases that you located that may not be the five best cases. Explain how you found them (but you do not have to go into detail about the case's relevance). Please also provide a full and correct citation for each of these cases (limit of 10 cases).

IV. Secondary Sources:

A. **Explain the steps** that you took to locate secondary sources and authority. **List at least three secondary sources** that you would use to analyze the issues raised in the problem. Briefly explain how you located each authority and why it may be useful to this particular issue for our client.

V. Am I Done Yet?

A. Did the authorities that you have located refer back to each other? Did the new authorities that you located fail to reveal any significant new information, i.e., this is one way to check that you've found all the relevant information.

VI. What was the most surprising thing about the research for this problem?

The Research Log allows you to begin your research in an organized fashion. Remember that research is a recursive process—it is not linear but cyclical. You may begin pursuing one avenue only to find out that it was a dead end. Begin again and take a different path. But try to record your different paths so you know where you've been and where you're heading.

B. Final Tips for Legal Research

The following section offers four final tips to improve your efficiency with legal research: (1) know when to stop researching; (2) limit the number of cases you ultimately choose to write about; (3) organize your research; and (4) begin to write.

1. The Biggest Challenge: Knowing When to Stop!

One of the most important skills to develop as a law student is to learn when to *STOP* researching your problem. As you become more practiced at the skill of legal research, you will gain an intuitive sense of when to stop researching, and when to begin outlining and writing. Until then, give yourself a firm deadline as to when you will stop your research. Choose a date on the calendar, e.g., one week after the date you receive your assignment, and do as much research as you can until that point, and then stop![1]

The biggest mistake I see *all* law students make is the tendency to believe that there is one 'right' case out there if only you can find it. The reality is that there is no 'perfect' case that answers the issue completely. As with most legal problems in real life, your job as a lawyer is to take the cases you *do* find and synthesize the cases (see how they fit together) into a rule that a lawyer can use. You then apply that rule to the facts of the case to predict a result. This is the *work* of lawyers.

2. You Cannot Write About 50 Cases!

Another issue that beginning law students tend to have is that they want to write about too many cases. When you begin to research your legal issue, you will likely find that there are hundreds of cases that may apply. Interestingly, however, when you actually begin to narrow down your

---

1. This doesn't mean that you won't go back and perform more research after you begin to write your assignment. In fact, it is likely that you will need to search for another case. My point here is that you need to begin writing so that you can learn where you have holes in your analysis such that you can fill those holes with more research.

list to the most relevant cases, you will rely upon only four or five cases in your writing assignment. Part of the *process* of legal research is to re-fine your issues as you go along. In other words, once you have that ini-tial pile (or list) of cases, you will need to sift through them to determine which ones truly help you resolve your problem—and which ones do not. If you are not going to use a particular case, write it on the top of the case: "Not Helpful." Put it into a different pile.

For the cases you think you will use, write on the front of the case why it's relevant: "Good Case for NIED Issue." This helps you stay or-ganized. Ideally, you want to end up with around three to six cases about which to write for each separate legal issue in your problem. You cannot write about many more than that number of cases and write about them *well*. Hopefully, your professor will guide you about the number of cases she expects you to use in your particular problem. If not, *trust* yourself that you can pick out the most relevant cases. You *will* be overwhelmed if you try to incorporate too many cases into your legal memorandum or brief.

3. Organization Is Key

Keeping organized can be particularly challenging for any law student given the demands on your time and energy. Some students believe they are conducting effective legal research when they sit down at the West-law or Lexis printers—and print off hundreds of cases. Perhaps these students are thinking that if they print off everything of potential rele-vance—then they will *have* everything. Yes, you may *have* the case—but the question is: will you be able to find it?

Organization is the key to effective legal research. If keeping organized is a particular challenge for you, make sure to address this right away. Get yourself a three-ring binder or a set of file folders. Divide your cases up as they relate to your different legal issues. If your first three cases support the negligence issue, then clip those cases together and write "Negligence Issue" on the top of the case. Divide the cases up based upon the issues they support. Write the main issues/holdings of the cases on the first page of the case as well. This will help you sort through and or-ganize your research. Instead of paging through cases to re-orient your-self to the case, you can locate the most relevant cases more efficiently.

Consider placing your actual writing assignment and your notes about the assignments into a binder or separate computer file as well. If you have all your information in one place (and not scattered about in your apartment), you'll feel much more in control of your assignment. And, BACK UP your computer files. Send yourself your work product in emails—keep multiple electronic copies. Having your computer crash (and losing your work) is not typically a reason for which professors give you extensions!

4. Begin to Write — Soon!

Finally, begin the writing process sooner than you want to! Legal research and writing is a cyclical process. In other words, you tend to go from one to the other, and then back again. You will research for awhile, then you will write your outline. You may realize that you need another case or two. So you'll go back to researching for awhile, but it will be more directed at this point. Then you'll work on writing the draft of the memorandum. This recursive cycle is a *good* thing. It ensures that you are actively involved in thinking throughout the problem — analyzing the issues critically — and realizing the need for further support.

Another reason to begin writing soon is to prevent yourself from getting stuck in the researching phase. Depending on your learning style, you may end up enjoying the research phase a great deal. For a kinesthetic learner, research is *doing* something versus sitting in the classroom. For the visual learner, research involves reading and examining cases and books. Some students want to stay in this phase forever! However, you need to give yourself enough to time complete the writing phase as well. If you have three weeks total for your entire legal writing assignment — give yourself at least two-thirds of that time for the writing process. In other words, limit your initial research phase to approximately one week. Don't worry — you can always do a bit more research later!

Chapter 8

Outlining: It's So Much *More* Than Simply Creating a *Really* Long Document on Your Computer

In law school, outlining seems to be something mysterious that all law students *do* in order to prepare for law school exams. Yet there is typically no explanation of how best to go about outlining or even what the purpose of outlining is on a basic level. Therefore, this chapter is devoted to discussing the purpose of outlining in law school and providing you with several approaches to law school outlining to help you maximize your exam preparation.

A. What Is the Purpose of Outlining in Law School?

Outlining in law school is a way to organize all the information you've accumulated throughout the semester in your classes. Outlining helps you prepare for law school exams in three specific ways: (1) you will be able to see the big picture and how the individual cases or rules fit into the big picture; (2) you will force yourself to practice your deductive reasoning, i.e., applying the general rules to a new factual hypothetical; and (3) you will organize all the information from your casebooks, class notes, case briefs and commercial outlines.

Keep in mind that most of your classroom experiences in law school involve *inductive* reasoning. Inductive reasoning is a type of reasoning which involves moving from a set of specific facts (the cases you read) to a general conclusion or application. In class, you begin with a case that sets out a rule. Your job is to read and understand the case, and then to pull the rule *out* of the case so you can apply the rule to future cases.

But when you take law school exams, you will actually use *deductive* reasoning. In other words, you do somewhat the opposite of what you do in class. In class, you read specific cases and extract general rules. When you take a law school exam, you will use deductive reasoning: you will reason from a general rule to a specific conclusion. Most law school exams require you to identify issues, state the general legal rules that apply, and then analyze a set of facts in light of the general rule to formulate a conclusion. Applying this general rule to a set of specific facts (that your professor gives you in the form of an exam hypothetical) uses *deductive* reasoning.

Therefore, one key to outlining successfully in law school is to recognize that you must prepare for your exams differently than you prepare for your law school classes.

B. Should You Make Your Own Outline or Use a Commercial Outline — or Both?

Law students often question whether or not they should make their own law school outlines, buy commercial outlines or borrow others' outlines. Realistically, you will likely use some content from all of these sources. Although some law professors will tell you that you must create your own outline, I have always felt that students benefit from seeing different perspectives, i.e., those perspectives from other students' outlines and commercial outlines. Sometimes seeing a concept explained differently is very helpful

However, your outline should be very course specific. When you begin outlining, use your course syllabus, your casebook (the table of contents, in particular), your class notes, *and* your favorite commercial outline.

C. How Do You Begin?

Begin by focusing on the larger picture. Start by looking at how your course syllabus divides the different segments of the course. Compare the course syllabus to the table of contents in your casebook. Look to see how your professor and the author of the casebook divide the concepts into larger categories.

For example, perhaps you studied Intentional Infliction of Emotional Distress in the first two weeks of the semester. A larger concept like this will become one of the main headings in your outline. Then proceed to add different levels of detail. After the main heading, your next level should be the specific rules or elements of Intentional Infliction of Emotional Distress. What is the majority rule? What is the definition of the rule? What are the elements? The next sub-level of your outline will include case examples that you've either read or discussed in class. Add material as you review your notes and put in as many examples or hypotheticals as you can find.

After you have the larger framework of your outline (including the rules and cases), the most important layer of your outline may be examples of the *application* of these rules. In law school, we test your application of the general rules to new factual situations. You need to train yourself to recognize these types of fact patterns. Commercial outlines are particularly helpful for this aspect of outlining because they often have examples of how to apply the rule.

When I review students' outlines, I often find that they fail to take this critical step in outlining: they fail to add in factual hypotheticals for every concept so they can *see* the application of the rule next to the rule itself.

When you find a commercial outline (or another student's outline) that you like, find specific examples or factual hypotheticals for each of the main concepts for that part of the course. For example, if the concept involves "proximate causation" from your Torts outline, find specific examples of factual hypotheticals that implicate this issue. For many students, they can teach themselves the legal concept through these examples.

In addition, adding in hypotheticals for each legal concept teaches you to see the issues as they relate to the legal concept. In other words, you are more likely to recognize or spot the proper issue in an exam because you have considered the most common factual hypotheticals that tend to "trigger" those issues. In addition to using outside sources such as outlines, you should also review your class notes. Insert into your outline any examples that your professor gave you to illustrate a particular concept.

The following example illustrates a section of a course outline in a first-year Property course. What do you notice about the outline? Is it simple to read? Does it incorporate examples? Evaluate the outline to see if it helps you understand the general rules and various specific examples to which the rule might apply. We will talk more specifically about how to make your outline an effective learning tool. Initially, however, I encourage you to spend a few minutes looking at this example and then progress to the general tips on outlining. We will then look specifically at how to create outlines and how to make them work *for* you!

Property Outline[*]

Obtaining and retaining ownership
Methods of acquiring title

Adverse possession is a method of acquiring title by using or possessing property. An action for adverse possession is by statute, incorporating common law elements—essentially, the statute of limitations for an action in ejectment.

If you bring a successful adverse possession claim you get title to the property in question that can be recorded.

Adverse possession:
Statute + 4 common law elements
1. Actual entry and exclusive possession
2. Open and notorious
3. Adverse, hostile and under claim of right
4. Continuous for the statutory period

> <u>Trigger facts:</u>
> **Boundary disputes**
> **Use of property without record of title**
> **Title is unclear or in dispute**
> **Long time squatters/trespassers**
> **Misplaced fences or encroachments**

Elements:
1. Actual entry and exclusive possession
Type of entry/use that true owner would make of that property such that neighbors and other observers would regard the occupant as exercising exclusive dominion (<u>Ewing</u>)

Sufficient acts depend on nature, character and location of land and potential uses
Camper, outhouse, fish rack, reindeer pen on northern portion (<u>Nome 2000</u>)
Cattle grazing OK (<u>Quarles</u>)
Gravel pit OK (<u>Ewing</u>)

> <u>Notes from review session:</u>
> **Likely on the multiple-choice section.**
> **Know case names.**

Can be demonstrated by residence or with fences and cultivation

Have to have entry with intent to **own.**

---

* This example outline was created by Alison M. Nissen, Director of Academic Success, Visiting Clinical Associate Professor, Rutgers School of Law—Camden. These materials were developed by Professor Nissen for the 2009 AALS Annual Meeting, San Diego, California, Academic Support and Teaching Methods Workshop: "Show Us Your Stuff" and they are used in this book with the author's permission.

Before we analyze the strategies for creating the most effective outlines, here are a few general tips.

1. Include appropriate defenses and remedies in your outline as well as principal claims.
2. Cover the application of the legal principles from every side (from both a pro side and a con side).
3. Consider the bigger picture or larger context of a principle or rule of law. Commercial outlines can be very helpful.[1]

---

1. You need to know how to apply the law in an exam, but you also need to consider social, political, economic, moral or policy arguments, too. These are secondary to the rules of law but they can be important in an exam answer.

4. Try *not* to simply type in all of your class notes into your outline or your document will become too detailed to be helpful.

5. Think about larger concepts and try not to get lost in the minute details of the cases—*specific holdings in most cases are not nearly as important as the larger legal concepts or claims.* Law school exams rarely ask you to discuss specific cases. It is far more important to ask yourself the following: for what *proposition* does each case stand? In class, you often discuss the details of the cases. This is because professors want you to grasp the basics of the case so you can extract the rule, i.e., inductive reasoning. However, on a law school exam, the details of a case are far less important than the application of the rule to a new factual hypothetical, i.e., deductive reasoning. Therefore, you want to prepare your outline with that reality in mind.

D. How Early Should I Start Creating My Outline?

As with everything else in law school, time management is very important. Like studying and attending class, you want to set aside specific blocks of time each week to work on your course outlines.

Begin outlining early in the semester. Consider your learning style. Consider your tendencies (or lack thereof) for procrastination. Make a specific plan of attack for changing your prior habits—*if* they need changing. Set a schedule. Determine what class you want to tackle first. Should you tackle your most difficult class? Probably yes. And just do a little bit each week. You will feel much better knowing that you've already started working toward your exams.

E. Specific Visual Outlining Strategies

Research has shown that they way in which we present information on a page or on a computer screen, i.e., the way information is presented *visually,* can have a large impact on how our brain processes and retains information. Many first-year law students will obtain course outlines from upper-level students. Having someone else's outline is often a good way to *begin* the outlining process. You can gain some valuable insights by examining how another student has organized the class material. However, the prior outline is only the beginning and you will want to add to this outline to create something that specifically enhances your own learning. The process of making an outline *yours* is particularly important in law school. Further, if you learn best in a particular way, i.e., visually, with flow charts, etc., tailor your outline to match your learning style. Do you like to work with mind maps? Do you need lots of examples to see how a principle works? Allow your learning style to guide the way in which you outline.

The example below is another section of a first-year Property outline dealing with the subject of Adverse Possession.[2] Even if you have not yet studied Adverse Possession, examine the outline. Do you find its organization logical? Do you like the way it looks? Examine the font and the use of highlighting. Does anything stand out? Is it easy to read? Does the outline incorporate examples of *how* the legal concepts apply to different factual scenarios?

PROPERTY OUTLINE*

FALL 2012

ADVERSE POSSESSION

1. ACTUAL ENTRY AND EXCLUSIVE POSSESSION

* type of entry/use that true owner would make of that property such that neighbors and other observers would regard the occupant as exercising exclusive dominion (Ewing)

* sufficient acts depend on nature, character and location of land and potential uses camper, outhouse, fish rack, reindeer pen on northern portion (Nome 2000)
  cattle grazing OK (Quarles)
  gravel pit OK (Ewing)

* can be demonstrated by residence or with fences and cultivation

* have to have entry with intent to OWN

* may have to occupy "whole" parcel; only to get title to what is actually used; if reside in a house then may get possession (b/c this is how ordinary owner would use a house) but if trying to possess multi-acre farm would have to cultivate just like ordinary owner would do

* possession must be exclusive — not shared with either true owner or public does not have to be absolute, occasional, isolated visits by third parties (think hunters; hikers) will not impact exclusivity

2. OPEN AND NOTORIOUS

* possession must be sufficiently visible and obvious to put reasonable owner on notice to true owner that someone is using the property with intent to claim possessory rights (Smith v. Hayden — garage on neighboring property)

* acts sufficient to satisfy open and notorious = residing; building fences; other improvements; cultivation
  wall enclosing property OK (Tippet)

---

2. Once again, my appreciation to Professor Alison Nissen for her permission in allowing me to use her examples. *See* Nissen, *supra* n.1.

* concealed use (like cave) does not equal open use

* how "open" the use needs to be is in keeping with the character of the property, however rural property that is extensive and wooded may require more than minimal activity to put owner on notice (<u>Nome 2000</u>)

3. <u>**ADVERSE, HOSTILE AND UNDER CLAIM OF RIGHT**</u>

→ THREE DIFFERENT APPROACHES:

OBJECTIVE STANDARD — WHAT THE ADVERSE POSSESSOR THINKS ABOUT TITLE IS IRRELEVANT, HOSTILITY WILL BE IMPLIED BY ADVERSE POSSESSOR'S ACTIONS IN USING/OCCUPYING THE PROPERTY

GOOD FAITH — ADVERSE POSSESSOR NEEDS TO BELIEVE THAT HE/SHE HAS TITLE TO THE PROPERTY, THAT ADVERSE POSSESSOR HAS MADE AN HONEST MISTAKE ABOUT OWNERSHIP

HOSTILE TRESPASSER — ADVERSE POSSESSOR KNOWS PROPERTY BELONGS TO ANOTHER, BUT INTENDS TO TAKE TITLE AWAY

Also, the possession must be continuous for the statutory period — number of years required varies from state to state.

---

* *Id.*

Although the substance of this outline is accurate, the *way* in which the information is presented could be improved.

In order to enhance the way in which you outline, consider adjusting your outlining strategy in three specific ways: (1) use summaries and roadmaps; (2) adopt visual strategies (font and contrast); and (3) use trigger facts.[3]

The next section of this chapter will discuss these three strategies and illustrate how to apply them to the example outline above.

---

3. Again, my appreciation to Professor Nissen as I adopted these terms from her presentation.

1. Use Summaries and Roadmaps

As you examine the 'before' and 'after' excerpts from the Property Outline below, what do you notice? What are the differences between them? Is the second outline easier to understand? Why? Is the second outline easier to read? The 'after' outline incorporates summaries and roadmaps. Can you pick out where these elements are?

Before	After
PROPERTY OUTLINE	Property Outline
ADVERSE POSSESSION	**Adverse Possession**
1. ACTUAL ENTRY AND EXCLUSIVE POSSESSION	Adverse possession is a method of acquiring title* by using or possessing property. An action for adverse possession is by statute, incorporating common law elements — essentially, the statute of limitations for an action in ejectment.
• type of entry/use that true owner would make of that property such that neighbors and other observers would regard the occupant as exercising exclusive dominion (<u>Ewing</u>)	If you bring a successful adverse possession claim you get title to the property in question which can be recorded.
• sufficient acts depend on nature, character and location of land and potential uses camper, outhouse, fish rack, reindeer pen on northern portion (<u>Nome 2000</u>) cattle grazing OK (<u>Quarles</u>) gravel pit OK (<u>Ewing</u>)	**Adverse possession:** **Statute + 4 common law elements**** **1.** Actual entry and exclusive possession **2.** Open and notorious **3.** Adverse, hostile and under claim of right **4.** Continuous for the statutory period
* * *	**1. Actual entry and exclusive possession** Type of entry/use that true owner would make of that property such that neighbors and other observers would regard the occupant as exercising exclusive dominion (<u>Ewing</u>)

   * Advance Organizer: Using a Summary Defining Adverse Possession.
 ** Advance Organizer: Using a Roadmap Laying out the Elements Clearly.

Summaries are simply short paragraphs of information that give you the larger picture of a legal concept before getting into the individual elements. In legal writing, we often call these types of summaries "roadmaps" because they give the reader a short synopsis or "roadmap" of where the text is heading. Summaries can help you learn the bigger picture of the concept as well as the individual elements.

The 'after' outline incorporates short summaries and roadmaps. In this outline, the summaries provide a brief snapshot of the concept of Adverse Possession. The 'before' outline does not contain summaries.

In addition, using summaries to define concepts in your outline will allow you to self-monitor your learning. In other words, because the concepts are clearly articulated, you will get a better sense of whether you truly understand the concept or not.

2. Visual Strategies: Changing Fonts and Contrast (Bold/Regular Text)

Research has found that our eyes focus better and read faster when we use some fonts over others.[4] For example, it is very time consuming for your eyes to read a sentence in ALLCAPS. In outlining, you may think initially that using ALLCAPS will emphasize a certain point or principle. In reality, it will take your brain longer to process that material. Consider the example outlines below. What are the differences between the 'before' outline and the 'after' outline? Which font is easier to read—the bolded text or the ALLCAPS? Does it take longer to read in ALLCAPS?

Before	After
PROPERTY OUTLINE	**Property Outline**
<u>ADVERSE POSSESSION</u>	* * *
1. <u>ACTUAL ENTRY AND EXCLUSIVE POSSESSION</u>	Elements:
	1. Actual entry and exclusive possession[*]
* * *	* * *
2. <u>ADVERSE, HOSTILE AND UNDER CLAIM OF RIGHT</u>	**2. Adverse, hostile and under claim of right**
→ THREE DIFFERENT APPROACHES:	3 different approaches:
OBJECTIVE STANDARD—WHAT THE ADVERSE POSSESSOR THINKS ABOUT TITLE IS IRRELEVANT, HOSTILITY WILL BE IMPLIED BY ADVERSE POSSESSOR'S ACTIONS IN USING/OCCUPYING THE PROPERTY	**A. Objective standard:** What the adverse possessor thinks about title is irrelevant, hostility will be implied by adverse possessor's actions in using/occupying the property
GOOD FAITH—ADVERSE POSSESSOR NEEDS TO BELIEVE THAT HE/SHE HAS TITLE TO THE PROPERTY, THAT ADVERSE POSSESSOR HAS MADE AN HONEST MISTAKE ABOUT OWNERSHIP	**B. Good faith standard:** Adverse possessor needs to believe that he/she has title to the property, that adverse possessor has made an honest mistake about ownership
	* * *

* *Id.* at 119 (describing how using bolded text increases comprehension).

---

4. Ruth Anne Robbins, *Painting with Print: Incorporating Concepts of Typographic and Layout Design Into the Text of Legal Writing Documents*, 2 J. Ass'n Legal Writing Directors 108, 114 (2004)(*citing* Miles A. Tinker, *Bases for Effective Reading* 15 (U. of Minn. Press 1965) (summarizing his scientific studies on reading and legibility of text)).

The 'before' outline uses ALLCAPS. Does it slow down your reading? The research illustrates that using ALLCAPS increases your reading time by 9%–19%.[5] This means that your eyes are working harder (and getting tired more easily) when you format your outline to look like the 'before' outline. In the 'after' outline, the headings use font with a light/dark contrast. The use of contrasting (**bolded** versus non-bolded text) maximizes readability and comprehension. Further, the 'after' outline uses lower case letters instead of ALLCAPS. Studies have shown that 90% of readers prefer lower case typeface over ALLCAPS.[6]

These small adjustments in the look of your outline may actually enhance the way your brain processes this information. This may be particularly helpful if you learn differently—if you are a visual learner—or if you simply take longer to process information overall.

3. Add "Trigger Facts" and Examples into Your Outline

Finally, a third technique for good outlining is to add "trigger facts" or examples into your outline. "Trigger facts" are nothing more than typical hypotheticals used to illustrate a particular legal concept.

As you know, law school classes tend to focus on extracting rules *out* of the case law (inductive reasoning). On an exam, you will need to recognize the issue and apply the general rule of law to the factual hypothetical (deductive reasoning). As part of your exam preparation, you will need to practice 'spotting' legal issues. In other words, you will need to be able to recognize the more typical fact patterns that fall within a particular rule or legal concept. These types of factual scenarios are rarely in your casebooks. Unfortunately, many law students fail to incorporate these types of factual hypotheticals or "trigger facts" into their outlines.

Yet it is precisely your ability to recognize the typical fact patterns that will determine your success on a law school exam. Therefore, you need to incorporate "trigger facts" or examples into your outline.

"Trigger facts" are those facts that will alert you to the application of a particular rule or cause of action. In the example outline below, one "trigger fact" is a boundary dispute. Boundary disputes often involve issues of Adverse Possession. Therefore, if you see an exam question that deals with a boundary dispute, it is likely that you will need to discuss some aspect of Adverse Possession. Having "trigger facts" in your outline will allow you to remember and spot these issues more easily.

The example below contains "Trigger Facts." The example also uses lower case letters and contrast (bold) in the headings. Does this outline provide additional information in a format that is more readable?

---

5. *Id.* at 115.

6. *Id.*

Property Outline

Obtaining and retaining ownership
Methods of acquiring title

Adverse possession is a method of acquiring title by using or possessing property. An action for adverse possession is by statute, incorporating common law elements—essentially, the statute of limitations for an action in ejectment.

If you bring a successful adverse possession claim you get title to the property in question that can be recorded.

Adverse possession:
Statute + 4 common law elements
1. Actual entry and exclusive possession
2. Open and notorious
3. Adverse, hostile and under claim of right
4. Continuous for the statutory period

> **Trigger facts:**
> Boundary disputes
> Use of property without record of title
> Title is unclear or in dispute
> Long time squatters/trespassers
> Misplaced fences or encroachments

Elements:

1. **Actual entry and exclusive possession**

   Type of entry/use that true owner would make of that property such that neighbors and other observers would regard the occupant as exercising exclusive dominion (Ewing)

   Sufficient acts depend on nature, character and location of land and potential uses Camper, outhouse, fish rack, reindeer pen on northern portion (Nome 2000)
   Cattle grazing OK (Quarles)
   Gravel pit OK (Ewing)

   > **Notes from Review Session:**
   > Likely on exam. Know the different cases here.

   Can be demonstrated by residence or with fences and cultivation

   Have to have entry with intent to **own**

   May have to occupy "whole" parcel; only to get title to what is actually used; if reside in a house then may get possession (b/c this is how ordinary owner would use a house) but if trying to possess multi-acre farm would have to cultivate just like ordinary owner would do

   Possession must be exclusive—not shared with either true owner or public
   Does not have to be absolute
   Occasional, isolated visits by third parties (think hunters; hikers) will not impact exclusivity

2. **Open and notorious**

   Possession must be sufficiently visible and obvious to put reasonable owner on notice to true owner that someone is using the property with intent to claim possessory rights (Smith v. Hayden—garage on neighboring property)

   Acts sufficient to satisfy open and notorious = residing; building fences; other improvements; cultivation

   Wall enclosing property OK (Smith v. Tippet)

   Concealed use (like cave) does not equal open use

How "open" the use needs to be is in keeping with the character of the property, however rural property that is extensive and wooded may require more than minimal activity to put owner on notice (<u>Nome 2000</u>)

3. Adverse, hostile and under claim of right

3 different approaches:

A. Objective standard:

What the adverse possessor thinks about title is irrelevant, hostility will be implied by adverse possessor's actions in using/occupying the property

Hypotheticals from Class:
Example of neighbor who placed fence over property line believing that it was on his property.

B. Good faith standard:

Adverse possessor needs to believe that he/she has title to the property, that adverse possessor has made an honest mistake about ownership

C. Hostile trespasser approach:

Adverse possessor knows property belongs to another, but intends to take title away

4. Continuous for the statutory period

Number of years — required varies from state to state
Exception: tacking
Successive periods of adverse possession by different Persons may sometimes be combined together to satisfy the statutory duration requirement

---

Final Tip: As you create your outlines during the course of the semester, make sure to add in any examples that your professor has given you in class. Write these examples into your outline — it is likely that these examples will clue you into what your professor sees as important. In addition, commercial outlines often provide good examples of hypotheticals associated with particular rules or concepts. Add in these examples as well!

Chapter 9

The Law School Essay Exam

There is no doubt that the law school essay exam is mysterious to most law students. You've likely heard the joke that law professors grade essay exams by simply throwing the pile of exams down the stairs and the paper that lands closest to the bottom gets the A. But the real difficulty in conquering the law school essay exam lies in understanding the format of the exam. There are two main differences between law school essay exams and other types of exams. First, the law school essay exam is a timed test; you have only a limited amount of time to put down all the information you've learned during the semester. For most students, if they had a full day to complete the essay exam, they would likely do well. However, law students typically are given between three and four hours to complete a final exam in a course. Answering all the questions in that limited amount of time is very challenging.

Second, law school essay exams ask you to *apply* the information you've learned in class to a new factual situation and come to a conclusion based upon that analysis. In other types of exams, you are frequently asked to *give back* all the information you've learned during the course. However, in a law school exam, we assume you can write down what you've learned in class. After all, you are very smart—you wouldn't be in law school otherwise! But law professors are asking you to go one step further. We want to see if you can *identify* a legal issue within a factual hypothetical, *apply* the rules you've learned in class to this factual situation, and *predict* a likely outcome based upon both the facts and the law.

In other words, the method by which we test you in law school is different than the way in which we teach you. In class, you talk about different cases and extract the rules out of the cases you read. You prepare for class by focusing on case reading and analysis (i.e., the Case Method). But the typical law school essay exam requires you to *apply* the rules you've learned to a new problem. Another way to think about this is that the exam assumes (in most cases) that you are an attorney *applying* the law to a new set of facts as if you're talking to a client that has come to your office (i.e., the Problem Method). Therefore, if you approach studying for your law school essay exams by simply reviewing the cases and their rules, you may not do as well as you would like. Instead, you need to go one step further and *practice* how to *identify* the legal issues in a fact pattern and *apply* the rules. This is what you will be asked to do on your essay exams.

The key to essay exam preparation is to prepare for your exams by concentrating on what your professors will *test* on the exams, i.e., you need to *practice* how to read through a fact pattern quickly, *identify* the key issues, *analyze* the law as applied to the facts, and *conclude*. Further, you need to *practice* how to quickly outline your answer before beginning to write.

Outside materials, including commercial outlines, can be a big help with exam preparation. Once you have chosen some helpful study aids (that match your learning style),[1] your job is to replicate the essay exam experience *before* you take exam. Quite simply, you need to teach yourself how to *take* the exam almost as much as you need to study the substance of the course material.

Generally speaking, law professors are testing two main skills in essay exams: first, whether or not you can *spot the legal issue* in the problem; and second, whether you can *analyze* the issue, i.e., apply the law to the facts of the hypothetical. In order to properly prepare yourself for your essay exams, you need to have a game plan in place early on in the semester. In addition, you will need to consider how your individual learning will affect your exam preparation. The way in which you learn will factor into the materials and methods you will choose to prepare for exams. This section will provide you with various strategies for understanding and mastering the law school essay exam.

A. The First Step: Issue Spotting

Most of your essay exam questions will begin with a lengthy factual situation commonly called a 'hypothetical.' In an exam, your job is to read through the hypothetical carefully and efficiently. Some facts will be very relevant to your analysis of the problem and other facts will not be relevant to your analysis of the problem. The purpose of these long (and sometimes silly) factual hypotheticals is to test your ability to spot the relevant issues.

Issue spotting requires you to identify the facts in a hypothetical that relate to a legal concept or claim that you've covered in class. A law professor packs a number of issues into any given essay question. Your job is to read the facts in order to determine whether the facts give rise to a particular legal issue. This is difficult to do—under pressure—and in a time-limited situation.

First, begin your exam preparation by understanding that there is no *perfect or right* answer to any given question on an essay exam. Your job

---

1. See Chapter 7 for a comparison of the different study aids, commercial outlines, etc.

is not to give the professor the *perfect* answer but to think creatively about the problem and give the professor all the potential *possibilities* that come from the hypothetical. In order to see all the possible issues that flow from an essay fact pattern, you need to train yourself in the skill of issue spotting.

In longer essay questions, there will be as many as ten to twelve different legal issues in a factual hypothetical. You are awarded points for each issue you spot and analyze; if you fail to spot and discuss the issue then you will not receive points for that issue. Therefore, it is essential that you become adept at issue spotting.

Consider the following issue spotting exercise.[2] The author of this exercise based the problem on a California Bar exam question. The purpose of this exercise is to sensitize you to the words that convey fact patterns and to discipline yourself to read the facts of questions carefully.

Step 1: Assume you have just completed your study of the crime of burglary. You are about to take your Criminal Law midterm and you receive the following factual hypothetical on the essay exam. Read the following factual hypothetical and circle all the facts that you think might be important as you analyze the problem for the elements of burglary.[3]

> One evening Albert was told that his estranged wife Zola was having overnight male guests in their residence. He immediately stormed out of the Sleezy Saloon, where he had been all evening, and drove his car wildly to the residence.

Step 2: Pull out (and rewrite) the key facts that may lead to legal issues. You should end up with a list of key words.

Key Words
evening
Albert
told
estranged wife
Zola having overnight male guests
their residence
he immediately
stormed out
Sleezy Saloon
been all evening

---

2. This example was adapted from an Issue Spotting exercise from http://www.law schoolsecretstosuccess.com/Issue_Spotting.html (last visited 2/24/09).

3. Assume that you studied common law burglary, which is typically defined as the breaking and entering of the house of another in the nighttime, with intent to commit a felony therein, whether the felony be actually committed or not.

drove car wildly
to residence

Step 3: Each of these key words could become a separate issue in your exam answer. At this point, you may not even need to look at the exam hypothetical again! You can simply refer to your list of key words. Now you will begin **issue spotting**. Your job is to recognize the legal issues presented or "triggered" by the key words. Remember that each key word or phrase *may* be a possible issue in the problem. But you cannot write about every word—so you must decide which terms are *relevant* to the crime of burglary and which are not. For example, you might analyze the first three key words from the list as follows.

> "Evening" represents the common law crime of burglary. The associated facts to burglary are "their residence" and "been there all evening," which suggest that it may still evening or it may be sunrise and also the issue of burglarizing one's own residence.

> "Sleezy Saloon" suggests intoxication, a defense, and is supported by the fact that he had "been there all evening" and "drove his car wildly." The latter indicates a charge of drunk driving and a possible mitigation to the provocation suggested by the fact that his "estranged wife" had "overnight guests." The fact that it took time to drive to the residence and that he might have had a chance to cool off or maybe a reasonable person would have done so would also mitigate the provocation.

> "Estranged wife" suggests the issue of provocation and is supported by the facts that he "immediately stormed out" and that she has "overnight guests," which on further analysis could also suggest a possible charge of adultery.

All of the individual facts relate to one another in various combinations. If you find that you're not using all of the facts presented, you may not be spotting all the issues.

Being able to spot the legal issues in an exam hypothetical is a necessary skill and it is also a skill that requires practice.

Pay attention to key words in any factual hypothetical that can trigger issues for you. For example, in the above hypothetical, there are some basic words that suggest an issue such as "evening" for burglary and the use of "the Saloon" for intoxication. Other words are used more subtly but also highlight potential issues such as the description of "storming" out of the Saloon, the "wild driving," and the "estranged wife."

Each of these phrases relates to the legal issues of burglary, provocation, drunk driving, intoxication, and adultery. Of course, there may be other crimes that come into play in this hypothetical as well—such as drunk driving, speeding, and adultery. Although these secondary issues may be of less significance when compared to the primary issue of burglary and murder, being able to spot sub-issues will show your professor that you have an in-depth understanding of the law.

Remember: all issues are derived from the facts in the problem. *Read the factual hypothetical very carefully.*

Once you feel like you've gotten a handle on the basic substance of the course, spend some time teaching yourself *how* to spot the legal issues in an exam situation. In other words, *practice* issue spotting explicitly.

Go through different hypotheticals related to the subject of the course. You can find hypotheticals in commercial outlines, study aids, prior exams, etc. The main point is that issue spotting is a skill—and you will need to set aside some specific time to acquire this skill in order to be successful on your exams. Practice as much as you can so you begin to develop a consistent plan for how you will approach issue-spotting on an essay exam.

B. The All-Important Analysis in the Essay Exam: A Mini-IRAC for Each and Every Issue

After you spot the issues in the factual hypothetical, you will analyze the issues and come to a conclusion. On an exam, you *will* receive some points for simply spotting the issue. However, the bulk of your points on an essay exam will come from a well-written analysis for each legal issue.

In law school, when we say that we want an *analysis* of a legal issue, we want you to apply the rule of law to the set of facts, and come to a conclusion. Does this sound familiar? This is the same type of analysis that you have done in your legal writing class. The main difference between a Legal Writing IRAC and an essay exam IRAC is that the essay exam IRAC is what I call a Mini-IRAC, i.e., it's shorter and more focused than the legal structure used in more formal legal writing. Law professors often complain that law students do not take the time to do a proper 'analysis' in their essay exam answers. What they really mean is that students forget to include *all* the necessary elements of a Mini-IRAC for a legal issue. Using an IRAC structure for your exam answers is helpful for two main reasons. First, IRAC helps you organize your writing so that your professor can more easily *see* the legal reasoning in your answer. Second, IRAC ensures that you won't forget to address important elements for any legal issue.

When your professors are reading your essay exams, they are evaluating whether you can (1) spot the legal issue; (2) understand and identify the applicable rule; and (3) analyze different possible arguments for the application of law to the facts; and (4) come to a conclusion. Again, you should not worry about an *absolute* right or wrong answer; instead, law professors are looking for your *analysis*.

Law school essay exams are typically made up of two types of questions: the short answer essay question and the long answer question. In a short answer essay question, the professor will ask you to review a shorter and more focused factual hypothetical (likely containing two or three legal issues). A long-form essay question contains a lengthy factual hypothetical. Typically, this type of essay question contains ten to twelve legal issues. Your strategy in answering either type of essay questions should be very similar.

1. Short Answer Questions

Typically, a short essay question will have a one paragraph factual hypothetical that is focused on one to three legal issues. If you spot the issue/s quickly in this type of question, you can write an efficient and concise answer and gain time to use on other questions. Here's an example of an actual short answer question from one of my Evidence exams.

Question A: Short Answer Example

Donald ran a red light and collided with Ellie. Donald died in the crash, and Ellie was severely injured. In the wreckage of Donald's car, police found a dozen boxes of Peppie's Take-Out. Ellie sued Peppie's, claiming that Donald was delivering the food and that Peppie's was responsible for Donald's negligence. Peppie's claimed that it had no connection with Donald and that he must have stolen the food boxes. In response, Ellie offers evidence that Donald was insured under Peppie's group health insurance plan. <u>Is this evidence admissible?</u>

The 'call of the question' is underlined here. Pay special attention to this part of the question. Many students read the 'call' of the question first to frame the way in which they read the facts.

How would you go about writing an answer to this type of question? The best exam answers are written with a coherent structure. Here is the IRAC structure which is often used in exam writing.

I = Issue	(State the legal issue.)
R = Rule	(State the main rule that applies to the legal issue)
A = Analysis	(Apply the rule to the facts of your case. Examine the issue from both sides of a possible argument, discussing the strongest argument and possible counterarguments.)
C = Conclusion	(Prediction of a likely result.)

The IRAC structure makes answering essay questions more efficient because you don't have to think about how to organize your exam answer. You know *ahead* of time how you will approach each exam question.

In addition, using the IRAC structure ensures you will discuss each essential part of a legal argument, i.e., you won't forget to state the *rule* or to *analyze* the issue as you are writing quickly in an exam setting.

The most important element in IRAC is the A (Analysis). Students sometimes forget to properly *analyze* the legal issue and provide reasons for their conclusion. Your reasoning is precisely what your law professors *want* to see!

Further, don't spend *too much time* answering short answer essay questions. You need to know when to *stop writing*—so you don't waste valuable time that takes away from other questions. Just because there *could be* a potential legal issue related to a factual hypothetical does not mean that you *must* take the time to write about it. You will not likely receive much (if any) credit for bringing up extra issues. Therefore, part of becoming an efficient test-taker is knowing when to *stop writing* and move on. This is particularly important for short answer essay questions.

Let's look at a student's answer to the above-referenced question from my Evidence exam. This student received full credit for her answer to this essay question. Below I indicate each component of the IRAC structure to illustrate how using IRAC helps organize an exam answer.

Question A: Student Example Answer 1

I: The issue in this case is whether Federal Rule of Evidence 411 will bar Ellie from using the fact that Peppie's insured Donald under its group health insurance. **R:** The rule is that FRE 411 bars evidence of liability insurance to prove negligence. **A:** In this case, we are dealing with group health insurance which is medical insurance and not liability insurance. Because these facts deal with medical insurance, it is quite possible our facts will fall outside the protection of FRE 411 and be admissible as evidence. However, some courts have construed FRE 411 to include medical insurance. If a court does consider medical insurance to fall within FRE 411, then we must apply FRE 411 to determine whether 411 will preclude admissibility on these facts. FRE 411 excludes evidence of insurance for liability, but not for other purposes, such as ownership or control. On these facts, Ellie offers the insurance to show agency or control. **C:** Therefore, this evidence will be allowed because it is offered for some purpose other than liability.

Issue

Rule

Analysis

Conclusion

I: Issue
R: Rule
A: Analysis
C: Conclusion

This was a concise, well-written answer and the student received 15 out of 15 points. Notice how the student was very economical with her words but still discussed each element within the IRAC structure.

Note also that there was a sub-issue involved in the answer to this question, i.e., whether Rule 411 applied to health insurance. This student picked up on the sub-issue and chose to address the sub-issue within her main issue analysis of Rule 411. Many students who answered this question failed to see this sub-issue.

Consider a different student's answer to this same question in Student Example 2. Does this second answer use the IRAC form? As a law professor, I had a more difficult time locating each IRAC element in this student's answer. In addition, this student added some *additional information* to her answer regarding the topic of relevance. I had not wanted relevance to be an issue in this exam question. Typically, law professors simply read over "extra" material that students add to an exam answer and move on to the issues that directly address the question. In other words, adding extra information will not likely help you but it will rarely hurt you either. The danger is wasting time that you could use for other questions.

Note that in the following IRAC example, I've added a new category for "extra information" in the key below. I have also inserted several comments that I had as I reviewed this exam answer.

Question A: Student Example Answer 2

X: First, we want to determine whether this evidence is relevant under rules 401 and 402. The fact that the pizza place had insurance may have some relevance, i.e., may help make more probable the fact that the company was able to pay for the claim and was potentially liable. Once relevance is established we can examine **I:** whether the evidence should be admissible. **C:** I don't think this evidence will be admissible because it is insurance. **R:** The federal rules do not allow another party to mention health insurance except in specific circumstances. **A:** Ellie probably wants to use the insurance to show that Donald was liable which is a restricted use. However, insurance can be used for other purposes such as ownership or control. **C:** Evidence will probably be excluded.

I: Issue
R: Rule
A: Analysis
C: Conclusion
X: Extra Information

Extra Information. The student addressed the relevance issue which was not an incorrect analysis, but it was also not exactly what I was looking for in this short answer. I simply read over the relevance issue until I got to the Rule 411 issue.

Rule. This is an accurate statement of the rule generally. But the student fails to identify which Federal Rule of Evidence governs the issue, i.e., Rule 411. Also, this rule statement needed more specificity with regard to what the rule states.

Analysis. This is the beginning of the student's analysis but it is not complete. True, Ellie may use the evidence of insurance for this purpose, but more likely it will be for another purpose, i.e., to establish that Donald worked for Peppie's Pizza. Partial credit. More analysis needed.

Issue. This is the larger issue, i.e., admissibility, but the issue is not specific enough. It should involve the particular rule at issue: FRE 411.

Conclusion. This is the writer's conclusion. It's fine to begin with a conclusion, and to end with one. However, this conclusion doesn't give me the reason why the evidence should be excluded. Is it because of Rule 411? This conclusion is too vague.

Conclusion. It's probably not a correct outcome given the facts of this case but I'm not as concerned with that as I am with the fact that the conclusion doesn't state any reasons for the result. In other words, there is no analysis here—just a result.

This student was able to identify some of the important issues in this question but didn't follow through with enough detail about the rule itself or the analysis as to why the general rule would not apply in this case, i.e., that the policy was really health insurance versus liability insurance. This was an average to below-average answer to this question. This student received 8 out of 15 points.

Consider another example of a short-answer essay question.

Question B: Short Answer Example

Susan sued Mark for stealing a pair of running shoes from her athletic supply shop. Mark took the stand at trial and denied that he took anything from Susan's shop. "I don't even shop there," Mark said. "She has shoddy, out-of-date merchandise." On cross-examination, Susan's attorney offered evidence that Mark had been convicted three years earlier for illegally downloading music from the internet. Mark's conviction was for a misdemeanor defined as "making unauthorized copies of audio recordings for commercial advantage or private financial gain." Is evidence of the conviction admissible?

A good student answer is reprinted below. I have also pointed out the different components of IRAC.

Question B: Student Example Answer 1

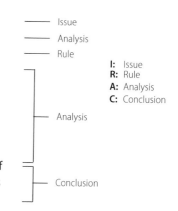

Conclusion — **C:** Possibly admissible. **I:** The main issue is whether or not the conviction is admissible under Rule 609. **A:** Here, it is a misdemeanor. Misdemeanors do not fall under Rule 609. **R:** Rule 609 addresses a felony that results in a year or more in prison. **A:** So it would be admissible under 609 ONLY if it was a crime of dishonesty. The question then becomes whether illegally downloading music could be considered a crime of dishonesty. Although courts come to different conclusions, there's a good argument that it IS such a crime. Congress recently tightened that definition; did not want theft to constitute "dishonesty." **C:** If this court agrees that it is a crime of dishonesty, then evidence is admissible without any balancing—not even under Rule 403.

— Issue
— Analysis
— Rule

I: Issue
R: Rule
A: Analysis
C: Conclusion

— Analysis

— Conclusion

Note that this answer contained mostly Analysis in the answer. Although there could have been a more specific and thorough rule statement, the analysis in this answer was quite good. The student was very concise in his answer but he hit all of the essential issues. The student received 23 out of 25 points.

Consider a different student's answer to this question. This student also received 23 out of 25 points. This answer contained more overall explanation of the rule and also addressed a few additional issues that were not necessarily required to receive full points—but the answer demonstrated an in-depth understanding of the legal issues.

Headings. Using Headings helps
your professor follow your answer.

Extra Information. The student
did a nice job discussing the
relevance of the evidence and a
possible FRE 403 argument. I
had not expected students to
go into this aspect of the question but I chose to recognize it
as an issue when grading the
exam.

Issue Missing: The student actually failed to
clearly state the issue
although I could tell
that the student was
discussing FRE 609
here. The student lost
two points for failing to
state the issue.

Rule

Analysis

I: Issue
R: Rule
A: Analysis
C: Conclusion
X: Extra Information

Extra Information. Here, the
student was discussing this
evidence as possible character
evidence. Once again, the student identified a different
issue, i.e., one that I wasn't
testing in this problem. This
discussion certainly didn't hurt
the student in her answer but
it wasn't necessary either.

Question B: Student Example Answer 2

Question 4: Is evidence of the conviction admissible?

X: First, evidence of the conviction may be admissible only if it is relevant. Relevant evidence (401) is any evidence that has any tendency to make a fact of consequence more or less probable. The governmental interest in allowing evidence in is evidenced by the words "any tendency" so evidence regarding a prior bad act that has something to do with the D's nature regarding truthful conduct is relevant. The evidence may be unfairly prejudicial to the D. The conviction does suggest an inference to the jury that if he stole music, he may steal shoes. Under 403, a defense attorney may be able to bar this evidence because its unfair prejudice outweighs the probative value.

Second, **R:** convictions are admissible against a witness under 609 if the conviction was one that resulted in more than 1 year in prison. **A:** I believe, as a misdemeanor, this crime would not result in a year or more in prison and therefore the evidence is likely to be overly prejudicial and therefore barred. Also, 609 applies to witnesses other than the accused (unless he is on the stand perhaps) and therefore the evidence may also not come in during under 609.

X: Third, because this is cross exam discussion, I assume that Mark is on the stand and therefore his character comes into play regarding his reputation and opinion. (404). Assuming that a person represents themselves to the best of their abilities, it is likely that his character is in play and the prosecutor could attack his character under 404(a)(1) with specifics. The prosecution may also attempt to avoid a character issue by admitting the evidence under 404(b) but there is little evidence to provide a MOPPIIK reason. The specific instance of conduct may be admissible under 405 to prove that his statement that he didn't steal the shoes and sporting gear should be treated with caution as to its truthfulness may come in under 405(b).

Note that the answer I was looking for with this question is located in the middle of the student's answer (the A: Analysis portion). Most of the other issues discussed in the answer were extra issues that the student was not required to discuss.

When it doubt, it may not hurt to address extra issues *as long as* you've fully discussed the main issue in the question (and you've given yourself enough time to complete all the other exam questions). *Sometimes students delve too deeply into a single question which takes far too much time away from answering the other questions on the exam.* Don't fall into this trap. Set yourself a time limit for short answer questions and move on once you have used up your time for that question!

In order to prepare for short answer essay questions, *practice* writing in an IRAC formula as much as possible prior to your exams. Find out how many short answer questions will be on your exam. Calculate the time you will spend for each. And practice, practice, practice! Use examples or hypotheticals from commercial outlines. Develop different questions with your study group. You can also write short answers to multiple-choice hypotheticals. Use the fact pattern and write out an answer before you look at the answer choices.[4]

2. Long Essay Exam Questions

Long essay exam questions can be more difficult for several reasons. First, longer essay questions have multiple issues within the lengthy factual hypothetical and it is challenging for anyone to spot all the issues in a timed situation. Second, you need to manage your time very carefully on long essays. In other words, you don't want to write several paragraphs about a few issues and fail to write anything about several other issues. By not addressing issues, you are guaranteed to lose points on the exam! And writing extensively about only a few issues will not earn you any extra points. In an essay exam, you need to ascertain exactly how much time you can spend on each separate question and stick to it! If you have three long essays in a one hour exam (or section), then you should budget 20 minutes per section. Once you hit 20 minutes on a question, wrap it up and move on. This is a hard technique to master so you need to begin *practicing* taking timed exams as soon as possible.

Here is a game plan to tackle longer essay exam questions.

Step 1: Page through the exam (or section). Note how many questions are on the exam. (Students often forget to answer *all* the questions!) Allocate your time carefully. Know exactly how much time you can afford to spend on each question in the exam.

Step 2: Skim the call of the question first so you know what the question is asking for specifically. You may be able to direct your reading of the factual hypothetical more efficiently if you know the issue beforehand.

Step 3: Skim the facts.

Step 4: Re-read the facts again and begin to pull out the different issues. Circle key facts that may lead to legal issues. Write a list of key facts on the margin of your paper.

Step 5: Draft Mini-IRAC's for each separate key fact and/or issue that stems from the factual hypothetical. Note your different issues specifically so your professor can identify the separate analysis.

Let's see how this works with another example.[5] The purpose of this example is to show you how to begin to outline multiple issues in a longer

---

4. This will also help you reason through answer choices for the multiple-choice questions.

5. Note that this question is likely a bit shorter than most long-answer essays but the process you use to read and pick apart the issues is the same.

essay question. Or in other words, after you have identified each issue, you will draft an individual IRAC for each issue.

Example C: Long Essay Question

Jane represents Roger, an unknown songwriter, in a copyright infringement action against the star singer Beyonda. Roger claims that Beyonda based one of her best-selling hits on an obscure song that he composed. Roger sends a fax to Jane's office that reads "I realize my infringement claim is far-fetched, but I'm relying on you to get me something in settlement. Beyonda has plenty of dough to spare. We can allege anything and get some money!" Hector, another one of Jane's clients, is standing near the fax machine when Roger's fax arrives. Hector has no connection with Roger or Beyonda, but he has always admired Beyonda's work so he calls her to tell her what Roger wrote. Beyonda moves to dismiss Roger's claim as frivolous, attaching an affidavit from Hector that relates the contents of Roger's fax. Does admission of the affidavit violate the attorney-client privilege under current federal law?

Example C: Answer Example 1

Here is *my* sample answer to this question.[6] As in the other examples, I have coded the answer to reflect the different parts of IRAC.

There are four overall issues in this question. **I:** The first issue is whether and how the attorney-client privilege applies in this case. **I:** Second, whether there was a "confidential communication" from the client (Roger) to the attorney (Jane) such that the attorney-client privilege attaches to the communication. **I:** And the third issue is whether there was an Inadvertent Disclosure of the document under Federal Rules of Evidence 502(b) of the Rules. **I:** Lastly, there may be a final issue involving the fraud exception to the attorney client privilege.

I: The first issue is whether the attorney-client privilege applies in this case. **R:** In order for the privilege to attach, the common law requires that there was a "confidential communication" from the client (Roger) to attorney (Jane). **A:** In this case, Roger was sending a fax to his attorney's office, so he did reasonably have an expectation that this was a confidential communication. Roger intended the communication to go to Jane, his attorney. It was not unreasonable to assume that since it was being faxed to Jane at her office that she or a representative from her office would pick up the document. **C:** This was a confidential communication protected by the attorney client privilege.

Margin notes:

An introductory paragraph laying out the four main issues is helpful for the professor. Therefore, even if you don't have time to get to all the details, you've at least outlined the main issues and you'll likely get partial credit.

Issue

Rule

Analysis

Conclusion

---

6. I hand out sample answers to my students after exams. Note that this is more organized than most of the actual student answers to this question.

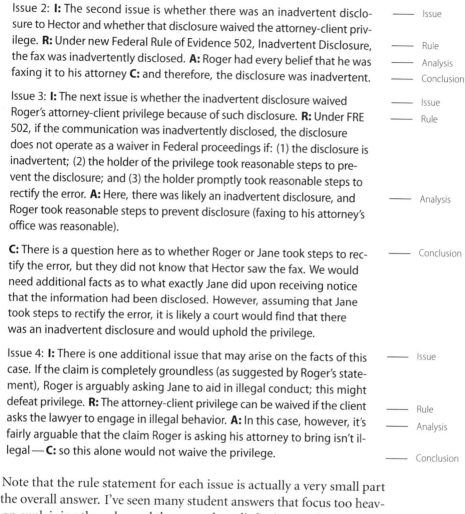

Issue 2: **I:** The second issue is whether there was an inadvertent disclosure to Hector and whether that disclosure waived the attorney-client privilege. **R:** Under new Federal Rule of Evidence 502, Inadvertent Disclosure, the fax was inadvertently disclosed. **A:** Roger had every belief that he was faxing it to his attorney **C:** and therefore, the disclosure was inadvertent.

— Issue
— Rule
— Analysis
— Conclusion

Issue 3: **I:** The next issue is whether the inadvertent disclosure waived Roger's attorney-client privilege because of such disclosure. **R:** Under FRE 502, if the communication was inadvertently disclosed, the disclosure does not operate as a waiver in Federal proceedings if: (1) the disclosure is inadvertent; (2) the holder of the privilege took reasonable steps to prevent the disclosure; and (3) the holder promptly took reasonable steps to rectify the error. **A:** Here, there was likely an inadvertent disclosure, and Roger took reasonable steps to prevent disclosure (faxing to his attorney's office was reasonable).

— Issue
— Rule

— Analysis

C: There is a question here as to whether Roger or Jane took steps to rectify the error, but they did not know that Hector saw the fax. We would need additional facts as to what exactly Jane did upon receiving notice that the information had been disclosed. However, assuming that Jane took steps to rectify the error, it is likely a court would find that there was an inadvertent disclosure and would uphold the privilege.

— Conclusion

Issue 4: **I:** There is one additional issue that may arise on the facts of this case. If the claim is completely groundless (as suggested by Roger's statement), Roger is arguably asking Jane to aid in illegal conduct; this might defeat privilege. **R:** The attorney-client privilege can be waived if the client asks the lawyer to engage in illegal behavior. **A:** In this case, however, it's fairly arguable that the claim Roger is asking his attorney to bring isn't illegal — **C:** so this alone would not waive the privilege.

— Issue

— Rule
— Analysis

— Conclusion

Note that the rule statement for each issue is actually a very small part of the overall answer. I've seen many student answers that focus too heavily on explaining the rules and they spend too little time explaining their analysis, i.e., applying the rule to the facts of the case—addressing the arguments and counterarguments. The majority of your discussion in most exam answers should be devoted to the *analysis* of the issue.

Certainly, however, the number of sentences you use to analyze the issue will depend upon the complexity of the issue (and the arguments surrounding it). If it's a straightforward resolution of an issue, less space is required. If it's a complicated issue that has authority to support both sides of an issue, then you need to spend more time developing the arguments and counter-arguments. Note that the sample above provides *at least* one sentence for each element of IRAC. Minimally, you want to write one sentence per IRAC element and often you want to provide *more* than one sentence per IRAC element (particularly in the analysis section) for more complex issues.

Under exam conditions, you probably won't write as coherently about every issue as I did in the example above. That's okay! Professors realize that you are under pressure and we do not expect perfection in your answers. The idea is to practice writing an exam answer like the sample answer and to try and identify and explain as many issues as you can in the time amount given. If you get confused and scratch out portions of your answer—don't worry. You can still get credit for your answer.

Here's an example of an *actual* student answer to Example C that received 19 out of 24 total points on this question. Although the student got the main issue correct, i.e., whether an attorney-client relationship existed, the student missed two of sub-issues, i.e., the inadvertent disclosure issue and the fraud issue.

But because the student identified the main issue, the student did fairly well on this exam question with regard to the total number of points received.

As you read through the student's answer, evaluate it as if you were the professor reading the answer. Did the student follow the IRAC formula? Can you identify the individual parts of IRAC? Did the student actually *see* an additional issue within the problem?

Example C: Answer Example 2

Question C: Does the affidavit violate A-C privilege?

Extra Issue. The student addressed a "relevance" issue. Although "relevance" was beyond the scope of what was originally intended with the question, I gave the student some credit for this addition. This offset slightly the points the student lost on the missing issues of inadvertent disclosure and fraud.

X: First, evidence of the plan to squeeze Beyonda may be admissible only if it is relevant. Relevant evidence (401) is any evidence that has a tendency to make a fact of consequence more or less probable. The governmental interest in allowing evidence in is evidenced by the words "any tendency" so evidence regarding a conspiracy to extort money and the fact that there is a bogus case is likely relevant to a judge when considering the validity of a case in a Motion to Dismiss.

I: Issue
R: Rule
A: Analysis
C: Conclusion
X: Extra Information

Issue —— **I:** Whether it violates A-C privilege depends on **R:** whether (1) the privilege existed and (2) whether it was violated. First, the privilege may
Rule —— have existed. **A:** Jane was an attorney, Roger was her client, he contacted her for legal advice regarding a (supposed) copyright infringement action, the fax was presumably meant to be confidential as a statement such as this if it were not would be very damaging to the person who communicated it to their attorney. The privilege only "may" exist rather than "certainly" exists because the communication seems to be sent to Jane in hopes that he can make a fraudulent claim (and likely
Analysis ——
Conclusion — an illegal act) with the help of his attorney. **C:** This action taken by Roger fits the crime fraud exception to A-C privilege voiding the privilege. **I:** The fact may also not be found to be privileged for the fact that
Issue — the statement was readily observed by another client. **R:** The presence
Rule — of a third party waives the privilege and although the privilege exists

for individuals under the attorney's employ, the presence of a client ob-serving the communication destroys the privilege. **C:** The admission of this likely does not violate A-C privilege.

X: Additionally, the statement by Hector would avoid hearsay and be admitted under 801(d)(2)(1) as an admission by a party (Roger); or it could be admitted as it is not meant to prove TMA under 801(c) but rather that R had knowledge that he does not have a viable claim against Beyonda.

Missing Analysis. The student jumps from the Issue to the Rule with no Analysis.

Conclusion

Extra Information

Note that the student's answer was not perfect but it did discuss the main issue of whether the attorney-client privilege had attached. Fur-ther, even though the student missed two sub-issues (inadvertent dis-closure and fraud), the student added two issues (relevance and admissions) which provided the student with a couple extra points. Note also that the student's answer wasn't in perfect IRAC form. For the most part, however, the elements were distinct enough that I could find the dif-ferent elements as I read through the answer. And the student did a nice job on the overall analysis, which is what law professors look for to as-sess your overall understanding of the legal issue.

In addition to using the IRAC formula in constructing organized exam answers, you may also want to practice the ability to quickly outline dif-ficult long-essay questions before you begin writing. This is particularly important if you learn differently or become easily overwhelmed with long fact patterns. Long-form law school essays tend to have *very* de-tailed and complex hypotheticals that are full of legal issues. Law pro-fessors are testing your ability to recognize the legal issues but also your ability to organize the issues and rules into a coherent discussion, and to note relevance information and discard irrelevant information.

For many students, if they fail to outline their answers before they begin to write, their essay answers are jumbled and difficult to follow, and they typically miss issues. The key to the outlining step in exam writ-ing is to become so familiar (and practiced) with your *process* for out-lining that you can know exactly what you will do when you get to this type of question.

Therefore, when you take your practice exams, work on outlining the longer and more difficult questions. Practice in a timed situation, i.e., limit the time in which you allow yourself to outline. For example, for a typical long answer essay, you have one hour to complete the entire essay. This means that you should spend approximately 15 minutes read-ing and re-reading the facts, and 5 minutes outlining your answer. This allows you 40 minutes to write your answer. Replicate this *process* of plan-ning your essay exams as many times as you can before your actual exam.

Consider the following long essay question from an Evidence exam. This was a difficult question that addressed several hearsay exceptions in both a criminal and civil context. Very few students got all the issues involved in this essay question. However, the students who did get most of the issues spent some time outlining the issues on their test booklet before writing. Consider the outline that follows this essay question.[7]

Example D: Long Form Essay Question

You will have one hour to answer this essay question.

Tricia Adams broke into John Vicker's house to steal his bobblehead collection. While Adams was in the house, Vicker came home with a man Adams recognized as Paul Brown. Adams hid behind a curtain; Vicker and Brown could not see her, but she could see them. Adams watched from behind the curtain as Brown killed Vicker with a knife. Brown then ran from the house.

Adams forgot about the bobbleheads and used her cell phone to call a friend named Fred White. Adams told White that she "desperately needed a place to hide out for a few days and chill from some major stress." According to White, Adams was "sobbing and hysterical on the phone."

White allowed Adams to stay at his apartment for four days. At the end of that time, Adams confided to White that she had broken into Vicker's house, intending to steal his bobblehead collection. While in the house, she told White, she had seen Brown stab Vicker to death. "I'll never forget the sight of his bleeding body," Adams said, starting to cry again. She composed herself and returned to her own home.

White was horrified by Adams' revelation. After thinking about the matter for a week, he called Adams and told her that he could not keep silent about the crimes. White then went to the police and reported everything Adams had said about breaking into Vicker's house and witnessing his murder. The police drove to Adams's house to interview her, but found that she had committed suicide shortly after receiving White's call about notifying the police.

In addition to White's report, the police gathered some circumstantial evidence linking Brown to Vicker's murder. A grand jury indicted Brown for homicide. Vicker's widow also sued Brown for the wrongful death of her husband.

    (A) In the civil suit against Brown, will Vicker's widow be able to call White as a witness to testify about Adams' statements (1) during the phone call to White, and (2) after she had stayed at his apartment? Explore all plausible bases for admitting these hearsay statements.

---

7. This example was created by Deborah Jones Merritt, John Deaver Drinko-Baker and Hostetler Chair in Law; Courtesy Professor of Sociology; Courtesy Professor of Public Policy and management, and Associate Faculty Member in Women's Studies, The Ohio State University, Moritz College of Law. Professor Merritt is a wonderful teacher and mentor. This example and the following outline are used with her permission.

(B) Can White testify for the prosecutor about Adams' statements during the homicide trial? In answering this subpart, build upon your previous answer. Focus, in other words, on how admissibility of the statements in the homicide trial differs from that in the wrongful death suit.

Here is an example outline of an answer listing the various issues in this essay. What do you notice? The outline is very detailed, and you may not have enough time to fill in all of the details. But having something to help you organize the many issues in any long form essay will be very helpful. In the end, you will write a better answer to your long essay questions.

(A) The Civil Suit

1. Statements made during the phone call. Hearsay: Does any exception apply?

    Exception for excited utterance

    - Witnessing murder is a startling event
    - Adams' statements related to this event
    - Was Adams speaking under stress of excitement? Subjective standard
      As a criminal, would illegal activity bother her less?
    ○ But sobbing and hysterical
    ○ Words suggest she was under stress
    ○ How much time passed before she called?
    ○ Cases suggest statement made within 30–40 minutes of major stress ok

    Exception for state of mind

    - Admits statements of emotion or feeling
    ○ "Desperate need" could be an emotion
    ○ "Stress" could be a feeling or a reason for feeling; latter inadmissible under this exception
      - Feelings must be contemporaneous with statement: Within confines described above, these statements fit

    Adams is not a party, so can't use party-opponent exception

    Others possibilities that people discussed were present sense impression.

2. Statements made after staying with White. Also hearsay: Applicable exception?

    Not excited utterance: four days is too long to sustain stress

    State of mind might admit "I'll never forget the sight of his bleeding body" as statement of contemporaneous feeling. But other statements are memory/explanation; inadmissible under this exception.

    Statement against interest

    - Adams is unavailable (dead)
    - Against interest

- ° Subjected her to criminal liability (breaking and entering)
- ° Reasonable person wouldn't have made unless true
- ° Against interest at time made
- ° She was open to prosecution
- ° No evidence that she then intended suicide
  - • Not offered to exculpate criminal defendant; don't need corroboration
  - • Judge might redact, limiting references to Adams' own crime
- ° Her attempted burglary was entirely separate from murder
- ° But Adams had no legal reason to be in the house; very fact she could see murder was against her interest
- ° Statement seems reliable, particularly valuable, and it's offered in civil case: all reasons supporting admission

Other points

No Sixth Amendment issues in civil case

Statements during phone call may not help plaintiff unless later statements are also admissible. Former statements alone could suggest that Adams, rather than Brown, committed murder.

(B) Criminal prosecution

1. Sixth Amendment's Confrontation Clause[8] applies.

   a. If the statement was testimonial, admissible only if Adams is unavailable and Brown had a previous opportunity to cross-exam. First condition is met, but not second.

   b. To admit statement, therefore, prosecutor must persuade judge it was non-testimonial. Prosecutor seems to have a strong case:
      - • Both statements were made to a friend, not a government official
      - • Circumstances surrounding statements were not formal
      - • First statement was made under stress, possible emergency
      - • Second statement was more factual
      - • No evidence that Adams intended either statement to be used for prosecution. In first, she asked friend for place to stay. In second, she sought comfort from friend
      - • Fact that Adams committed suicide when White went to police supports conclusion that she did <u>not</u> intend statements to be used prosecutorially

Whether or not you outline (and how much time you spend on an exam outline) depends in large part on how you learn. Some students hate outlining—either for papers or for exams. Obviously, you will

---

8. Note this example does not take into account recent case law involving the Confrontation Clause and the Sixth Amendment.

not want to outline your exam answer before you begin to write if you find that it does *not* help you. But even if you are not inclined to write a detailed outline, it *is* beneficial to write at least a list of issues that you intend to cover as you write. Minimally, having a list of the main issues in a problem will prevent you from *missing* issues as you write your exam.

The next example is a long answer essay question from my Professional Responsibility class.

Example E: Long Form Essay Question

Please read the following hypothetical and discuss the ethical issues that may arise under the Model Rules of Professional Responsibility. For each issue, please discuss the ethical issue involved, state the rule, and analyze whether the lawyer's conduct is in violation of the rule. Please use an IRAC structure for each issue that you discuss. You have 60 minutes.

Dylan was a 75-year-old widower, his wife having died in 2002. Their two children, Brenda and Brandon, lived nearby, but contacted Dylan infrequently. Dylan spent most of his time with Donna, a 55-year-old woman he called his "companion." Dylan had suffered from the beginning stages of dementia. In November of 2007, Dylan called his only brother Steve, who was an attorney, to prepare his will. Steven was a trial attorney by training and has been retired for the past 10 years — although he is still licensed to practice law. Dylan instructed Steve to divide his estate as follows:

Brandon (Dylan's son)	40%
Brenda (Dylan's daughter)	40%
Steve (Dylan's brother)	10%
Help For Hounds (a local charity)	10%

Steve was to be Executor of the estate.

In April 2010, Dylan had a stroke and died. At Dylan's funeral, Donna showed Brandon a photocopy of a "revised" will his father (Dylan) had allegedly signed in March 2010. In the new will, Dylan left his entire estate to Donna.

Brandon called Steve the next day asking him to represent the estate in the probate process. Brandon also informed Steve that he and Brenda wanted to dispute Donna's "revised" will, and specifically, they wanted the November 2007 will to control. Brandon asked Steve to handle the case. Brandon also mentioned that he probably should receive more of the estate than Brenda — since she's a little bit "crazy." Brandon brought Steve $10,000 in cash that he found in his father's house as a fee retainer. Steve wasn't sure whether he should take the money since it was not really Brandon's money but he decided it was okay for the time being. Since Steve hadn't practiced law in the last decade, Steve put the retainer fee in his personal bank account.

Steve had never really probated an estate. Therefore, Steve asked one of his more experienced colleagues for advice, and his colleague, David, said that a reasonable fee for a simple probate case would justify a fee between $1,500 and $2,500; a complicated probate representation would justify a fee of $5,000 to $7,000. Steve decided to charge the entire $10,000, assuming he would need to spend more time on it than would a more-experienced estate lawyer. Steve called Brandon and said "Look, I don't have any experience in probating estates, but I think I can handle this, as long as you agree not to come after me later for malpractice." Brandon then responded, "Uncle Steve, I would never sue you! Okay, $10,000 for this sounds good. Go ahead and get started." Steve responded, "Good. But I need you to sign something to make sure I'm not sued!" Brandon agreed.

Two days later, Donna stopped to visit Steve. She asked Steve whether he might represent her in the will contest. She stated that she felt he was the "best lawyer" for the job, and she would pay him a fee of $20,000. Donna was very persuasive and said that she really considered Steve "her lawyer." Steve really wanted the extra money and he felt that he could competently represent Donna, as well as Brandon and Brenda. As per the instructions above, please address whether Steve has violated any of the Model Rules of Professional Responsibility.

This was a long factual hypothetical that triggered quite a few Professional Responsibility issues. Yet the length of this factual hypothetical is fairly typical for law school essay exams. For this question, I created an issue list of the issues I wanted the students to address in the essay. The students should have identified the following issues:

1. Dylan is older and suffers from dementia. 1.14 Potential capacity issue.

2. Steve is a trial lawyer. 1.1 competence. Older lawyer, perhaps 1.14 capacity.

3. Steve will receive a testamentary gift. 1.8 prohibits, although may fit within exception of close sibling.

4. Steve agreed to represent in probate process, without 1.1 competence.

5. Steve took money that was not Brandon's, in violation of 1.2 (helping a client perpetuate a fraud/crime against the estate).

6. Steve's taking someone else's money may be a violation of 1.8 (someone else paying for services).

7. Steve violates 1.7 conflict, because of his own personal interest in the outcome of the case. Must discuss ramifications of limitations of representation with Brandon and Brenda, and obtain informed consent confirmed in writing.

8. Brandon stating that Brenda is "crazy" suggests a 1.7 conflict issue because Brandon and Brenda may have different interests as beneficiaries in the will contest.

9. Steve violates 1.5 because fee of $10,000 is unreasonable.

10. Steve violates 1.15 by placing funds in his personal account versus a client trust account.

11. Steve violates 1.1 again because he cannot charge for his additional time in "learning" and gaining competence in the probate issue/s. Steve should associate with other counsel.

12. Steve violated 1.8(h) because he seeks to limit his malpractice liability prospectively, and asks Brandon to sign such a document.

13. Steve violated 1.4 because he didn't fully discuss the limitations of his representations with Brandon (due to his incompetence/inexperience re: wills).

14. Steve cannot represent Donna at all because this is direct adversity prohibited by 1.7, and also there is no way to make it consentable because it violates 1.7(b) relating to the requirement that you cannot represent two parties in the SAME litigation.

15. Has Steve violated 1.18 relating to a prospective client? Shouldn't he have told Donna instantly that he could not represent her, so she limited any confidential information? Donna thinks of him as "her attorney" which suggests that he has created an attorney/client relationship. Serious violation of 1.18 and 1.7.

The following is a student's actual answer (unedited) for this essay question. I am giving you an example of a student's answer so you see exactly what students are capable of (and do!) write. No student saw every issue, but many students saw a majority of the issues.

Student A.

1.1 Competence

Steve (S) was a trial attorney by training and had not practiced for 10 years. Additionally the facts show he was unaware of what to charge and had never probated a case before. This brings his overall competence to perform his duties as an attorney regarding what will likely be a complicated probate case. Rule 1.1 states that a lawyer must reasonably believe they can have the legal knowledge and experience or that they can acquire the legal knowledge through study or associate to effectively represent their clients' interests. Regarding the writing of his brothers' will, its probably reasonable that S could believe he could acquire the legal expertise necessary to write a will. The will does not appear to be completed and one would assume most attorneys are capable of doing the necessary research to learn how to write an effective will. Regarding S's representation of Brandon (BO), Brenda (BA), and possible Donna (DO), it may be questionable whether, after not having practiced law for 10 years and never having probated an estate, S could reasonably believe he was capable of effectively presenting these complicated, conflicting issues. There is no indication that Steve did additional research regarding the actual probate process, although the facts do show that he asked a more experienced colleague for advice regarding fees. Additionally, its mentioned that Steve charged more because he thought it would take longer for him, than for an experienced probate attorney, but there isn't any indication of whether that additional time was pent researching or whether S would just take extra time because he wasn't familiar with the process. Its likely that Steve was fine under 1.1 when he wrote Dylan's (DY) will, but that he was likely no competent to provide effective representation to the Estate, BO, BA, and DO without lots of additional assistance from other attorney's and a lot of additional research/study. Since there is no indication S associated in any, more experienced attorney's or did extensive research/study, it is likely that S violated 1.1 and would be subject to discipline.

There is an exception to 1.1 if a family member comes to an attorney in an emergency requesting representation. In such a case, despite a belief that they are not competent to represent the client until the end litigation, an attorney may represent their family member or close friend in an emergency situation until the emergency has passed and they can either associate in a more experienced attorney or withdraw from the case and hand the case over to a more experienced attorney. This exception does not apply in this case.

1.6   Confidentiality of Information

There are a number of confidentiality risks present in the current facts. At the end of the facts, S is representing up to 4 different parties, each with potentially confidential facts that cannot be shared with any of the other parties. Rule 1.6 states that any confidential information that an attorney learns during the course of representing a client may not be disclosed unless under very specific exceptions, none of which are present in this case. If S were to actually consent to representation of all four clients he would have to write one doozy of a confidentiality waiver because as the sole attorney there could be no screening and no way of limiting his exposure to confidential, material facts. The waiver would have to say, essentially, that because S is acting as the attorney for all four parties that any confidential information the four parties give him will be used in an overall calculation of the probate process. Each client would have to be advised to consult another attorney regarding the waiver and then provide written consent. This situation is comically impractical and no mater what waiver S got, if he represented all 4 parties there would be so much confidential information floating around that there would be almost no way for him to effectively represent each client. Based on 1.6 alone, S would probably have to withdraw form the case.

1.7   Conflict of Interest (COI): Current Clients

There are a number of Conflicts of Interest in this case. S may have a conflict arising from him being a beneficiary of the will, BO's, BA's, and DO's interests may all conflict with on another and in addition to all that, S must effectively execute the will as the official Executor.

A. A's Conflict as a Beneficiary

Generally, an attorney may not write a will in which they are a beneficiary. Once exception is if the attorney is a family member of the person requesting the will. Since S was DY's brother, this exception applies, and S is likely fine to write DY's will and execute the estate.

B. BO's Conflict of Interest

BO has conflicting interests with all three other parties. As the person who first approached S after DY's death, BO has established that he (1) wants more money than BA; (2) doesn't think DO should get any money; and (3) that he should get more money than the original will says he should. This puts BO's interests in conflict with BA, DO, S and the Estate. Rule 1.7 states that if one current client's interests are directly, materially adverse to the interest of another client that an attorney must withdraw from representation unless he receives informed, written consent from both clients that they are aware of the conflict and still want the attorney to represent them. It's probable that despite informed, written consent given in this case, that S should still not have accepted BO as a client initially as he was already representing DY's estate as executor. Its possible tat a waiver could allow S to represent the estate and BO, but regarding A and DO, a waiver would likely be insufficient and S should have communicated to DO that he could not represent her zealously based on his representation of the original estate of BO, and of BA.

C. BA's Conflict of Interest

Its safe to assume that BA wants at least what was originally allocated for her in her father's will. The fact that S has not even spoken with BA regarding his theoretical representation of her interests indicate that there is a lack of communication going on. Rule 1.4: Communication states that a lawyer must effectively communicate with clients regarding their interests and how the case is proceeding. In this case, we can assume because a lack of communication that BA's interests are being damaged by the whole process and that S must speak with he and get her to either waive the COI or possibly find a different attorney to represent her. The face that BO wants to get more money from the will than BA adds to the likelihood that this would be a good idea.

D. DO's Conflict of Interest

DO interests directly conflict with those of BO and BA, who Steve is already representing. This type of direct adversity cannot be waived and even if S believes that he can represent all four clients effectively and zealously, this is not a reasonable belief and S should have declined representing DO based on 1.7.

E. S's Conflict as Executor

I believe Executor's are charged with executing the will as written and that any challenges to the written will have to be decided in court with the Executor representing the estate. Probate law may imply certain COI's regarding S's position as executor of the will.

1.14 Client With Diminished Capacity

This rule states that an attorney must act when he believes that his client's diminished capacity is leading him to make decisions that materially harm his own interests and those interests are related to the lawyer's representation. While DY may have believed his brother was fine when he spoke with him, it may have been his duty to ensure that his brother was of "sound mind" when he wrote the will and instructed S to execute it. There are insufficient facts to indicate that S actually conducted himself unprofessionally, but it still may have been a good idea to verify DY's soundness of mind before agreeing to write and execute the will.

1.15 Safekeeping Property

When brought S the 10K he found in his father's house, S should have put it in a client trust account rather than accepting it as payment. It's likely that the money was part of DY's estate and is therefore in direct dispute as a result of the actions from all the beneficiaries of the will.

1.16 Duties to Prospective Clients

When S was approached by BO, and later by DO, he should have advised them of his representation of current parties. By not telling both BO and DO that he was already representing clients with potentially conflicting interests he violated his professional duty and could be disciplined.

1.5 Fees

S probably overcharged BO based on his consultation with a more experienced attorney. Rule 1.5 states that lawyers must come up with a fee agreement, preferable written, that presents a reasonable level of compensation for the services they're providing. In this case, while S is an inexperienced probate attorney, he's charging BO more for his service. This likely is unreasonable and would subject S to discipline. Additionally, getting BO to waive any future malpractice claims was likely misconduct because S did not advise BO to seek additional, outside counsel before making such a sweeping waiver.

S definitely overcharged DO regarding his representation of her interests. According to his more experienced attorney friend, S was accepting nearly three times the going rate for an experienced probate attorney representing a difficult probate interest. Despite the fact that DO offered this fee and the fact that DO's interests conflicted directly with BO's and BA's, its probably that S acted unprofessionally in accepting an unreasonably high payment without disclosing to DO that the fee was unreasonably high.

1.18 Duties to Prospective Clients

When DO came in to seek representation from S he should have told her up front that he was representing interests that were directly adverse to hers and that she should not disclose any confidential information to him. S probably also should have immediately advise DO to seek another attorney to represent her. Rule 1.18 states that an attorney must disclose to unrepresented third persons (or is that 4.3) if he is an interested party. Its apparent from DO's statement that she thought of S as her attorney. This belief was probably unreasonable and S's belief he could effectively represent all 3 people is probably even more unreasonable.

The bottom line is that when DY came to S, S should have said that he would represent DY's will but that the will would hold more weight if S subjected himself to a psychological evaluation in order to verify his soundness of mind. When BO called S, S should have told him that there were likely to be pieces of confidential information and certain interests that conflicted and that BO should seek outside counsel before signing any waiver regarding these conflicts. S then should have told BO to have BA contact him independently to verify that he was representing them jointly. S also should have disclosed that he was not an experienced probate attorney and that he would likely need to do additionally research and seek outside advice. If BO then still chose to hire S, S should have done additionally research and sought outside advice. S also should not have charged as much as he did to BO or accepted the 10K from DY's house as payment BO. Additionally, BO's waiver was a bad idea as BO had not been advised to seek outside counsel on the matter. When DO came to S, he should have told her of the conflicting interests and that because of these conflicts that he could not represent her.

This student did an excellent job with issue spotting and with analyzing the issues. Although there were a couple of possible issues/rules that the student missed, overall this was a very strong exam answer. The student received 90/100 points.

3. How Do We Grade?

It's worth considering how law professors grade before you begin taking your exams. Law professors typically come up with a point system for grading. Your professor will develop a checklist for each issue and assign a certain number of points per issue. Although style, grammar and readability do matter, these factors do not carry as much weight as substance. In other words, you don't usually accumulate additional points for writing well. However, you may lose points for not writing well. Consider that writing an organized, grammatically correct exam answer will make sure that your professor *sees* all of your issues and analysis, and this will maximize your points on the exam.

Law professors read through exam answers quickly but we often read them two to three times each. The first time we read an answer is more of a 'skim' to get a gut feeling as to whether the student got the main issue/s or not. The second time, we may go through and actually check off the major issues you've identified and analyzed. The third pass is to ensure that we haven't missed any of your issues! A third read through is often necessary in a poorly organized exam answer. If at all possible, you want write clearly and concisely so your answer can be easily read — so it doesn't require that your professor read it again to search for issues.

So, for example, in a long essay, there may be 100 total points for the entire essay question. But the essay is likely divided into 10 different issues—each with a different Mini-IRAC. So each issue will be worth 10 points each. Again, under this system—time management is an important key to success. If you write beautifully on only six issues, you will still get points for only those six issues (and miss almost 40 points on the exam!). Make sure you leave enough time to address all of the issues in the essay question. Write down the time allotted for each overall question and try to stick to it.

Over the course of law school, you will develop your own method for taking essay exams (and all of your exams). The key is to develop your game plan early on in the first semester of your first year. Many students wait until after their first semester midterms or exams (or even into their second year) before they consider *how* to take exams. Perhaps you scored below average on your first set of midterms and you feel like there's no way to improve. Or you may think that you received the grade you did on an exam simply because you didn't understand the substance of the course well enough—or that your professor was less than fair on the exam, etc. Any or all of these things may be true. However, you should also consider that you might need to spend some of your time preparing for the *taking* of the exam itself. The key to success in taking law school exams it to develop a specific strategy for the exam and to practice your strategy or plan *before* the exam. You don't have to write a perfect answer—you simply need to catch the major issues and write an IRAC analysis for most of the issues. If you can accomplish this, you will perform well on your law school essay exams.

Chapter 10

Taking the Multiple-Choice Law School Exam

Law school multiple-choice exams are very different than any multiple-choice exams you have taken before law school. In your prior multiple-choice exams, the questions most likely tested your ability to *recall* information. However, the law school multiple-choice exam (and the multi-state bar exam as well) tests your ability to *analyze* a fact pattern and come to the correct conclusion. Like the law school essay exam, law professors are asking you to perform the same type of skills in a multiple-choice exam: read a factual hypothetical, identify the legal issue, and apply an IRAC analysis to come to the correct conclusion. Although you have a closed universe in a multiple-choice exam, the questions themselves are quite complex and time-consuming.

Law professors often justify their use of multiple-choice exams by claiming that they want to simulate bar exam questions. This may be partly true. We do want to prepare you for the bar exam after you graduate from law school. But law professors also like multiple-choice exams because they are objective and they are easy to grade! That being said, however, drafting a good multiple-choice question is very difficult. So, as with any other type of exam, I would suggest trying to obtain copies of your professors' prior multiple-choice exams early on in the semester.[1] You will need to practice taking multiple-choice exams as a separate skill set in law school. The types of multiple-choice questions used in a law school exam are unique. So even if you do not have access to a particular professor's prior multiple-choice exam, consider asking your professor if there is a particular study aid that the professor recommends.[2] Minimally, you need to simulate the types of questions you might find on multiple-choice exam in that particular course.

---

1. This may be somewhat difficult, however, because many law professors have policies that prevent them from giving students copies of the multiple-choice questions so that we can reuse multiple-choice questions on different exams.

2. For example, I often suggest the Q & A Series which has hundreds of multiple-choice questions for any subject. You can practice writing Mini-IRACs with the questions, or use them for multiple-choice practice as well. This series is a good supplement to your own outline. It's not a bad idea to have many different study sources. They each give you a different but helpful perspective.

Law school multiple-choice questions are very difficult for several reasons.[3] First, the factual scenarios or hypotheticals that precede the answer choices are complex and detailed. Second, several of the answer choices seem equally correct. Third, the answer choices often contain distracting information designed to lure you away from the real focus of the question.[4] Therefore, to do well on these exams, you must not only understand the rules applicable to a given issue in the question, you must also understand the formula a law professor uses to create multiple-choice questions. You are less likely to feel ambushed by your first series of multiple-choice exams if you become familiar with the types of questions used in a law school multiple-choice exam.[5] This chapter will explain these different types of multiple-choice questions and provide you with important strategies for mastering this type of exam.

A. The Terminology of Multiple-Choice Questions

First, let's begin with some basic terminology of the different components of a multiple-choice question. There are three parts to any multiple-choice question: the 'root' or factual hypothetical; the 'call' of the question (sometimes called the question or 'stem'); and the 'options' (or answer choices).[6] First, the 'root' is the fact pattern that precedes the actual task being demanded of the law student. The root likely contains all of the facts needed for a knowledgeable examinee to answer that question. A well-written root uses concise language and minimizes extra characters, names or information. However, law professors may not give you a "well-written" factual hypothetical. Sometimes, we will use silly names or put in extra information in the fact patterns (which is not helpful to you but fairly typical). So you should be prepared to distill the *relevant* facts from the 'root' as quickly as possible. Like the factual hypothetical in an essay exam, you want to begin reading the root by circling any key phrases or words that signal issues.

---

3. Rogelio Lasso, *Taking Multiple Choice Exams,* (*citing* Michael Josephson, *Evaluation and Grading in Law School,* (1984)) (updates to Professor Josephson's work on multiple-choice exams provided by Rogelio Lasso, John Marshall Law School, Chicago and Professor Vernellia Randall, University of Dayton Law School. Professor Lasso's handout is at Appendix D at the end of the book.)

4. *Id.*

5. *Id.*

6. Michael Josephson, *Learning and Evaluation in Law School, Volume 2: Test Construction, Scoring, Grading, and Ranking Institutional Policies* (1984), Submitted to the Association of American Law Schools Annual Meeting; January 4, 1984 Teaching Methods Sections.

Second, the 'call' of the question is a short, focused question that asks you to perform a particular task. Sometimes the call of the question will add facts to the initial hypothetical. Other times, the call of the question will require you to make certain assumptions before answering the question. Or the call may specify what cause of action or theory to advance. Whatever the particular call, make sure to read the call very *carefully* so that you know precisely what you are being asked to do!

Third, the answer choices or 'options' are the lettered choices given to you as potential answers to the call of the question. One of the answer choices, called the 'key,' should be clearly better than the other options (called 'distractors'). A well-written series of answer choices or options should be parallel in language and structure; should be as concise as possible; should not contain new facts; and should not contain additional conditions. Once again, however, since not all law professors are trained to write *good* multiple-choice questions, you may see questions on your exams that do not always follow these rules.

In the following example,[7] I have labeled each of these parts in a typical law school multiple-choice question:

Root or Factual Hypo — 1. Pam sues for injuries after her car is struck by a truck driven by Reginald. On direct examination, Pam's lawyer asks her: "Isn't it a fact that you were driving well within the speed limit prior to the collision and keeping a careful lookout for other cars?

Call or Stem — The defense attorney objects. The judge should:

Options A–C are distractors.

A. Sustain the objection because leading questions are never allowed on direct examination.

B. Overrule the objection because leading questions are permissible in some introductory situations on direct examination.

C. Sustain the objection because the witness should testify in a narrative form.

D. Sustain the objection because leading questions are generally not allowed on direct and the attorney is not asking simply introductory material.

Key (correct answer). Although leading questions are sometimes allowed for introductory material, in this situation, the lawyer is planting the information and the leading question goes too far under Rule 611.

Why do law professors use multiple-choice questions? The multiple-choice exam is a very flexible form of objective testing that is similar to the essay exam in terms of analytical requirements and substantive knowledge. Essay questions can be converted into multiple-choice questions and professors can alter multiple-choice questions easily to make them more or less sophisticated by adjusting the complexity of the facts or by changing the manner in which the call of the question is worded. In addition, a law

---

7. *Id.* at 349–378.

professor can make a question more challenging by posing options which are both complex and close to each other in terms of similarity between answer choices. It is then up to the student to read carefully and closely in order to determine the subtle differences between the listed options.

B. What Are the Different Forms of Multiple-Choice Questions?

There are several different forms of multiple-choice questions but the most common form types are as follows: (1) the simple fact pattern; (2) the complex fact pattern; (3) the two-tiered option; (4) overlapping options; and (5) the question series.[8] Having a sense of the different types of multiple-choice forms (and becoming comfortable with them) will help you reduce test anxiety. In addition, you may want to develop a strategy where you can spot easier multiple-choice questions versus more difficult forms of questions. Keep in mind that the typical law school multiple-choice exam will have some of each of the five types of questions. In my experience, approximately 25% of the multiple-choice questions are of low to moderate difficulty; 50% of the questions are of moderate difficulty; and approximately 25% of the questions are of high difficulty. The remainder of this sub-section will describe the different forms of law school multiple-choice questions and provide you with an example of what they look like.

1. The Simple Fact Pattern

The simple fact pattern is comprised of a straightforward factual hypothetical that focuses on a single legal issue. Your strategy for this type of question is to read the question carefully in order to make sure you get it right! This question form is likely a lower difficulty question type so you want to maximize your opportunities for getting these types of questions correct. Here is an example of a 'simple fact pattern' type of multiple-choice question.

> John was fired from his job. Too proud to apply for unemployment benefits, he used his savings to feed his family. When one of his children became ill, he did not seek medical attention for the child at a state clinic because he did not want to accept what he regarded as charity. Eventually,

---

8. These remaining examples in this chapter are based upon prior bar exam questions; *see* Josephson, *supra* n.6 at 352 (noting that the illustrations used in the book are taken from "Multistate Bar Examination Questions VI" (1981) by the National Conference of Bar Examiners).

weakened by malnutrition, the child died as a result of the illness. John has committed:

(A) murder
(B) involuntary manslaughter
(C) voluntary manslaughter
(D) no form of criminal homicide

In this example, the answer choices are fairly straightforward as well. Therefore, if you know the answer fairly quickly, fill in the answer and move on to a more complex question. Sometimes you can efficiently answer these types of questions which will leave you more time for higher difficulty questions.

2. The Complex Fact Pattern

This type of multiple-choice question involves a more complex factual hypothetical that may take you a bit longer to read and digest. Some students can be overwhelmed by the details of these longer factual scenarios. Take your time reading the question and don't panic. The challenge of this type of question is to sort through the facts carefully and methodically to pick out the relevant facts from the less relevant facts. One effective strategy is to read the "call" of the question early on so that you know what to focus on. Here is an example of a complex fact pattern type of multiple-choice question.

> Homer and Purcell entered into a valid, enforceable written contract by which Homer agreed to sell and Purcell agreed to purchase Blackacre, which was Homer's residence. One of the contract provisions was that after the closing Homer had the right to remain in residence at Blackacre for up to 30 days before delivering possession to Purcell. The closing took place as scheduled. Title passed to Purcell and Homer remained in possession. Within a few days after the closing, the new house next door which was being constructed for Homer was burned to the ground, and at the end of the 30-day period Homer refused to move out of Blackacre; instead, Homer tendered to Purcell a monthly rental payment in excess of the fair rental value of Blackacre. Purcell rejected the proposal and that day brought an appropriate action to gain immediate possession of Blackacre. The contract was silent as to the consequences of Homer's failure to give up possession within the 30-day period, and the jurisdiction in which Blackacre is located has no statute dealing directly with this situation, although the landlord-tenant law of the jurisdiction requires a landlord to give a tenant 30 days notice before a tenant may be evicted. Purcell did not give Homer any

such 30-day statutory notice. Purcell's best legal argument
in support of his action to gain immediate possession is that
Homer is a:

(A) trespasser ab initio
(B) licensee
(C) tenant at sufferance
(D) tenant from month to month

Note that the answer choices are fairly straightforward; the difficulty
lies completely with the factual hypothetical itself. Some law students
handle these types of multiple-choice questions using the following
strategy.

First, skim the facts to get a general idea for the subject matter; second, read the call of the question first to get the focus on the question;
third, re-read the facts more carefully, actively marking key words and
phrases that relate to the legal issues; and fourth, begin going through answer choices to eliminate wrong answers and narrow in on the correct answer. Note that these types of multiple-choice questions may require a bit
more time to work through the factual hypothetical so keep that in mind
as you work through your exam.

3. The Two-Tiered Option

In this type of multiple-choice question, there is an initial factual hypothetical that is fairly straightforward. Following the hypothetical, you
will see a two-tiered option section which provides *two possibilities* that
might reasonably flow from the factual hypothetical.

Your task is to assess whether the options in either I. or II. are correct
based upon the information given in the factual hypothetical. And there
is one additional step to this type of question. After reviewing the options, you then need to go to the answer choices to evaluate the different choices. The answer choices will ask you to determine if none, either
or both options are correct.

This type of question is challenging because is adds an additional
step in your reasoning process. Therefore, although the factual hypothetical is not overly complex, the additional requirement of reasoning
through the two options (I. and II.) and *then* moving to the answer
choices can make this type of multiple-choice question challenging.
Here is an example:

On March 1, Zeller orally agreed to sell his land, Homestead,
to Byer for $46,000 to be paid on March 31. Byer orally
agreed to pay $25,000 of the purchase price to Quincy in sat-
isfaction of a debt which Zeller said he had promised to pay
Quincy. On March 10, Byer dictated the agreement to his sec-
retary but omitted all reference to the payment of the

$25,000 to Quincy. In typing the agreement, the secretary mistakenly typed in $45,000 rather than $46,000 as the purchase price. Neither Buyer nor Zeller carefully read the writing before signing it on March 15. Neither noticed the error in price and neither raised any question concerning omission of the payment to Quincy. In an action by Quincy against Byer for $25,000, which of the following is (are) correct?

I. Byer could successfully raise the Statute of Frauds as a defense because the Byer-Zeller agreement was to answer for the debt of another.

II. Byer could successfully raise the Statute of Frauds as a defense because the Byer-Zeller agreement was for the sale of an interest in land.

(A) I only
(B) II only
(C) Both I and II
(D) Neither I nor II

Strategically, if you can determine that one of the options is definitely *wrong*, you can narrow down your answer choices immediately to eliminate any reference to that option. For example, if you determine that option I. is incorrect in the above example, then you can eliminate answer choices (A) and (C) immediately. The challenge is to focus on the options first and then move on to evaluating the answer choices. These types of questions are very typical on law school multiple-choice exams so it is important to recognize this type of question.

4. Overlapping Answer Choices

The fourth type of multiple-choice question is the "overlapping answer choices" type of question. In this multiple-choice question type, you are presented with a simple fact pattern and you are given a series of answer choices that overlap. Therefore, the challenge inherent in these types of questions is to reason through the overlapping answer choices. Typically, the answer choices will ask you to decide between two different possibilities, one possibility or neither option. Here is an example:

Defendant was tried for robbery. Victim and Worth were the only witnesses called to testify. Victim testified that Defendant threatened her with a knife, grabbed her purse, and ran off with it. Worth testified that he saw Defendant grab Victim's purse and run way with it but that he neither saw a knife nor heard any threats. On this evidence the jury could properly return a verdict of guilty of:

(A) robbery only
(B) larceny only
(C) neither robbery or larceny
(D) both robbery and larceny

One good thing about this type of multiple-choice question is that you are being asked to assess *only* two options. Therefore, you will focus your analytical process on whether the answer is both options, one option, or possibly neither option. Typically, you can eliminate at least two of the answer choices very quickly which will allow you to focus on the answer choices if you must choose quickly.

5. The Question Series

Finally, there is a fifth type of multiple-choice question called the question series. Like its name implies, the question series multiple-choice question begins with an initial factual hypothetical that will apply to more than one multiple-choice question. In one sense, this is an economical type of question; you can read through the initial hypothetical and apply the factual scenario to more than one question. One key to answering this type of multiple-choice question is to read the initial hypothetical very carefully and write out notes in the margin so you can refer back to key issues quickly without re-reading the facts. Here is an example of a question series.

Questions 53–55 are based on the following fact situation.

Harry met Bill, who was known to him to be a burglar, in a bar. Harry told Bill that he needed money. He promised to pay Bill $500 if Bill would go to Harry's house the following night and take some silverware. Harry explained to Bill that, although the silverware was legally his, his wife would object to his selling it.

Harry pointed out his home, one of a group of similar tract houses. He drew a floor plan of the house that showed the location of the silverware. Harry said that his wife usually took several sleeping pills before retiring, and that he would make sure that she took them the next night. He promised to leave a window unlocked. Everything went according to the plan except that Bill, deceived by the similarity of the tract houses, went to the wrong house. He found a window unlocked, climbed in and found silver where Harry had indicated. He took the silver to the cocktail lounge where the payoff was to take place. At that point the police arrested the two men.

53. If Harry were charged with burglary, his best argument
for acquittal would be that:

(A) there was no breaking
(B) he consented to the entry
(C) no overt act was committed by him
(D) there was no intent to commit a felony

54. Bill's best argument for acquittal of burglary is that he:

(A) acted under a mistake of law
(B) had the consent of the owner
(C) reasonably thought he was in Harry's house
(D) found the window unlocked

The question series is a fairly common type of multiple-choice question on a law school exam. Keep in mind, however, that the question that follows the initial factual hypothetical may add *additional* facts for you to consider. Therefore, you will need to apply the facts from the initial hypothetical to any additional facts given to you in the separate question. Finally, if you find yourself running out of time on your exam, you may want to look for this type of question. It may be possible for you to move through a question series more quickly.

C. What Are the Different "Calls" to a Law School Multiple-Choice Question?

In the last section, we examined the different types or *forms* of multiple-choice questions. In this subsection, we will consider the most typical question stems or calls of the question. In other words, there are four typical tasks that a law school multiple-choice question will ask you to complete. Becoming familiar with each of these tasks may help you move faster through your multiple-choice exam.

A multiple-choice question will typically ask you to find: (1) the "one correct answer;" (2) the "one incorrect answer;" (3) the "best answer" (relative to the choices given); and (4) the "best reasoning" (among the choices given). This subsection will give a short explanation of each type of question call or task.[9]

1. One Correct Answer

In this type of call, only one of the answer choices is correct and it is *absolutely correct*. The remaining options are incorrect. Your job is either to locate the correct answer immediately (because you know that it

---

9. Adapted from Josephson, *supra* n.6, at 355–366.

is clearly the correct answer) or to eliminate the answers you know are incorrect. The exact language used in the call of the question may vary somewhat, e.g., see the two examples below, but these types of multiple-choice questions always ask you to find the one correct answer. Consider using the following strategy with this type of question. As you read each answer choice, think of the answer choice as a true/false question. Thus, you can derive the correct answer either by knowing it when you see it or by the process of elimination (i.e., eliminating answers you know are incorrect). In the following examples, I have highlighted the call of each question as it represents the one correct answer variety.

Example 1:

Which of the following statements is most accurate?

(A) Payment of Daniel of the $100 was a condition precedent to Paul's duty of performance.
(B) The performances of Paul and Daniel under the contract were concurrently conditional.
(C) Payment by Daniel of the $100 was a condition subsequent to Paul's duty of performance.
(D) Performance by Paul under the contract was a condition precedent to Daniel's duty of payment of the $100.

Example 2:

In a collision case, Plaintiff offers in evidence a photograph showing the scene of the accident while the cars were still in place. **A proper foundation must include, as a minimum, testimony by which of the following?**

(A) The photographer
(B) A person who was present at the time the photograph was taken
(C) A person who observed the cars while they were still in place
(D) A person in whose custody the photograph has been since it was developed

2. One Incorrect Answer

The second type of question stem or call of the question involves a variation of the single correct answer but it is the negative form of the question. The one incorrect answer stem asks you to pick out the one incorrect answer from a set of options. The remaining options, the distractors, are all correct statements. Like the strategy described above for the one correct answer question type, you can use a process of elimination to narrow down your answer choices. The only difference: eliminate the *true* statements and select the *false* statement. In the following two examples,

I have highlighted the call of the question that illustrates the one incorrect answer format.

Example 1:

> Which of the following crimes is **LEAST likely** to result in a felony murder conviction if the victim dies during the perpetration of the crime?
>
> (A) rape
> (B) robbery
> (C) larceny
> (D) kidnapping

Example 2:

> Which of the following statements regarding the legal effect of Daniel's illness is **LEAST accurate**?
>
> (A) Daniel's illness and the related development excused Paul from his obligation to deliver the cards on or before December 15.
> (B) Prompt notice by Daniel to Paul of Daniel's recovery from illness was an implied condition of Paul's duty under the circumstances.
> (C) Paul was under a duty of immediate performance of his promise to deliver the cards, as of December 15, by reason of the express language of the contract and despite the illness of Daniel and the related developments.
> (D) Daniel's conduct after his illness constituted a waiver of the necessity of Paul's performing on or before December 15.

3. One Best Answer

The third variety is the one best answer question stem, which is also the most common multiple-choice question because it provides law professors with the most flexibility in creating subtle differences between answer choices. In other words, law professors can make the answer choices sound very similar and it's up to the student to determine which answer choice is the best answer.

Thus, this question stem or call tests a student's relative judgments and does not require the law professor to draft answer choices that are absolutely true/correct or false/incorrect. Instead, this form allows for a wide variety of question types that can test students' understanding in several different ways. Consider the following list of possible question stems within this category of one best answer.

a. Which is the **best, more likely or most probable** result?

b. What is the **best reasoning** supporting a stated result?

c. What is the **best argument** supporting a particular position or party?

d. What is the **best defense** under these circumstances?

e. What is the **best cause of action** that applies to the fact pattern?

f. Which facts will **most help** a particular party advocate for a particular argument/position?

Consider the following two examples of this variety of question stem.

Example 1:

Roofer entered into a written contract with Orissa to repair the roof of Orissa's home, the repairs to be done "in a workmanlike manner." Roofer completed the repairs and took all of his equipment away, with the exception of a 20-foot extension ladder, which was left against the side of the house. He intended to come back and get the ladder the next morning. At that time, Orissa and her family were away on a trip. During the night, a thief, using the ladder to gain access to an upstairs window, entered the house and stole some valuable jewels. Orissa has asserted a claim against Roofer for damages for the loss of the jewels. **In her claim against Roofer, Orissa will**

(A) prevail, because by leaving the ladder Roofer became a trespasser on Orissa's property.
(B) prevail, because by leaving the ladder Roofer created the risk that a person might unlawfully enter the house.
(C) not prevail, because the act of the thief was a superseding cause.
(D) not prevail, because Orissa's claim is limited to damages for breach of contract.

Example 2:

The State of Rio Grande entered into a contract with Roads, Inc., for construction of a four-lane turnpike. Prior to commencement of construction, the legislature, in order to provide funds for parks, repealed the statute authorizing the turnpike and cancelled the agreement with Roads, Inc. Roads, Inc., sued the state to enforce its original agreement. **In ruling on this case, a court should hold that the state statute canceling the agreement is:**

(A) Valid, because constitutionally the sovereign is not liable except with its own consent.
(B) Valid, because the legislature is vested with constitutional authority to repeal laws it has enacted.
(C) Invalid, because a state is equitably estopped to disclaim a bid once accepted by it.
(D) Invalid, because of the constitutional prohibition against impairment of contracts.

These types of questions tend to be fairly challenging on a law school exam because students are required to read through each answer choice to evaluate both the stated *conclusion* in the first part of the answer and the *reasoning* that lead to that conclusion in the second part of the answer choice. So, in the above example, a student must first determine whether the court's decision is either valid or invalid; and second, the student must analyze the reasons justifying the end result. These types of questions tend to take more time because students need to read the answer choices very carefully.

4. Best Reasoning Supporting a Stated Position

The fourth and final type of question stem asks the student to analyze the best reasoning for a particular position or conclusion. Once again, like the one best answer variety described in (3) above, the best reasoning question can be equally time-consuming because it requires you to evaluate the reasoning of each answer choice. Consider the following two examples of the best reasoning variety:

Example 1:

> Tess occupied an apartment in a building owned by Len. She paid rent of $125 in advance each month. During the second month of occupancy, Tess organized the tenants in the building as a tenants' association and the association made demands of Len concerning certain repairs and improvements the tenants wanted. When Tess tendered rent for the third month, Len notified her that rent for the fourth and subsequent months would be $200 per month. Tess protested and pointed out that all other tenants paid rent of $125 per month. Thereupon, Len gave the required statutory notice that the tenancy was being terminated at the end of the third month. By an appropriate proceeding, Tess contests Len's right to terminate. **If Tess succeeds, it will be because:**
>
> (A) a periodic tenancy was created by implication.
> (B) the doctrine prohibiting retaliatory eviction is part of the law of the jurisdiction.

(C) the $200 rent demanded violates the agreement implied by the rate charged to other tenants.
(D) the law implies a term of one year in the absence of any express agreement.

Example 2:

The State of Missoula has enacted a new election code designed to increase voter responsibility in the exercise of the franchise and to enlarge citizen participation in the electoral process. None of its provisions conflicts with federal statutes.

Which of the following is the strongest reason for finding unconstitutional a requirement in the Missoula election code that each other must be literate in English?

(A) The requirement violates Article I Section 2 of the Constitution, which provides that representatives to Congress be chosen "by the People of the several States."
(B) The requirement violates Article I, Section 4 of the Constitution, which gives Congress the Power to "make or later" state regulations providing for the "Times" and "Manner" of holding elections for senators and representatives.
(C) The requirement violates the due process clause of the Fourteenth Amendment.
(D) The requirement violates the equal protection of the laws clause of the Fourteenth Amendment.

For this type of question, try to eliminate wrong conclusions quickly. This will eliminate at least two answer choices. Then work to analyze the reasoning and determine which answer choice contains the most thorough and accurate reasons for the stated result.

D. Pay Attention to the Role That the Question Asks You to Play

In addition to the different forms of multiple-choice question types (and the different varieties of question stems), you should also pay attention to the role that the question asks you to play.[10] You may be asked to assume a certain role in the call of the question. Typically, you will be asked to assume one of three roles: a judge; a lawyer (or advocate); or a scholar (or policy-maker). You may answer the question differently depending on the role to which you've been assigned. If you learn to recognize these different roles, you can use your role to eliminate wrong answer choices quickly.

---

10. *See* Professor Lasso, *supra* n.3, at 4.

1. The Judge[11]

One common role that a multiple-choice question will ask you to assume is that of a judge. Many multiple-choice questions use this type of format. For example, consider the following question stem: "If John sues Mary for battery, **the court should** find in favor of …." Once you recognize this type of question, you want to make sure to begin your analysis with no particular result or conclusion in mind. A judge will be open to both sides of any argument. Second, try not to decide questions of fact (in the answer choice) because judges focus on questions of law. In addition, be alert for misstatements about facts in lawyers' arguments. As a judge, you want to wait to resolve any issue until you have considered all the arguments presented in the answer choices. Examine each option in turn. Ask yourself whether the facts and law are accurately stated. Is the conclusion offered consistent with the argument advanced? The correct option is the one where the argument advanced is based on *accurate* statements of fact and law, and is consistent with the conclusion offered. Select such an answer choice even though you may not personally agree with the result.

2. The Lawyer[12]

You may be asked to assume the role of a lawyer or advocate. The following example illustrates this type of multiple-choice question: "Which of the following is the most effective argument in favor of Mary's position?" For these types of questions, make sure to examine each answer choice in turn. Is the law accurately stated? Are the inferences on which the answer choice is based supported by the facts given? Could the argument result in victory for the client? The correct option is the one where the argument advanced is based on accurate statements of fact and law and is consistent with the conclusion offered. Once again, select that answer even if you don't really believe that your client can win.

3. The Scholar[13]

You may also be asked to assume the role of a scholar or academic, i.e., someone who considers the policy of the law more than its application. Here is an example: "The interest in Blackacre which John had on the day after Testatrix's death is best described as a …"

In answering these types of multiple-choice question, try to refrain from determining or trying to determine the actual outcome of the fac-

---

11. *Id.*
12. *Id.*
13. *Id.*

tual hypothetical. Use your knowledge of the law to recognize the legal significance of a particular fact or to select the most applicable rule. Try to focus on the specific and limited issue that you're being asked to consider. Resolve the issue in your own mind first, and then examine each of the options carefully and select the one which comes closest to the selection you have already formulated. And once again, select the answer even if you don't really believe it's the best or just result.

E. Answer Choices: Recognizing Distractors[14]

One key skill in taking multiple-choice exams is to eliminate wrong answer choices or distractors. Consider that three out of the four answer choices in *every* multiple-choice question will be a wrong answer. A wrong answer or distractor is an answer that initially may seem correct but either ends up having faulty reasoning or the answer choice is incorrect but it uses the correct *reasoning*. Law professors want to test your knowledge and analytical abilities with multiple-choice questions but they do not want to be too obvious with the correct answer. Therefore, several of the answer choices will look correct on a superficial level. Your goal is to read each answer choice carefully so you can eliminate distractors as you move through the answer choices. All of the answer choices are designed to give a look of plausibility. Therefore, you must read them carefully!

Here are some potential pitfalls as they relate specifically to *distractors* in a multiple-choice context and some suggested approaches to deal with them.[15]

1. Watch Out for Incomplete Definitions and Arguments[16]

Sometimes an answer choice or a definition will seem correct superficially but it actually contains an incomplete definition. Don't accidentally add in the remaining definitional components or arguments to the answer choice. Focus on the text given. Here's an example. Assume that the answer choice states: "Murder is the unjustified killing of a human being." Although there doesn't seem to be anything wrong with this definition, it is likely an incorrect answer choice. The full definition of murder is as follows: "Murder is the unjustified killing of a human being *with malice aforethought*."

Try not to complete the definition or argument in your mind and conclude mistakenly that an incomplete answer choice is correct.

---

14. *See* Lasso, *supra* n.3 at 2–4; *see also*, Josephson, *supra* n.6 at 350.

15. *Id.* at 3.

16. *Id.*

2. Deal Only with the Facts Given: Don't Add Facts and Don't Ignore Facts![17]

In examining answer choices, you want to assume *nothing* in addition to what has been established or given in the answer choice. For example, if the question states: "The Prosecutor proves that John shot Mary and that Mary died an hour later. Is John guilty of murder?" The answer is likely, "No." You must also prove that John's bullet *caused* Mary's death. The facts, as given, may not demonstrate murder.

In addition, don't *ignore* facts either. Typically, you will find facts in an answer choice for a particular reason. For example, you may have been taught in criminal law that an intoxicated person cannot usually drive a car in a reasonable manner. Assume that the factual hypothetical states that "although Mary drank two quarts of whiskey, she was driving her car in a reasonable manner when she collided with Paul." The call of the question asks: "Was Mary negligent?" Mary is not negligent. Negligence is *unreasonable* conduct. Since the facts tell you that Mary was driving her car in a *reasonable* manner, you must conclude that she was not negligent.

3. Don't Overlook the Obvious[18]

Sometimes the answer choice is so obviously correct that there is no rational excuse for missing it. Don't ignore an obviously correct answer. Remember that some of the questions on the exam will be easier than others.

4. Watch Out for Unfamiliar Phrases[19]

As you've no doubt learned in law school, there are many legal phrases to learn. But be careful of an answer choice that seems to suggest a familiar but slightly 'off' legal theory. For example, on a property exam, the following characterization is incorrect despite the fact that it uses a legal phrase: "A plaintiff could not be the holder of a certain easement because an incorporeal hereditament lies only in grant." If you've never heard of a doctrine or a rule then the answer is probably incorrect. Note also that you might encounter answer choices that describe familiar concepts in non-traditional words. For example, instead of saying: "John owed Mary a duty of reasonable care only if he created a foreseeable risk to her," a correct option would say: "John had no obligation to Mary unless it ap-

---

17. *Id.*
18. *Id.*
19. *Id.* at 4.

peared that John's conduct would injure her." Remember that *substance is more important than form.*

In summary, as you skim through answer choices on your multiple-choice exam, make sure to keep in mind the following rules: (1) watch out for incomplete definitions or reasoning; (2) deal with only the facts given; (3) don't overlook the obvious answer; and (4) be wary of unfamiliar language or phrases.

F. Final Strategies to Enhance Your Performance on the Law School Multiple-Choice Exams

This final sub-section will address some specific strategies for taking multiple-choice exams. Although you will know the material in your course well, you may experience other issues that affect your exam performance. Perhaps you have test anxiety or time management issues that prevent you from illustrating your true understanding of a subject. Or perhaps you are a slower reader and struggle to make it through the factual hypotheticals. I've had many students over the years that have scored perfectly on the essay portion of my exam but did poorly on the multiple-choice section of the exam. I know these students worked very hard in the course and that they knew the material. But something about the multiple-choice questions tripped them up. When I talk with students about their exam performance, they often state: "I'm just bad at multiple-choice exams!" I respond: "You may feel that way, but you need to figure out how to get better at them because you will see these type of exams throughout law school and on the bar exam."

For students who have trouble with multiple-choice questions, I try to encourage them to go on a 'multiple-choice' diet. I recommend that they work on multiple-choice questions at least one hour per week (beginning the second or third week of the semester) per course. The reality of the situation is this: if you have difficulty with multiple-choice questions, you may need to spend some additional time teaching yourself *how* to take these types of exams. Although you may struggle *more* with multiple-choice exams than essay exams, you *can* get better at taking them.

For some law students, one of the biggest roadblocks to multiple-choice exams is time management. On the bar exam, you will have only about two minutes per multiple-choice question. In this type of 'timed' test, you need to become *so* comfortable with the types and format of the questions that you can read through the questions and answer choices efficiently. So — decide to put yourself on a 'multiple-choice diet' and commit yourself to improving your comfort level with the types of questions in a law school multiple-choice exam.

The remainder of this section offers ten strategies for practicing and taking multiple-choice exams. Try to integrate these strategies into your practice sessions as much as possible and then you will internalize the strategies before the exam.

1. Control Your Test Anxiety (as Much as Possible)

We all get nervous when taking exams. For any law student, the pressure of doing well on an exam that counts for 50% to 100% of your course grade is enormous. It is particularly important for you to control your test anxiety as much as possible. Panicking will inhibit your memory and make it impossible to read and comprehend the questions.[20] One way to control your test anxiety is by being as prepared as possible. Another way to control your test anxiety is by simulating the exam experience as much as possible before the exam. This means you need to begin 'practicing' taking the exam early and often during the semester. Try to obtain some past bar exams questions, commercially prepared multiple-choice questions, and/or prior multiple-choice questions from the professor teaching your class. It's not enough that you know the rules or the law. You must train yourself to analyze the fact patterns and answer choices of multiple-choice questions carefully and efficiently. The more comfortable you are with the different types and forms of multiple-choice questions (in addition to knowing the substance of your course), the less anxious you will be on your exam.

2. Spaced Practice Is Better Than All-at-Once Practice

Research has shown that spaced practice is generally superior to 'massed' practice, i.e., practicing for fewer but longer sessions. For example, if you have only one remaining day to study for your Torts exam, you'll get more mileage out of several two-hour blocks of time than studying for 12 hours straight. Cramming is a recipe for poor retention, mental and physical fatigue, and test anxiety. Try your best to schedule how and when you will study for your multiple-choice exams. Plan to spend one to two hours per week simply working on multiple-choice questions in each of your courses. Doing a little bit each week will relieve some of your stress about multiple-choice exams because you are *doing* something early on in the semester to become *better* at taking this

---

20. Test anxiety can have a significant effect on one's performance. *See* Keith A. Kaufman, V. Holland LaSalle-Ricci, Carol R. Glass, Diane B. Arnkoff, *Passing the Bar Exam: Psychological, Educational, and Demographic Predictors of Success*, 57 J. Legal Educ. 205, 207 (2007). In studying how test anxiety affects performance on the bar exam, Kaufman states, "Test anxiety, for example, is characterized by the disposition to react with intrusive thoughts, mental disorganization, tension, and physiological arousal when exposed to evaluative situations." *Id.*

type of exam. The reality is that the more you practice any skill—the better you become at it. And this holds true for taking multiple-choice exams as well!

3. Budget Your Time for Each Test Question and Stick to It!

You will often know ahead of time how many multiple-choice questions will be on your exam. For example, I will often give students 25 multiple-choice questions in a one-hour period for my exams. Therefore, students know that they have between two and three minutes per multiple-choice question for that section of the exam. On easier questions, try to stick to the two minute mark. On more difficult questions, you may need three minutes or more to answer the question. As much as you can, try to stay within that average of two to three minutes per question. Remind yourself to check your progress every five questions or so (no more than 15 minutes should have passed). If you run across a question where you have no idea how to answer it, try not to waste valuable time. You could be using that time answering questions in which you *do* know the answers. If you're stuck, choose your best guess and move on.

4. Develop a Plan for Attacking the Factual Hypothetical of Each Question

As you practice, you will get a sense about the way that you like to approach multiple-choice questions. For example, some students like to skim the facts of the hypothetical first. Next, they read the 'call' of the question. Then they go back and read the factual hypothetical again in detail—circling the key phrases and issues. Or perhaps you are a visual learner. You may want to draw a diagram or picture of the facts on the margin of your exam. When you develop an approach that you can use throughout the exam, you will feel more comfortable with taking the exams. Another tip for dealing with factual hypotheticals includes focusing *only* on the facts given. For example, in a breach of contract case, if someone was talking on the telephone—this may be an important fact. Circle it. In addition, try to use a simple interpretation of the facts—do not make them more complex than they are. Pay attention to your instincts. And pay special attention to seemingly meaningless details—it's possible they are in the fact pattern for a reason.

5. Reword the Call of the Question

Sometimes rewording the call of the question can be very helpful. This allows you to rewrite the task of the question so you understand more clearly what the question is asking you to do. This may be particularly helpful as you work through your practice exams. Consider the following examples:

Actual Question Call	Revised Call
What is the most likely outcome?	What is the result and why?
Which claim is most likely to succeed?	Which is the only claim that can succeed on these facts and why?
What is the defendant's best defense?	Why won't the defendant be guilty on these facts?
If party X loses, the most likely basis	Party X lost because ...

You probably won't have time to re-write all the question calls but you may choose to use this strategy if you run across a call that is particularly confusing to you.

6. IRAC Your Answer before Looking at the Choices

After reading through the factual hypothetical, consider doing a quick IRAC of the factual hypothetical before you go through the answer choices. This is the same process that you'd use in an essay exam. The idea behind this suggestion is that doing an IRAC *before* looking at the answers will help you solidify your reasoning. In addition, it may prevent you from being seduced by a distractor because you have already thought through a possible answer. It's good to get a gut sense of the correct answer before you look at the different options.

7. Eliminate Incorrect Responses

In a perfect world, the correct answer to the multiple-choice question would simply jump out at you. However, law school is *not* a perfect world! Therefore, the best (and sometimes only) way to arrive at the correct answer to some multiple-choice questions is to use a process of elimination. Go through the answer choices of the three questions you believe are wrong and determine specifically *why* the answers are wrong. Hopefully, you can eliminate incorrect answers. Read very carefully. Check the *reasoning* of each option. If the reasoning is not correct then the answer cannot be correct. How are options likely wrong? An answer choice is likely wrong if it mischaracterizes the facts; misstates the law; or ignores a central issue. If an answer choice does *any* one of these three things, you can eliminate the answer choice and move on.

8. Choosing between Two Possible Answers

Many students tell me that when answering a multiple-choice question, they can usually narrow down the answer choices to two likely possibilities. How do you choose? Sometimes answers can both be *technically* correct but one answer is a *better* answer choice. Note that an answer ultimately can be the wrong choice even though it's factually and legally correct; but it may not be as precise or effective as another option. For example, an option that is easier to prove is more likely to be correct than an option that is difficult to prove. A more precise answer is better than a less precise answer. Also double-check the reasoning of the choices: does one overstate the requirements of the law or cite rules that do not apply? Does another option assume a particular fact is true when it is actually in dispute?

9. Okay, Sometimes You Gotta Guess!

Let's face it. Between time constraints and anxiety, you may have to guess at some questions. Try to eliminate wrong answers. Then go through your remaining choices. Be wary of answer choices that have language of certainty, i.e., "always," "never," "cannot," "must." Be wary of answer choices that focus on the results. Be wary of answer choices of theories or doctrines that seem unfamiliar to you. If two answers are opposites, one is probably true. Remember that some questions test your knowledge of rules; but others test your knowledge of exceptions. Don't waste too much time. If you don't know, guess. Then come back ONLY if you have time. If you waste too much time guessing, you may be missing points on questions where you DO know the answer.

10. Final Tips

Don't skip questions without filling in an answer choice. You might forget to come back. Write on your exam—note facts, issues, rules. Make the fact patterns visual; create flow charts to match your learning style. Do not let one question influence your answer on the next question. And remember to breathe. You have studied hard and you can reason through the questions to get to the correct result.

Multiple-choice questions are indeed difficult in law school. However, with diligence and practice, you can become more proficient at taking these types of exams. Get as many example exams and/or questions as you can and begin practicing now. You can succeed in law school!

Chapter 11

Managing "Dead Week"

There is a mysterious law school phrase called "dead week," and it is the term given to the week before final exams (or the three or four days between the end of classes and the beginning of final exams). Hopefully, by the week before your final exams, you've completed all your reading, reviewed your class notes, and have your outlines up to date for all your classes. In other words, by the time you get to "dead week," you want to be able to focus exclusively on preparing for your exams.

This chapter addresses how to use your time during those precious four, five or more days between the end of the semester's classes and your final exams. The pace is grueling because you are attempting to cram an entire semester's worth of material into your head for up to five substantive classes. And you have to maintain your stamina to get through the five exams—from the first to the fifth.

But what if you aren't up to date with your outlines? Or you missed a few classes because you were sick? Try to evaluate realistically where you are in terms of your preparation for final exams. Don't panic—you simply need to develop a plan.

A. Two–Three Weeks *before* "Dead Week"

Let's assume that it is a couple weeks before "dead week" (or approximately three weeks before the beginning of final exams). Plan to complete your outlines (and input your class notes into your outlines) within the next two weeks. If you've missed a couple of classes or reading assignments, you need to make completing these tasks a priority.

Get the missing class notes from a friend and make up your reading assignments. Stay home on the weekends until you get these basic but essential tasks done. Figure out exactly how many classes behind you are for each outline and determine how much time it will take to make it up. You have three to four weekends left so you need to plan your makeup time on these weekend days. Although its no fun, force yourself to stay disciplined so you don't get further behind. If you make a diligent effort in these last weeks of the semester, it will make finals preparation all the easier. And it will reduce your anxiety substantially!

In some classes, you may find that the reading becomes lighter as the semester moves towards the end. Remember: this isn't an excuse to catch up on all the television shows you've recorded throughout the semester! Rather, use this extra time to make sure you are caught up with your outlines and classes.

1. Okay, You're Panicking. You're Way Behind!

It may be that you're simply behind. You need to change gears immediately. All the reading and color-coded tabbing and briefing isn't going to do a thing for you if you cannot give yourself enough time to learn it in the end. The reality is that if you're way behind in your reading, you simply will not be able to cram it all in during one week. At this point, you need to make the most of your time. Minimally, you want to start "Dead Week" with good outlines for your each of your classes.

If you have a great deal of reading left, you may have to switch gears and work on outlining and rules. You need to learn the black letter rules first and foremost. Hopefully the outlines you have made (or are able to obtain) will contain these rules. Use commercial outlines. These are excellent resources for the basic rules. Another useful source is the practice exams that you should have already obtained (or will obtain!) from your professors. Often your professor's issue analysis to the practice exams (or the student answers the professor provides) will give you a rule statement for at least some of the rules so you can add these to your outlines as well.

In addition, you need to ask yourself honestly: "How far behind am I in my outlining?" Calculate the number of hours it will take you to complete your outlines for each class, and budget your time. You may need to cut down on your class preparation during these last couple of weeks before "Dead Week" in order to complete outlining.

Further, if you are really behind in your outlines, it may be too late for you to start writing your own. You can gain some extra time by reading good commercial outlines and/or by working with an already completed student outline that you've gotten from a friend. With these outlines, you need to make them your *own* as much as you can. In other words, you need to add in your own class notes. This allows you to internalize the concepts as you write them and simultaneously learn what your professor wants you to emphasize. Compare the student outlines with the commercial outlines and add noteworthy hypotheticals and examples from the outlines that help clarify a concept for you. Focus on clear rule statements. That is what you'll need to write down in an exam. Make sure the person from whom you've gotten the outline had the same professor that you have now and that the material covered in class is the same as when this student had the professor.

If you are in a rush, you are looking to achieve a *basic understanding* of the material. You want to understand how the material fits together so you'll be able to apply the law to a new set of facts with a slightly different fact pattern in your exams. As discussed, your exams will test how you analyze a new set of facts based on the law and underlying social policies you learned during the semester. At this point, do not worry about subtle details. Weed out minor rules and/or distinctions and *focus on the main rules.*

2. Obtain Copies of Practice Exams

Spend the last couple of weeks before "Dead Week" obtaining copies of at least three to four old exams and model answers for each of your classes. Try to find the actual exams that your professor has given in the past—as each professor is slightly different in the way that they teach and test a subject. If you have a newer professor, then go to the Internet to find copies of exams and/or rely on other professors' exams at your school that teach the same subject. Even if your professor may test the subject differently, it will still be helpful.

At this point, do not actually begin working through or even reading sample answers. You are not ready yet because you have not mastered the law well enough to be able to apply it. If you begin working on practice exams now, you will simply cause yourself to panic unnecessarily. You will wait until "Dead Week" to use the practice exams but you want to have them ready to go!

Make sure you also understand the format of each of your exams. This may affect the way you prepare. Will there be multiple-choice and essay questions on the exam? What percentage of the exam will each cover? Does the professor have examples of multiple-choice questions? Will the individual sections be timed? Or can you divide the total exam time however you see fit? Is the exam open book, i.e., can you use outlines on the exam? Can you bring in your rules book? Knowing the details of your exams will help you plan accordingly. You will feel more in control if you get to the exam already having planned out how much time you'll spend on each multiple-choice question or short answer essay. There are so many uncertainties in law school exam-taking that the more you can do beforehand, the better.

B. The "Dead Week" Schedule

One of the keys to making the most of your "Dead Week" is careful scheduling of your time. While you might like to think you can live entirely on energy drinks and 30-minute power naps during finals, the truth is you're going to need to take a break. With a well-organized study plan—you can study effectively and schedule time for refueling as well.

Most schools release the final exam schedule either at the time of registration for classes or at the beginning of the semester. Make sure to look at this information early on in the semester and plan accordingly. Do you have more than one exam scheduled in one day? If you wait until the week before exams to figure that out, it may be too late to change it. Check your school's student handbook to see what the policy is on taking multiple exams in one day. Many law schools will permit you to change your exams if, for example, you are scheduled to take two exams within a single 12-hour period. If needed, ask if your schedule can be modified as soon as possible. Many law schools will not allow students to take final exams early or late, so take this into consideration when picking your classes each semester. While it is not essential to plan your class schedule around final exams, be realistic with yourself: is the idea of taking multiple exams on the same day something you are comfortable doing?

1. Organizing Your Schedule

All students take a different approach to organizing their finals study schedule. But there is one thing that all experienced law students agree upon: having a planned schedule will help reduce stress and increase productivity during "Dead Week."

Creating an actual schedule can be done in a number of ways, but the most important thing is that you do it in a way that is both clear to you and easily accessible. Many students carry a hard copy of their schedule with them so they can reference it when they need to; others input the schedule into their computer, cell phone, or other mobile device. If you choose to have a digital copy of your schedule, there are several computer software programs that can help create a calendar for you. Some students prefer color-coding their calendars by class and activity. This can be particularly helpful for visual learners. The level of detail and intricacy is entirely up to you.

When filling out your calendar, start from the date of your last exam and work your way backwards to the current date. For example, if your last final takes place on May 16th—make that the last date of your calendar and work backwards from that date to the current date. Make sure to take into account any papers or final assignments that may be due at the end of semester. If you organize your schedule hourly, make sure to allot the proper amount of time to arrive at school and set up for your exam. Determine when you are allowed to enter the classroom before an exam and give yourself plenty of time to set up your computer and get comfortable before the exam begins.

After filling in the dates of your exams on your calendar, start filling in other important dates. These other dates include the last day of classes, review sessions, due dates for projects and any other due dates you need to meet. From this point, the detail of your schedule will be determined by how much you want to put down in writing. Many students find it helpful to identify specific classes each day where they will concentrate their time. Other students break up their day by focusing on multiple subjects, allotting a specific number of hours for each subject. Regardless of how you choose to organize your days, identify your plan on your calendar and stick to it. Adjust your calendar as you go. And be realistic about how much time you will need for each class. Many beginning law students make the mistake of focusing too much time and energy on their first final; they fail to realize the importance of at least beginning to study for their other classes during the days prior to their first final.

Another important consideration: when do you study best? Are you a morning person? Perhaps you need to map out your day and study for a larger block of time in the morning. This will leave some time in the evenings open for exercise or relaxation. Other students like to sleep in and then study later into the night. Whatever works for you is completely acceptable as long as you figure it out well in advance of your first final exam!

In addition, test out several study locations and make sure you are comfortable with your choices of where to study. Consider the noise level, seating, internet access, and the hours. Make sure you are in a place where you won't be distracted and where you can study comfortably for several hours. Your law school, apartment, local law library, or a neighborhood coffee shop may all be great places for you to try out. Regardless of where you choose to study, make sure it works for you and *your* needs.

2. Convert Your Outlines to Flashcards

One of the most helpful ways to learn your outline (yes, you *do* need to learn the whole thing!) is to break it down into more manageable pieces and learn them one at a time. After you finish your outlines, you might consider taking the substance of the outlines and breaking them into smaller parts—and placing these onto flashcards.

This method works particularly well for the memorization of rule statements and other legal tests that contain elements or factors. While the substantive material in your outline and flashcards will be the same, using flashcards will give you a more portable version of your outline and provide you with a way to improve the effectiveness of your studying. Using flashcards provides immediate feedback on how well you know the individual rules and their components. And using flashcards (instead of your 100 page outline) can be less overwhelming.

Further, flashcards can make the most out of small windows of time. Keep your flashcards with you in your bag, backpack or purse. When you have a few minutes waiting in line for coffee, outside before class, in between classes or even while grabbing a bite to eat, you can review your flashcards. While it may not seem like you are doing that much at the time, you are actually adding hours of study time to your finals preparation. Doing this a few times a day can make a huge difference!

Making Flashcards. The first step to making flashcards is to determine the size you need to write out fully your rules and any examples or explanations that are helpful. This usually requires index cards of 3x5 size or larger. Also, make sure you have enough index cards to cover the material from your whole outline. This may seem like a lot; but remember, you're not making your outline any longer; you are breaking it up into smaller pieces.

Remember also that handwriting your flashcards (rather than simply cutting and pasting the rules from a typed outline) is the most effective approach to learning. While this takes considerably more time than simply cutting and pasting the rules, the *process of writing out the rules and elements helps you learn the material*. However, if you are very short on time, then cutting and pasting the rules may be your best option. You can still get the benefit of using flashcards.

For classes that will test you by using an essay exam format, you want to begin your flashcards by taking the first level of your outline (the main headings) and write these on your flashcards without any explanation. This will look like a skeletal version of your outline.

For example:

- Front side: *Negligence Cause of Action (elements)*

- Back side:

> A. *Duty*
> B. *Breach*
> C. *Causation*
> D. *Damages*

On the next series of four flashcards, take each of these elements and break them down individually. By organizing your flashcards in this manner, you can keep in mind both the larger structure of the rule and the specific definitions of the individual elements.

Try to limit the material on any one flashcard to one or two definitions (or rule statements) per card. This will allow you to flip through them more efficiently.

3. Using Practice Exams

When should you begin using practice exams? It is not advisable to use practice exams until you have a good feel for the rules (and you've completed your outlines and flashcards). Most professors have a data bank of prior exams that you can access to obtain prior exams and sample answers.

After you learn the rules, then you can move onto practice exams. Looking through the exams will not only help you figure out the pattern of your professors' testing style, it will also help you become familiar with the common factual hypotheticals that you are likely to see on your exams.

You should try to have minimally two to three exams for each class (ideally, three to four exams). During "Dead Week," you want to schedule to take these exams in a timed setting. This process allows you to fully assess your understanding of the material and get accustomed to the actual form of the examination. How much can you expect to write in an hour? How will you format the exam? In the days leading up to your final exam, try to create a realistic testing scenario. Select a location and a block of time where you can fully dedicate yourself to the practice exam with no distractions. Further, ask your professors if they will look over practice exams and give you feedback. If they do offer this assistance, take them up on it! Not only will your professors appreciate your dedication and effort, they will often help you focus in on points you are missing and direct your attention to the areas where you can actually gain more points. And you will learn how each professor wants you to write for *their* exam. Most professors want to help students improve their essay taking skills and are happy to work with you to improve your scores.

Another way to improve your score on the essay portion of any exam is to go through the sample answers that are provided (hopefully) with the exam. Do you notice any specific phrases that the professor seems to like or recommend? Are the sample answers formatted or organized in a particular way? Focus not only on the substance of the answers but also the way they in which they are organized. Go through each of the answers and look for the way your professor uses bullet points, subtitles, underlining, and other methods of organization in the sample answer. Do they expect you to list case names or cite directly to a specific rule? All of these are questions that you may not have thought about during the course of the semester. Make sure to ask your professors! Once you have the answers to these questions, write them down on your outlines or flashcards. Understanding *how* to write each exam *before* you take the exam will allow you to save crucial time during the examination itself that you can use on your analysis section/s rather than outlining your answer.

Note that when you first review practice exams, however, the questions may seem overwhelming. But you have to start somewhere! Begin by using your outlines as you go through practice exams. One of the biggest challenges of law school exams is to spot all the issues hidden in the factual hypothetical. By allowing yourself to use your outlines when you first begin using practice exams, you will train yourself to look for the fact patterns that trigger specific rules. As you go through the exams, underline the facts that trigger a specific rule and write those down in your outline next to that rule or section. Then go through the elements of that specific rule or test, matching facts from the practice exam to each element of the rule. By doing this, you are helping your brain learn the facts that *trigger* a specific issue. Until you are comfortable with the fact patterns and elements of the rules, it is more productive to use your outlines while answering questions.

Once you become comfortable with spotting the issues for a subject, then you can move on to doing practice exams without your notes or outlines. Do not worry about imposing time restrictions the first time you complete practice exams for a course. Your main focus should be simply to spot the issues and try and write down the elements that match up to the rule you are applying. Try *not* to look back at your outline but if you are stuck—examine your outline (making sure to mark that spot in your outline so you can review it again). Once you finish the practice exam, go through and compare your answer to the issue analysis provided. Can you fill in any of the gaps or missed issues? Compare the way you organized your answer with the way the sample answer is structured. As you do more problems you will grow comfortable with a style you prefer. Remember to IRAC as you go along and send your essay into your professor for review.

The final step in using your practice exams is to take an exam in a testing environment that closely resembles the actual test setting. Use a timer and take a full examination with no notes or assistance. Practice truly makes perfect when working with past exams; the more you do, the better prepared you will be. Finally, always be sure to double-check that the rules and explanations provided in past exams are still up to date and good law. If a new court decision has come out since the time your professor gave the exam, it is possible that the rules have changed. Make sure to check the most recent notes you have been given during the semester.

4. Effective Use of Study Groups during Crunch Time

Study groups are another resource that may or may not be helpful to you as you prepare for your final examinations. Some students find it easier to study by themselves—while others feel that group studying will help them to have a better understanding of the material. If you choose to study with a group, make sure to determine who the members of this group will be early on in the semester and become comfortable with these students. Remember that different people learn in different ways and sometimes your group members will need you to review material with which you are already familiar. Patience is the key! Remember that just as you will have questions about certain topics, your classmates will also have questions. As a member of a successful study group, you must be prepared to take the time to ensure that each member of the group understands the principles.

Determine a set schedule of hours when you will study together and stick to that schedule. By maintaining a set schedule, you can both study with the group but also leave time to study by yourself too.

One of the best ways to utilize your study group during "Dead Week" is to harness the creativity of each group member and create original study materials. For example, you can split up the material and create multiple-choice questions for each main subject; create factual hypotheticals to simulate an essay exam; develop study games (like Jeopardy), etc.[1] In addition, you can go over past essay exams with your group members.

If, however, you find that the dynamics of the group are a little "*off*" (and you are not being as productive as you need to be), assess honestly whether this is the best way for you to study. Determine whether your group's productivity level is something you can fix or whether it would be more beneficial for you to each take some time on your own before coming back as a group. Make sure each member of the group is pulling their own weight and if someone isn't doing so—try to speak to them about it. Remember that ultimately you need to focus on what will be best for you.

5. Incorporating Multiple-Choice Questions

Most professors incorporate any number of multiple-choice questions into their midterms and final exams; therefore, it is important to figure out how to best study for this type of question. Because professors often use a data bank of multiple-choice questions (and often times recycle the fact patterns) most schools do not post past multiple-choice exams. You will need to find a different way to prepare. While the information presented in these types of questions is often the same as your essay questions, the *way* the information is tested is quite different. Refer back to the multiple-choice chapter in this book to review the different type of questions that are most commonly used on law school exams. Become familiar with types that make sense to you and those on which you need to spend more time.

Now it's time to get your hands on multiple-choice questions for the particular subjects of your classes. Your law school library should have multiple-choice resources that you can check out to help you practice these types of questions for all your subjects. Ask your professor which publishers they prefer and which supplements are closest to their testing style. For example, I tell students to use the Q&A series for my classes because they organize questions by topic. Students can study questions as they relate to a specific topic, i.e., such as character evidence or relevance.

Start by taking multiple-choice questions by topic. This allows you to test your knowledge of each section of your outline. This is also a good way to assess your level of understanding of the different topics to de-

---

1. For example, in creating a Jeopardy game, assign each group member a topic from the outline and ask her to create the questions for that section. Compile all of the questions together on your game board and then take turns selecting and answering the questions from the categories of the Jeopardy game. There are several good Jeopardy templates on the Internet. This is a fun way to review concepts—particularly on a Friday night!

termine which ones to which you need to pay extra attention. If you see yourself missing a number of questions on a specific topic, stop—and go back to your outline and review your notes. It is detrimental to continue to go through questions without fully knowing the information. Go back to your outline and review the information until you feel comfortable enough with it to try the multiple-choice questions again.

Also pay attention to the time it takes you to work through questions. You do need to eventually stay on pace with the amount of time your professor is going to give you. It makes no sense to give yourself five minutes to answer each question when on the exam you will only have two minutes. Make sure to ask your professor how many multiple-choice questions they are planning on asking and then plan your time according to the range they give you.

In addition, make sure to go through the answer explanations at the back of the books. Often these explanations will provide you with insight into fact patterns that are commonly used in exam situations. Reviewing the explanations will also help you remember the information in a way that will allow you to recognize the issues in a factual hypothetical. Read the explanation entirely, including the reasoning behind the *wrong* answers.

If you find that you have run out of published multiple-choice questions, try developing questions of your own and test yourself in this new way. You may find that if you change one slight fact in the question, your answer will change entirely. This is something you can work on with your study group. Assign each member a topic from your outline and create five to ten multiple-choice questions each, then quiz each other including going through your explanations as to why certain answers are wrong.

Doing well on the multiple-choice sections of your exams is a skill you must acquire—both for law school and for taking the bar exam. Work with your professors and study groups—and use whatever other resources you have available in order to prepare for this section of the exam.

6. A Take-Home Exam?

You may have a professor that assigns a take-home examination instead of an in-class final. It is equally as important to prepare and study for this type of exam. Often the hardest part about a take-home exam is the time-restraints that come with this type of examination.

Setting a clear timeframe for your take-home exam is the key to doing well. Your professor will give you a maximum time limit. Know exactly when your exam is due; make sure you give yourself plenty of time to complete it in a way that shows your hard work. For take-home exams, your professors will be looking for a well-edited examination that shows your thorough work. Use all of the resources available to you, making sure to *follow all directions explicitly*.

While following directions may seem to be obvious, *many* law students lose points on take-home exams by missing a question or misreading instructions. Double-check your professor's policy on the following: (1) working with other students; (2) whether and how you are required to cite to sources; (3) which sources you can use; (4) organization and structure; and (5) *exactly* when and where you are supposed to turn in your exam. Failing to follow instructions is a wasteful way to lose points. If you are in doubt about a specific instruction in your take-home exam, make sure you clarify that with your professor well *in advance* of when your examination is due!

7. The Night before the Exam

The night before an examination is a stressful time for any law student but with proper preparation you will be able to face these nights with confidence. Sleep is essential for strong exam performance; you must allow yourself to sleep the night before your exam. Set a time at which you will stop studying (and stick to it). Then try and relax for an hour before you go to sleep. Watch your favorite television show, make a nice meal, or take a walk or bath. Your brain needs a break to allow it to refuel before the exam.

If you absolutely *must* study the night before the exam, limit yourself to those materials that will reinforce your knowledge and comfort level—rather than test them. For example, consider reading through practice exams and sample answers or go through your flashcards. Focus on the elements of rules rather than the specifics that you may not have fully memorized. Comfort yourself with the knowledge that you have put in a sufficient amount of time to master the material and allow yourself time to take a deep breath, eat a good meal, and rest before you go into the exam.

8. Other Do's and Don'ts

The proctor has just called time so you've survived your final exam! Now what? The answer depends largely on where you are in your finals schedule. If you've just finished your last exam, then congratulations! Go out and celebrate and let your mind wander as far away from exams as possible—at least for a little while. If you've still got exams to finish, then you might need to scale the celebration back a bit.

First things first: as soon as you finish your exam, make sure all your items are turned in properly. Check to make sure you've successfully uploaded your exam (if you are using a computer). There is nothing worse than getting an email from a school administrator saying there was something wrong with your test, so listen closely to instructions.

Next, as tempting as it might be, try your hardest to avoid discussing the exam with your fellow classmates. It's not only likely that your school has official rules against this that might result in an ethics violation, but it is also extremely likely that you will unnecessarily upset either yourself or another student through these conversations. Your answers are your own, and no amount of discussion will change what you just turned in. Whether you are feeling confident or as though you bombed the exam, keep your opinions to yourself and remove yourself from the testing area as quickly as you can. If you absolutely feel the need, you can go and review your outlines and check back on your answer, but be cautious in doing so. Sometimes looking back over notes directly after an exam can lead to added stress because you'll suddenly remember something you think you should have written or realize you might have stated a rule slightly wrong. Try not to focus on these minute details and look instead to the bigger picture—that you are one step closer to finishing up this semester.

Allow yourself ample time to unwind after each exam that you have taken. Law school finals are high-pressure situations, and depending on the exam, you may have just subjected your brain to an intense workout for several hours. Just as your body needs to rest and recover after a long session at the gym, your brain needs to recover as well. Hopefully if you're on track with your schedule, you've given yourself at least a couple of hours to relax after each exam before you begin studying for the next exam.

After all of your exams are over and you have given yourself time to relax, determine when you will be able to review your performance. Most schools allow examinations to be released once professors have reviewed them and grades have been posted. When this opportunity is presented, make sure to take it. Reviewing your exams, regardless of your grades, will not only help reinforce your mastery of the material—it will also help you gain skills that you can apply to all of your future exams. Schedule appointments with your professors to review your performance and see how you can improve.

Chapter 12

Test Anxiety in Law School

Let's face it. If you think about how much time you actually spend studying for and taking exams in law school, these exams have a disproportionately large role in the course of your academic career. How you perform during a few short hours hunched over your computer in some strange classroom can have major consequences. A good or bad score on an exam may determine your ability to apply for jobs, internships—or clerkships. Realistically, there is plenty about which to be anxious.

The way test anxiety presents itself varies—it can be emotional, physical or psychological. Symptoms of anxiety can range from slight jitters to full-blown blank-out, deer-in-the-headlights syndrome while taking an exam. Other symptoms that may suggest you experience test anxiety include:

- Difficulty getting started with studying;
- Becoming easily distracted even after you have started studying;
- Concerns that you will not do well regardless of your best efforts;
- Symptoms such as lack of focus, sweaty palms, upset stomach, or headaches;
- Difficulty concentrating, following instructions, or understanding test questions; or
- Remembering material and/or test strategies *after* the test is over, but forgetting them while taking the test.

Test anxiety is real and measurable. There are many ways to understand the main causes.[1] From a behavioral perspective, anxiety can be learned from a prior negative experience. For example, if you have done poorly on tests in the past, you may be anxious and hesitant about taking a test in the future. You might even avoid or resist tests at all costs, and when you're forced to take them, you feel your behavior shift and change to create opportunities to avoid going through the experience again—usually physical manifestations of anxiety such as feeling sick before an exam.

---

1. *See, e.g.*, TEST ANXIETY: THEORY, RESEARCH, and APPLICATION (Irwin G. Sarason ed., Hillsdale, NJ, 1980); Charles D. Spielberger, *Conceptual and Methodological Issues in Anxiety Research*, *in* Anxiety 481 (Charles D. Spielberger ed., New York, 1972).

The idea of repetitive behavioral responses to stimuli was exemplified in B.F. Skinner's famous 'pigeon and superstition' experiments. Skinner placed hungry pigeons in a cage attached to an automatic mechanism that delivered food to the pigeon at regular intervals with no reference whatsoever to the bird's behavior.[2] He discovered that the pigeons associated the delivery of the food with whatever chance actions they had been performing as the food was delivered—for example, lifting a wing or a leg. He was able to deduce that the pigeons mistook their associated movements for a technique to ensure that they received food. Likewise, if a student feels anxiety going into an exam, but yet he or she still performs well, the student will assume (on some level) that anxiety contributed to the good performance. This motivates the student to become more anxious before the next test, and so on.

From a psychoanalytic view, anxiety may result from the conflict between your unconscious desires and the expectations others place on you—for example, anxiety would be felt by someone who doesn't fully want to go to law school, but feels the pressure and expectation to do so, anyway.[3] They might rebel against studying or manifest any of the aforementioned symptoms of test anxiety.

Everyone will feel somewhat anxious before they begin to take a law school exam. Anxiety becomes a problem when it begins to interfere with your ability to think logically or remember facts. So one of the first questions to ask yourself is whether your anxiety is "normal" or whether it is something *more*.

A. Normal Anxiety or Something More?

Anxiety or nervousness about stressful events is certainly a part of life. It is perfectly natural or "normal" to be anxious about any event that is important to you, especially one that could make a difference in your future life or job situation. Let's face it: law school exams are important landmarks in your career path, so it is expected that you would be a bit apprehensive about this experience.

But how do you know if your text anxiety is a normal reaction to the stress of the exam or something that might endanger your ability to pass the test—or even stay in law school? This depends largely on the symptoms you experience, as well as their severity.

---

2. *See generally* B.F. Skinner, SCIENCE AND HUMAN BEHAVIOR (1953) (explaining the "scientific validity" of behaviorist theory).

3. Sigmund Freud was the founder of psychoanalysis and the psychodynamic approach to psychology. This school of thought emphasized the influence of the unconscious mind on behavior.

1. Typical Symptoms of Normal Test Anxiety

Test anxiety produces symptoms that can affect you physically as well as mentally.[4] Physical symptoms might include:

- Headache
- Nausea
- Feeling queasy or faint
- Rapid breathing and heart rate
- Muscular tension

Symptoms of test anxiety that affect you mentally (in other words, they affect your ability to think) include:

- Inability to focus
- Thoughts focused on negative past experience
- Drawing a blank on answers

While all of these symptoms are natural if they are mild, extreme symptoms can cripple your ability to complete the test successfully. If your test anxiety is severe enough to affect your performance, there are steps you need to take in order to help you make it through the test.

2. Managing Normal Test Anxiety

The key for most law students in managing test anxiety is to be fully prepared for your exams. Granted, in law school, that is almost impossible because you often feel like you could study endlessly and still not be fully prepared. But you will have a sense of good preparation if you have kept up with your reading, gone to class, prepared your outlines and done practice exams. For most students, you have to rely on your good preparation as an objective management tool for test anxiety. You tell yourself: "I've done all I can." The unique challenge of law school exams is that students often feel like they have little control over what is on the exam. That is often true. Law school is different than other graduate school (or college exams) in that you are being tested on

---

4. Anxiety is a psychological, physiological and behavioral response similar to fear but a consequence to some unknown internal trigger or stimulus, inappropriate to the reality of an external stimulus or concerned with a future stimulus or event. These symptoms are not just randomly associated with some cases of anxiety. They are so fundamentally related to the mental condition in anxiety that they are considered some of the diagnostic criteria for anxiety. *See* John A. Talbott et al. eds., TEXTBOOK OF PSYCHIATRY 479–82 (1988). Examples of anxiety symptoms include anorexia, feeling "butterflies in the stomach," chest pain, diaphoresis, diarrhea, dizziness, dyspnea, dry mouth, faintness, flushing, headache, lightheadedness, muscle tension, nausea, pallor, palpitation, presthesias, sexual dysfunction, shortness of breath, stomach pain, urinary frequency and vomiting. *See id.*

an entire semester's worth of material. You have two or three hours to illustrate your knowledge of the entire course. This is difficult. But no one will score perfectly in law school; and remember that you are judged against the curve and there is no way to know how this will pan out. So, if you have prepared well, you need to rely upon that as much as you can.

But there are a few simple things you can do to help manage the physical and emotional symptoms most commonly experienced by law students when taking an exam. The key is to break the cycle of anxiety—and relax. This sounds overly simplistic, doesn't it? But if you can control the physical symptoms of anxiety, you can also gain more control over the mental aspects of anxiety as well. In other words, most students can learn to "calm" themselves during the exam so they can focus on recalling the information they have studied. When you are feeling anxious right before the exam, consider:

- Counting to 10 or 20 to distract and focus your mind;
- Tensing every muscle in your body and then relaxing them;
- Scanning the test to assess the questions;
- Starting with easy questions before tackling harder ones in order to build your confidence.

In many cases, test anxiety is a minor roadblock. After all, most people are a little nervous when taking a test, but that apprehension usually disappears once you become focused on and involved in the test. This kind of mild test anxiety is more easily overcome and rarely affects the final results of the test.

However, in more extreme cases, the anxiety experienced when taking law school exams factors into a student's final scores more than his or her knowledge of the topics being tested. Some students are so paralyzed by test anxiety that they feel no amount of study or preparation will enable them to pass an exam, regardless of how important that exam might be. Because of the difficulty of law school exams (and the volume of information you are expected to retain and apply for *each* exam), this feeling is not atypical.

The remainder of this chapter is designed to help provide you with strategies for dealing with test anxiety, from test preparation to coping strategies that will help both before and during your actual exams. Some of these strategies will be specific to the actual task of taking a test, while others will help you to improve your outlook and even your overall health. Factors you might not consider, such as exercise, stress and diet, can have more of an influence on your ability to perform well on a test than you might think.

B. Attitude and Mental Preparation

We tend to create either positive or negative feelings about ourselves through the thoughts we create or allow in a given situation. Anxiety is created by a person's thoughts or expectations about what is likely to happen. The remedy for dealing with the cognitive or mental aspects of test anxiety is cognitive restructuring. Cognitive restructuring is a process of examining the irrational messages one sends to oneself concerning the outcome of tests and replacing the irrational negative messages with positive messages.

What one *feels* is a by-product of what one *thinks*. The meaning of an event lies not within the event itself but rather in your interpretation of the event. In other words, test anxiety is not caused by the test itself but rather by the meaning that you attach to the test. If you mentally tell yourself that you are not going to do well or that you have not studied enough, then you will have an emotional reaction that is consistent with that message. The emotional message will be anxiety because the messages are negative or threatening.

In order to change your thoughts about yourself, you must first realize that your thoughts are actually negative. Negative thoughts can lead to a negative self-image. Consider the following questions. Do they seem familiar? Before a test, do you feel guilty for not having studied enough? Do you feel that others in the class know more than you do? Do you feel that other students seem to get better grades without as much effort? Do you question whether you should be in law school?

If you find that you have subconscious doubts about your ability, or you find yourself thinking negative thoughts before a test, then you need to change your thinking about yourself. In order to have a positive self-image, you need to find things that you can feel positive about. In dealing with test anxiety you have to *really* feel that you have studied all you can and that you are *really* prepared for the test. Initially this may mean that you have to study harder than you have ever studied before in order to feel positive about your preparation. But the key is to *not* let self-doubt to creep in.

C. Engage in Efficient and Consistent Studying

As we discussed earlier in this book, learning and studying in law school is different than the studying you did in college. Studying in law school is not just reading the casebook and reading your notes over and over. Law students who just read over the material may think that they have studied, but then find out during their first set of exams that they do not know the material with the specificity and detail required for law school. If, for example, on a law school multiple-choice exam, you find that two or three of the answers look right in several questions, then you did not learn the material well enough. In reality, there is only one right answer and the other possible answers are wrong for various reasons. In law school, you are expected to know and understand concepts, theories, and how various things are related. Further, you are being asked to apply the law and policy to the facts of a new hypothetical. You have to know the rules and cases very, *very* thoroughly in order to be successful on a law school exam. Often beginning law students do not spend the time required to really understand the material thoroughly. *Real* law school studying involves thinking, analyzing, writing things down, organizing the material in a meaningful way, and figuring out ahead of time what will be on the test.

D. Anxiety over Law School Multiple-Choice Exams

After your first law school multiple-choice exam, the mere sight of page after page of multiple-choice questions can cause test anxiety in any law student—especially if you felt like you didn't have enough time to finish the test—which occurs often in law school.

If you feel yourself becoming instantly overwhelmed when you examine the multiple-choice section of an exam, take a deep breath and consider the following general tips to keep you focused.

Do Not Rely on "Tricks." When it comes to multiple-choice questions, many people seem to think there is a "secret" to passing the test. They claim to know the best way to answer questions according to a pattern or a specific strategy, such as always choosing "C" if you do not know the answer. Relying on these strategies and patterns are more likely to help you fail the test than help you pass it. The only "secret" to answering multiple-choice questions is to choose the correct answer. If you do not know the answer, guessing is an option but usually a last resort. Make sure to review the Chapter in this book dealing with how to effectively prepare for multiple-choice exams.

Go With Your Gut. If you are unsure of the correct answer, your first instinct may in fact be the right one. Trust your instincts. Often you know more than you think you know, and by second-guessing yourself—you end up sabotaging that knowledge.

Avoid Perfectionism. Yes, you have a career plan, and that plan includes completing law school. Perhaps you even have expectations of doing *really well* in law school. Of course you want to do your best on every exam, but it is also possible to become overly concerned with achieving a perfect score.

When you sit down to take a law school exam, chances are that you *will* encounter questions to which you do not know the answers. If you are determined to get a perfect score, this could trigger test anxiety before you have actually begun the test. While it is good to want to do well, perfectionism in an exam situation (or in law school generally) is detrimental.

E. Anxiety over Essay Exams

Some people who are comfortable with multiple-choice exams freeze up when they approach essay exams. Because law school essay questions require an extremely detailed recall of test material, as well as the ability to apply complex concepts thoroughly and logically, they can be the most intimidating part of any exam experience.

If you find yourself experiencing test anxiety when required to answer essay questions, there are measures you can take both while studying for an exam and during the exam itself to help get your anxiety under control.

Studying for Essay Questions. The best way to prepare for essay questions is to study specifically for this type of question *and* for your *particular* professor. Rather than simply reading through numerous factual hypotheticals and having your study group ask questions that can be answered with a few sentences, focus on the specific types of questions that will appear on your professors' specific exams. As I discussed in the essay exam chapter, each professor will test concepts differently. Therefore, part of your preparation must be to figure out *how* your professors test the concepts. If you can obtain prior exams for each of your classes, incorporate those exams into your studying. Weave the questions within your review of outlines, notes and rules—so you have energy to replicate the exam experience. In other words, you want to have the energy to go through the real process of writing an exam answer—spotting the issues, thinking through the organization, and writing the answer.

Managing Essay Questions During the Test. If you have studied and prepared for essay questions, they should be less likely to trigger test anxiety when you encounter them on the actual exam. However, if you find yourself drawing a blank due to test anxiety when attempting to read through the fact pattern, do not panic. Consider the following techniques:

1. Read the fact pattern slowly. Circle each fact that may present an issue. If it is a short fact pattern, almost *all* the facts will present an issue. Know that for each fact you circle—this likely will become

a separate issue. Circling facts is active—it allows you to do something and this is essential to controlling test anxiety.

2. Brainstorm a few ideas about the hypothetical by jotting down
anything and everything that comes into your head regarding law
or issues until you have several ideas written down. Then, work
from this pattern of information to organize and formulate your
answer.

3. If you freeze or if your mind goes blank, move on to another question or part of the exam. DO NOT WASTE TIME if you are truly
blocked on a particular question. MOVE ON! Sometimes working on the answers to other questions will allow your mind to access ideas about the troubling question.

4. Try to formulate a brief outline of the answer, and then flush out
the outline to form your final answer.

The key to these techniques is they get you *doing* something instead
of staying stuck in your head—wrapped up in your anxiety and worry.
The other key is that these techniques do not require you to produce fully
formed answers on the first pass. By breaking questions down during
the exam and allowing yourself to work in a more free-form manner,
you can reduce or bypass test anxiety regarding essay questions.

F. Avoiding Perfectionism

Finally, as you prepare for exams, you must learn to avoid perfectionism. You need to remind yourself that it is okay to miss points—or
to get a B or C. Remember that the majority of students in law school *will*
receive a B– to comply with most first-year curves! Statistically—you are
more likely to receive that grade!! Promise yourself that you will do the
very best you can, but do not be too hard on yourself if you are unable
to answer every question on the exam. Of course you want to make a
passing grade, but seeking out perfection in law school simply cannot
be achieved.

And by giving yourself permission to perform less than perfectly, you
will reduce the stress you face while taking the exam and thus reduce the
likelihood of test anxiety. In fact, by accepting the fact that you will not
get a perfect score, you might actually create a mental environment in
which you are able to perform at your very best—and you might end
up getting that decent score after all.

But sometimes you do everything you can in order to prevent test anxiety, yet you may still find yourself freezing up or going blank when the
test is put in front of you. In these situations—which hopefully will be
rare—you need to have a set of coping tools available to manage test
anxiety while you are actually taking the test.

G. Controlling Your Thoughts during the Exam

One of the most effective ways to control test anxiety is to control your thoughts during your exam preparation and during the exam itself. This is easier said than done—and you need to begin thinking about the messages you're sending yourself early on in the semester. It is amazing how many negative thoughts we send to ourselves (particularly during law school!!) on a daily basis. Consider the list of self-verbalizations below. The list contains some common thoughts and worries that many test-anxious students have.

Grab a pen. Circle those statements that you identify with most. Are there additional statements that reflect what goes on in your head? Then study this list (and any statements you've added) and consider whether you can change any of your worrying thoughts. Ask yourself: "How rational is this thought?" "How much evidence do I have for such a belief?" "Can I change my thought to something reasonable or more positive?" We tend to create the things that we believe. In other words, if you are focused exclusively on the negative, you are more likely to create that reality. Although this is difficult in law school, try to find some positive thoughts to balance out the concerns or worries you have. Remember that you were a talented and intelligent person *before* law school! Those essential facts have not changed! What *has* changed is where you are right now—you are in law school. And although what you do each day has changed—*you* have not changed! You are still that worthy, excellent, talented, brilliant person who got into law school only a few months before.

Check or circle any of the following phrases that describe how you feel.

1. Thoughts or Concerns about My Performance

___ I should have studied more … I'll never get through.

___ I just want to finish and get out of here and hope for the best.

___ I don't know anything … what's the matter with me?

___ My mind is going blank … I'm going to fail.

___ I'll never get the answer … I must really be stupid.

___ I can't figure out what the professor wants.

___ There is no way I'll do well on this.

___ I can't remember a thing … this always happens to me.

___ I never do well on anything.

___ Only 10 minutes left … I'll never get through everything.

___ I just can't think … why did I ever go to law school?

___ It's no use … I might as well give up.

___ I knew this stuff yesterday … what's wrong with me?

___ My mind's a blank … I'm just not cut out for law school.

___ I have to get an A ... if I'm going to get a job—I need A's.

___ This is terrible, absolutely the worst exam I've ever had.

___ I'm just a worthless person.

2. Thoughts and Concerns about My Bodily Reactions

___ I'm sick ... I'll never get through this exam.

___ I'm sweating all over ... it's really hot in here.

___ My hands are shaking again ... I can't even type.

___ My stomach's going crazy ... churning and jumping.

___ Here it comes ... I'm freaking out again.

___ Normal people just don't get like this.

3. Thoughts and Concerns about How Others Are Doing

___ I know everyone's doing better than I am.

___ Everyone is working faster than I am.

___ It's taking me too long to read this.

___ I must be the dumbest one in the class.

___ I'm going to be the last one done again ... I'm going to fail.

___ I must really be stupid. No one else seems to be having trouble.

___ I need to get an A to compete with everyone else.

4. Worry about Possible Negative Consequences

___ If I fail this test, I'll never get a job.

___ If I fail this class, I'll get kicked out of law school.

___ If I fail this exam, I'll never get the kind of job I want.

___ If I fail this exam, my family (or friends, boyfriend/girlfriend, teacher) will really be disappointed in me.

___ Everyone will think I'm stupid ... I'll really be embarrassed.

___ If I fail this exam, I'll never be able to pay back my student loans.

If you found yourself checking a number of these statements, consider the effect these statements have on your beliefs about yourself and your performance. Are all of these statements rational? Of course not. Most of these statements are based completely on fear. And the fear may seem reasonable at the time of the exam—but your fears are not *reality*. Here's the main point: if you are psyching yourself out—you may actually create the very thing you are trying to avoid. If you create or heighten your test anxiety by telling yourself you will fail, you may create such anxiety that it blocks your ability to recall the information you studied. What will happen? You may in fact score low on the exam—precisely because you were overwhelmed and anxious.

The key to dealing with test anxiety is to stop the irrational, negative thoughts. Analyze each of the thoughts you checked above. Is the thought or feeling reality or do they represent your fears? Could you replace each one of those negative thoughts with a positive thought?

Positive affirmations yourself and your law school experience can be used to reprogram your thought patterns and change the way you think and feel about things. The following list of short positive statements can help you focus on goals, get rid of negative, self-defeating beliefs and re-program your subconscious mind.

- I accept myself and am true to myself.
- I have confidence in myself and my abilities.
- I am intelligent and successful.
- I eat well and exercise regularly.
- I forgive myself for not being perfect because I know I'm human.
- I work very hard in law school.
- I never give up.
- I forgive myself for not getting A's (or B's) in law school.
- I accept what I cannot change.
- I have control over my thoughts, feelings and choices.
- I have control over the people with whom I choose to associate.
- I stand up for my beliefs, values and morals.
- I treat others with respect.
- I contribute my talents and knowledge in various ways.
- I make a difference to this world.
- I practice patience, understanding and compassion with others as well as myself.
- I am committed to learning new things, remaining open-minded and I am the best that I can be.
- I choose to live in the moment while learning from the past and preparing for the future.

Positive statements that replace negative statements can truly change the way in which you approach law school. Select several of the above statements (or create your own) and agree to tell yourself several of these each day. By focusing on the positive—you can actually make the positive happen.

H. Setting Realistic Goals

When you began law school—or likely even before—you set goals for yourself. In fact, you've likely had the goal of getting into law school for quite some time. And clearly you are a talented and intelligent person; here you are in law school. Once you get to law school, however, it is likely that your goals will change. For example, perhaps you thought you would go into Intellectual Property Law—or you thought you'd be a litigator or trial lawyer. Maybe after your first year, you know for sure that you despise Copyright Law. Or you loathe the idea of preparing for trial. This is good information—but its time to revise your goals.

Often beginning law students set unrealistic goals for themselves. For example, a new student comes to law school with the goal of getting all A's in every class. This may seem reasonable, right? Likely you received almost all A's throughout your undergraduate career. But in law school, getting all A's is often an unreasonable goal. In essence, to have that goal would be setting yourself up for failure. In these next couple of paragraphs, take a minute and consider your goals. If your goals are unrealistic and impossible, this can only increase your anxiety about law school generally—and about exams specifically.

A few thoughts about setting *realistic* goals for yourself.

- Be sure your goals are your own. It's your life. Do what means most to you. Self-set goals are better motivators than those imposed by others.

- Put goals in writing. This will lessen the odds of you losing sight of your goals in the shuffle of daily activity. Writing goals also increases your commitment.

- Make your goals challenging but attainable. Good goals are neither too easy nor impossible. They should cause you to stretch and grow. A challenging, attainable goal will hold your interest and keep you motivated.

- Goals should be as specific and measurable as possible. Don't say, "I want to do well in law school." Ask yourself: How can I improve? How can I study differently? How can I obtain practical experience? Specify clearly what you want and you will save an enormous amount of time and effort.

- Every goal should have a target date. Never think of a goal as a goal until you set a deadline for accomplishment.

- Check your major goals for compatibility. Don't fall into the trap of setting major goals where the achievement of one will prevent the attainment of another.

Frequently revise and update your goals. As a growing and evolving person, your needs will change over time, and this means your goals will have to be modified, discarded and added from time to time. Plan flexibly. Don't think of your goals as carved in stone. You will change as a result of your law school experience!

I. Learning How to Relax

A state of anxiety is incompatible with a state of relaxation, so training in relaxation techniques is by far the most commonly recommended treatment for dealing with any type of anxiety. Systematic relaxation and desensitization have been used successfully by psychologists for many years. These procedures involve only learning two things: (1) learning to relax all of your muscles and (2) while you are in a relaxed state—you imagine the anxiety-producing situation. A simplistic version of this procedure is outlined below. And if you find that even these relaxation techniques do not help your anxiety, you will likely need to consult a professional psychologist for additional help.

The relaxation procedure described below involves systematically tensing and then relaxing different groups of muscles in your body. Follow this procedure and practice it many times before exam time.

1. Begin the procedure by either sitting in a comfortable chair or lying down. Move your arms toward the center of your body and bend both arms at the elbow. Tighten your hands into fists and simultaneously tense the muscles in your upper arms and shoulders. Hold for 10 seconds and then relax for 15 to 20 seconds.

2. Tense your face muscles by wrinkling your forehead and cheek muscles. Hold for 10 seconds then relax.

3. Tense the muscles in your chest for 15 seconds and then relax. Repeat this procedure for all the different parts of your body while telling yourself that you are becoming more and more relaxed. Pay particular attention to the muscles in your neck and back since these muscles become tense easily.

4. After 10 or 15 minutes you will find that your body is completely relaxed.

If you practice this technique over a period of weeks you will find that it becomes easier and easier to achieve a state of complete relaxation. While you are in a state of complete relaxation, you then need to begin to visualize yourself in a law school exam situation. For example, while you are relaxed, imagine yourself the night before the exam. If this does not produce anxiety, then imagine yourself the morning of the exam or walking to the room where the test will be given. Imagine yourself starting up your computer and setting up your materials. If any of these images begin to produce anxiety, you will need to actively use your relaxation techniques and calm yourself back down. Eventually you should get to the point where you can imagine yourself actually taking the exam while remaining completely relaxed.

This technique has been shown to be better than 90% effective if it is used properly; however, the technique needs to be practiced for several weeks to attain maximum effectiveness. You cannot wait until you experience an episode of test anxiety and then try to relax. It will not work.

Along with the relaxation technique described above, here are some additional (and very practical) things that may help reduce your test anxiety:

Plan your studying so you are not cramming. Your school may offer study-skills classes or other resources that can help you learn study techniques and test-taking strategies. You'll feel more relaxed if you systematically study and practice the material that will be on a test.

Establish a consistent pre-test routine. Learn what works for you, and follow the same steps each time you're getting ready to take a test. This will ease your stress level and help assure you that you're well prepared.

Learn and practice relaxation techniques. There are a number of things you can do right before and during the test to help you stay calm and confident, such as deep breathing, relaxing your muscles one at a time, or closing your eyes and imagining a positive outcome.

Don't forget to eat and drink. Just like muscles in your body, your brain needs fuel to function. Eat the day of the test so that you're not running on empty when test time arrives. Also, drink plenty of water. Avoid sugary drinks such as soda pop, which can cause your blood sugar to peak and then drop, or caffeinated beverages such as energy drinks or coffee, which can increase anxiety.

Get some exercise. Regular aerobic exercise, and exercising on exam day, can release tension.

Get plenty of sleep. Sleep is directly related to academic performance. You need to get an adequate amount of sleep. You cannot perform well if you are sleep-deprived.

Talk to your professor. Make sure you understand what's going to be on each test and know exactly how to prepare. In addition, let your teacher know that you feel anxious when you take tests. He or she may have suggestions to help you succeed.

Don't ignore a learning disability. Test anxiety may improve by addressing an underlying condition that interferes with the ability to learn, focus or concentrate, for example, attention-deficit/hyperactivity disorder (ADHD) or dyslexia. In many cases, a student diagnosed with a learning disability is entitled to help with test taking, such as extra time to complete a test or having questions read aloud.

See a professional counselor. Talk therapy (psychotherapy) with a psychologist or other mental health provider can help you work through feelings, thoughts and behaviors that cause or worsen anxiety. Check to see if your school has counseling services available or if your students services department can recommend a therapist familiar with the particular stresses of law school.

Lastly, and most importantly, consider the following: we all create our own reality. The more you're worried about being 'consumed' by anxiety, the more likely you'll create that as a part of your reality. Once you find out what 'form' your test anxiety takes—find ways to create an alternative and believable scenario. For example, your inquiry might involve unpacking and understanding *why* you didn't finish the timed sections of an exam in the past (or perhaps it was how you went about the essay section, or not being prepared, etc.) and then identifying a better behavior to achieve your end result—through practicing writing essays and becoming accustomed to the timing you're dealing with to shifting your mindset. The goal is to defuse the anxiety-producing situation by imagining that things *can* be different, and to create a new reality that is believable and achievable.

Chapter 13

Law School Stress and Depression

There is no doubt that beginning law students experience more stress and anxiety during law school than at any other time in their lives. The current research documents that law students are likely to exhibit signs of psychological distress at some point in time during law school, including "elevated levels of depression, stress, and anxiety."[1] It is probably not surprising to you that 44% of law students in one study met the criteria for "clinically significant levels of psychological distress."[2]

> Law students also report significantly higher levels of alcohol and drug use than college and high school graduates of the same age, and their alcohol use increases between their second and third year of law school. Moreover, these problems seem unique to law students and are not generalizable to other overworked populations of graduate students. For instance, one study showed that compared to medical students in a similarly demanding academic situation, law students have significantly higher levels of stress, stress symptoms, and alcohol abuse.[3]

There is a popular anecdote among law students that rings true: "During the first year of law school, they scare you to death. During the second year of law school they work you to death. And during the third year of law school, they bore you to death!" Although many law professors would debate the validity of the third premise (i.e., certainly we do *not* bore students to death!!!"), the other statements tend to be true. In other words, the stress and anxiety you feel during your first semester of law school will likely continue throughout your law school career and into the practice of law. In fact, law student stress levels may even "increase as the years pass, and levels of depression and anxiety [may be] … signifi-

1. Todd David Peterson and Elizabeth Waters Peterson, *Stemming the Tide of Law Student Depression: What Law Schools Need to Learn From the Science of Positive Psychology*, 9 Yale J. Health Pol'y, L. & Ethics 357, 359 (2009).

2. *Id.* (n.10).

3. *Id.* (n.11).

cantly elevated two years after graduation."[4] The research also suggests that the problems law students endure are tied directly to the law school experience.[5]

There are many leaders in legal education who are trying to make the law school experience more "humane." Yet for now, the way in which law schools teach and test their students is not likely to change. Therefore, it is imperative that you find the best way for you *personally* to deal with the stress and anxiety that is inherent within legal education.

The fierce competition for grades makes law school extremely competitive. This will change peer relationships dramatically. During the first semester of law school, (before students have had exams), students are very collegial and friendly. However, after exams, the friend you thought would help you out is now in competition with you. It is one of the most interesting transformations that will occur between your first and second semester of law school. Further, the way in which you are asked to think and communicate in law school is highly analytical. Many students have never been asked to read, reason and write in this challenging way. Another reason for increased stress: law students tend *not* to be rewarded for creativity in the classroom. In other words, all of the answers in a course seem to be boiled down to one correct or incorrect response. If you are a particularly creative problem-solver, you may not understand why the universe of correct answers in the law school classroom is so small. Finally, law school is almost entirely "performance oriented." In other words, students cannot get away from the fact that there is a "singular emphasis on achievement."[6]

It is very clear that law school will be stressful and full of anxiety. But when does this stress transform into something more serious?

This chapter will address the possibility that stress and anxiety may lead to law student depression. What are the signs and symptoms of actual "depression" and where can you go for help? How do you know the difference between sadness and depression? How can you avoid depression in law school? If you are aware of the likelihood of stress, anxiety and depression in the law school environment, you can help yourself cope with all of these challenges.

A. Why Are Lawyers (and Law Students) More Prone to Depression?

In the past several decades, there has been significant research into understanding more about depression. Depression can be defined as: "a

---

4. *Id.* (n.12–13).

5. *Id.*

6. *Id.* at 360 (n.19).

psychoneurotic or psychotic disorder marked especially by sadness, inactivity, difficulty in thinking and concentration, a significant increase or decrease in appetite and time spent sleeping, feelings of dejection and hopelessness, and sometimes suicidal tendencies."[7] Interestingly, some of the research suggests that lawyers are more prone to depression than members of any other profession. If lawyers are more prone to depression—then it is not surprising that law students are more prone to depression, too. Consider these numbers:

A 1990 study at Johns Hopkins University found that of 28 occupations studied, lawyers were the most likely to suffer from depression, and they were more than 3.6 times more likely than average to do so.[8] A research study of 801 lawyers in the State of Washington found that 19% suffered from depression.[9]

Left untreated, depression can be fatal. Surveys of lawyers in Washington and Arizona showed that most lawyers suffering from depression also have suicidal thoughts.[10] One study found that lawyers have a much greater risk of acting on their suicidal thoughts and succeeding in doing so.[11] In fact, suicide ranks among the leading causes of premature death among lawyers.[12]

Why are lawyers (and possibly law students) more prone than anyone else to this dangerous disease? Psychologist Lynn Johnson points to two personality traits many lawyers (and law students) tend to have: perfectionism and pessimism.[13] Consider most of the law students you know and you will likely agree that law school attracts perfectionists and rewards perfectionism. Perfectionism drives students to excel in college and this same drive appears in law school as well. But perfectionism has a dark side; it can produce "a chronic feeling that nothing is good enough."[14] Perfectionists "are driven by an intense need to avoid failure.... [T]hey are unable to derive satisfaction from what ordinarily might be considered even superior performance."[15] According to John-

---

7. *Merriam-Webster.com.* 2012 at http://www.merriam-webster.com (last visited 2/22/12).

8. W.W. Eaton, J.C. Anthony, W. Mandel & R. Garrison, *Occupations and the Prevalence of Major Depressive Disorder*, 32 J. Occupational Med. 1079, 1079 (1980).

9. G.A.H. Benjamin, E.J. Darling & B.D. Sales, *The Prevalence of Depression, Alcohol Abuse, and Cocaine Abuse Among United States Lawyers*, 13 J. Law & Psychiatry 233, 233 (1990).

10. Joan E. Mounteer, *Depression Among Lawyers*, 33 Colo. Lawyer 35 (Jan. 2004).

11. *Id.*

12. Richard G. Uday, *That Frayed Rope*, Utah State Bar, at www.utahbar.org/barjournal2000/html/august_september_2003.html (last checked 2/22/12).

13. Lynn Johnson, *Stress Management*, Utah State Bar J., Jan./Fed. 2003.

14. *Id.*

15. Don P. Jones & Michael J. Crowley, "*I wish I would have called you before ...*" (*citing* Blatt, Sidney J., Ph.D. "*The Destructiveness of Perfectionism: Implications for the*

son, perfectionism raises levels of the stress hormone, cortisol, and chronically high levels of cortisol lead to various health problems, including depression.[16] And when perfectionists make the inevitable mistake, perfectionism magnifies the failure. "Perfectionists are more vulnerable to depression and anxiety, harder to treat with either therapy or drugs, and much more likely to commit suicide when things go very wrong."[17]

What is more problematic, however, is that lawyers tend to mix that desire for perfectionism with a healthy dose of pessimism. In 1990, a Johns Hopkins study showed that in all graduate school programs except one (i.e., law school), optimists outperformed pessimists.[18] In law school, optimists did not perform better—pessimists did.[19] The study seems to suggest that pessimism helps lawyers excel: perhaps it makes lawyers skeptical of what their clients, witnesses, opposing counsel, and even judges tell them. This may actually help lawyers anticipate the worst, and thus prepare well for it.

The problem, however, is that although pessimism may be good for a lawyer's or law student's career, pessimism is bad for your health. And combining perfectionism and pessimism can lead to stress and disillusionment, which makes lawyers (and law students) more vulnerable to depression.

B. What Is the Difference between Sadness and Depression?

Although depression is often thought of as being an extreme state of sadness, there is a vast difference between clinical depression and sadness. Sadness is a part of being human—a natural reaction to painful circumstances. All of us will experience sadness at some point in our lives. Depression, however, is a physical illness with many more symptoms than an unhappy mood.

The person with clinical depression finds that there is not always a logical reason for her dark feelings. And statements from well-meaning family and friends for her to "snap out of it" provide only frustration— for a person with depression can no more "snap out of it" than a diabetic can *will* his pancreas to produce more insulin.

Sadness is a transient feeling that passes as a person comes to term with his troubles. Depression can linger for weeks, months or even years.

Treatment of Depression," American Psychologist, Vol. 49, No. 12, pp. 1003–1020 (1997)).

16. Johnson, *supra* note 12, at *2.

17. *Id.*

18. Uday, *supra* note 11 at *1.

19. *Id.*

The sad person feels bad, but continues to cope with living. A person with clinical depression may feel overwhelmed and hopeless.

To further clarify the differences between normal sadness and depression, there are specific, defined criteria for the diagnosis of major depression:

- A person who suffers from a major depressive disorder must either have a depressed mood or a loss of interest or pleasure in daily activities consistently for at least a two-week period. This mood must represent a change from the person's normal mood and impair his functioning in his daily life.

- A depressed mood caused by substances such as drugs, alcohol, or medications is not considered a major depressive disorder, nor is one that is caused by a general medical condition.

- This disorder is characterized by the presence of five or more of the following symptoms:

  1. Depressed mood most of the day, nearly every day. An individual may express feeling sad or empty, or others may observe it (e.g., appears tearful).

  2. Markedly diminished interest or pleasure in all, or most, daily activities most of the day, nearly every day.

  3. Significant weight changes (e.g., a change of more than 5% of body weight in a month), or a decrease or increase in appetite nearly every day.

  4. Insomnia or hypersomnia (sleeping too much) nearly every day.

  5. Psychomotor agitation or retardation nearly every day.

  6. Fatigue or loss of energy nearly every day.

  7. Feelings of worthlessness or excessive or inappropriate guilt nearly every day.

  8. Indecisiveness or diminished ability to think or concentrate nearly every day.

  9. Recurrent thoughts of death, recurrent suicidal ideation without a specific plan, or a suicide attempt or a specific plan for committing suicide.

If you think you might have depression, you need to get help. Talk to therapist. Look one up online and go in for an appointment. Or talk to your family doctor; after all, depression is a health problem—and it has physiological components. Don't be ashamed or afraid of the treatment, whether it's antidepressant medication, therapy, or both. When treated, depression typically goes away. When untreated, it can kill you.

If you are still uncertain as to whether you (or a friend) may be suffering from depression, screening tests exist that can help you determine whether seeking a professional evaluation is advised. Simply go on the Internet and search for "Depression Screening Test" and you will locate many options. If the screening test indicates you may have depression, it is imperative that you get help immediately.

C. Treatments for Depression

Luckily, there are numerous treatments for depression. Medications and psychological counseling (psychotherapy or "talk" therapy) are very effective for most people. If you need a referral, check with the student services department at your law school.

In some cases, a primary care doctor can prescribe medications to relieve depression symptoms. However, many people need to see a doctor who specializes in diagnosing and treating mental health conditions (a psychiatrist). Many people with depression also benefit from seeing a psychologist or other mental health counselor. Usually the most effective treatment for depression is a combination of medication and psychotherapy.

The following describes various depression treatment options.

1. Medications. A number of anti-depressant medications are available to treat depression. There are several different types of anti-depressants. Anti-depressants are generally categorized by how they affect the naturally occurring chemicals in your brain to change your mood. Types of anti-depressants include:

- **Selective serotonin reuptake inhibitors (SSRIs).** Many doctors start depression treatment by prescribing an SSRI. These medications are safer and generally cause fewer bothersome side effects than do other types of anti-depressants. SSRIs include fluoxetine (Prozac), paroxetine (Paxil), sertraline (Zoloft), citalopram (Celexa) and escitalopram (Lexapro).[20]

- **Serotonin and norepinephrine reuptake inhibitors (SNRIs).** These medications include duloxetine (Cymbalta), venlafaxine (Effexor XR) and desvenlafaxine (Pristiq).[21]

- **Norepinephrine and dopamine reuptake inhibitors (NDRIs).** Bupropion (Wellbutrin) falls into this category.

---

20. The most common side effects include decreased sexual desire and delayed orgasm. Other side effects may go away as your body adjusts to the medication. They can include digestive problems, jitteriness, restlessness, headache and insomnia.

21. Side effects are similar to those caused by SSRIs. These medications can cause increased sweating, dry mouth, fast heart rate and constipation.

It's one of the few anti-depressants that doesn't cause sexual side effects. At high doses, bupropion may increase your risk of having seizures.

- **Tricyclic antidepressants.** These anti-depressants have been used for years and are generally as effective as newer medications. But because they tend to have more numerous and more-severe side effects, a tricyclic antidepressant generally is not prescribed unless you've tried an SSRI first without an improvement in your depression.[22]

Other medication strategies. Your doctor may suggest other medications to treat your depression. These may include stimulants, mood-stabilizing medications, anti-anxiety medications or anti-psychotic medications. In some cases, your doctor may recommend combining two or more anti-depressants or other medications for better effect. This strategy is known as augmentation.

Finding the right medication. Everyone's different, so finding the right medication or medications for you will likely take some trial and error. This requires patience, as some medications need eight weeks or longer to take full effect and for side effects to ease as your body adjusts. If you have bothersome side effects, don't stop taking an antidepressant without talking to your doctor first. Some anti-depressants can cause withdrawal symptoms unless you slowly taper off your dose, and quitting suddenly may cause a sudden worsening of depression. Don't give up until you find an anti-depressant or medication that's suitable for you—you're likely to find one that works and that doesn't have intolerable side effects. Working together, you and your doctor can explore options to get your depression symptoms under control.

2. Psychotherapy. Psychological counseling is another important depression treatment. Psychotherapy is a general term for a way of treating depression by talking about your condition and related issues with a mental health provider. Psychotherapy is also known as therapy, talk therapy, counseling or psychosocial therapy.

Through these talk sessions, you learn about the causes of depression so that you can better understand it. You also learn how to identify and make changes in unhealthy behavior or thoughts, explore relationships and experiences, find better ways to cope and solve problems, and set realistic goals for your life. Psychotherapy can help you regain a sense of happiness and con-

---

22. Side effects can include dry mouth, blurred vision, constipation, urinary retention, fast heartbeat and confusion. Tricyclic antidepressants are also known to cause weight gain.

trol in your life and help ease depression symptoms such as hope-lessness and anger. It may also help you adjust to a crisis or other current difficulty.

There are several types of psychotherapy that are effective for depression. Cognitive behavioral therapy is one of the most commonly used therapies. This type of therapy helps you iden-tify negative beliefs and behaviors and replace them with healthy, positive ones. It's based on the idea that your own thoughts— not other people or situations—determine how you feel or be-have. Even if an unwanted situation doesn't change, you can change the way you think and behave in a positive way. Inter-personal therapy and psychodynamic psychotherapy are other types of counseling commonly used to treat depression.

3. Electroconvulsive therapy (ECT). In ECT, electrical cur-rents are passed through the brain. This procedure is thought to affect levels of neurotransmitters in your brain. Although many people are leery of ECT and its side effects, it typically offers im-mediate relief of even severe depression when other treatments don't work. It's unclear how this therapy relieves the signs and symp-toms of depression. The most common side effect is confusion, which can last from a few minutes to several hours. Some peo-ple also have memory loss, which is usually temporary.

ECT is usually used for people who don't get better with medications and for those at high risk of suicide. ECT may be an option if you have severe depression when you're pregnant and can't take your regular medications. It can also be an effec-tive treatment for older adults who have severe depression and can't take antidepressants for health reasons.

In some people, depression is so severe that a hospital stay is needed. Inpatient hospitalization may be necessary if you aren't able to care for yourself properly or when you're in im-mediate danger of harming yourself or someone else. Getting psychiatric treatment at a hospital can help keep you calm and safe until your mood improves. Partial hospitalization or day treatment programs also are helpful for some people. These pro-grams provide the support and counseling you need while you get symptoms under control.

D. What Can You Do to Avoid Depression in Law School?

When you feel that your mood has changed in a negative way, its im-portant to think about how you can counteract that frustration or sadness. The following is a short list of things you can do every day to avoid having that stress, frustration and/or anxiety turn into something more serious.

1. **Don't equate your self-worth to your grades.** Your worth as a human being is *not* determined by your law school grades. Remember that you came to law school as a successful, intelligent, interesting person. That person is still there!

2. **Stop comparing yourself to others.** It is difficult not to compare yourself to your peers in law school. The reality is that your grade is—at least in part—determined by how everyone else does. Try to make a sincere effort to stop comparing yourself to your classmates. Whenever you compare yourself to others, you are always going to lose. There will always be someone who's better than you. Just focus on working hard and achieving your personal best.

3. **Exercise.** Start an exercise plan and stick to it. Try to get in at least three workouts a week. Exercise is a great way to let off some steam from law school. Also a sound body means a sound mind that will come in handy on test day.

4. **Eat right.** Don't feed yourself out of the vending machine. If you eat junk, you'll feel like junk. Make sure to eat breakfast everyday and bring a nutritious lunch to school.

5. **Sleep.** Adequate sleep is an important part of avoiding depression. Ideally you should be getting between seven to eight hours of sleep. Sleep is especially important during finals. Insufficient sleep has been shown to cause a decrease in mental abilities. So, do not pull all-nighters. *You're probably better off sleeping an extra five hours than studying an extra five hours.* Don't let the students who boast about pulling all-nighters get to you. They're not going to do better than you. In fact, you'll probably do better than them.

6. **Don't drink.** Alcohol is not the answer to your law school problems. Your bad grade will still be there after the hangover. Lawyers are notorious for having a high percentage of alcoholics. Often the problem began while in law school. Avoid becoming another statistic by not drinking.

7. **Maintain your hobbies.** Many law students give up their hobbies once in law school in order to devote more time to studying. This is a big mistake. It's good to do things that aren't associated with law school to keep balance. Having a hobby is great for rejuvenating your mind and body—which actually helps you to tackle law school. While you may not be able to devote as much time to your hobby while in law school, don't abandon them completely.

8. **Make time for friends and family who aren't going to law school.** While it's nice to have friends in law school, you usually just end up talking about law school! You need to get away from law school as much as you can. Non-law school friends and family keep you grounded. If you're married, make sure to have a night where you just hang out with your spouse. Don't talk about law school! Talk about normal things—it will remind you of what's really important in life.

9. **Don't study all the time.** Many law students have the false belief that that *how much* you study determines your success. The reality is that success in law school is determined by *how* you study. The best advice is to treat law school like a job. Put in your nine hours at school, come home, and leave the books in the bag. It will help keep you sane.

10. **Seek help.** If you feel like law school's getting you down more often than not, it is important to talk to someone. Many schools offer academic support programs that have counselors that can help you. Also, try talking to your professors. You'll be surprised how many are willing to listen and help if you're struggling. Often times, they will tell you that "they have been there, too."

Conclusion

Law school will be one of the most challenging experiences of your life. The key to success, however, is to believe in yourself and to maximize your potential. Everyone has unique gifts—the key is to use your gifts to your advantage and to limit your weaknesses to the extent possible. I hope that this book has given you some helpful advice about how to approach law school learning, studying and test-taking. Now the rest is up to you—but you *can* do it! Good luck!

Index